The African Informal Economy

Studies in the Political Economy of Global Labor and Work

VOLUME 5

The titles published in this series are listed at *brill.com/pelw*

The African Informal Economy

Structure, Dynamics, and Resilience

Edited by

Ayokunle Olumuyiwa Omobowale

BRILL

LEIDEN | BOSTON

Cover image courtesy of Wikimedia Commons. Fish market in Lagos, Nigeria (2014).

The Library of Congress Cataloging-in-Publication Data is available online at https://catalog.loc.gov
LC record available at https://lccn.loc.gov/2024020470

Typeface for the Latin, Greek, and Cyrillic scripts: "Brill". See and download: brill.com/brill-typeface.

ISSN 2667-288X
ISBN 978-90-04-69264-0 (hardback)
ISBN 978-90-04-69265-7 (e-book)
DOI 10.1163/9789004692657

This book is printed on acid-free paper and produced in a sustainable manner.

Contents

List of Figures and Tables VII
Notes on Contributors IX

Introduction 1
Ayokunle Olumuyiwa Omobowale

1 Women's Involvement in Keke and Boda Boda Transport Business in Nigeria and Kenya 7
Molatokunbo A. S. Olutayo and Mojisola A. Adeyemo

2 Female Commercial Three-Wheel Tricycle (*Kèké Marwa*) Riders in the Ibadan Metropolis, Nigeria 23
Dauda Aderemi Busari

3 The Traffic Space and the Context of Emancipated Adolescents' Involvement in Unsolicited Vehicle Windscreen-Cleaning in Ibadan, Nigeria 47
Mofeyisara Oluwatoyin Omobowale and Olugbenga Samuel Falase

4 Business Networking among Auto-artisans in Ibadan Mechanic Villages, Nigeria 64
Olufikayo Kunle Oyelade

5 Coconut Oil Processing, Marketing Network and Challenges in Badagry, Nigeria 85
Adebimpe Oluwabukade Adefila and Ayokunle Olumuyiwa Omobowale

6 Border Markets and Traders in Seme 106
O. S. Raji

7 Medicinal Herb Traders in Southwest Nigeria 129
Seun Mauton Ajoseh, S.O. Raji and I.O. Odejimi

8 Indigenous Usury Finance System and Informal Trader-Lendees in Ibadan Nigeria 148
Bernard Adeniyan and Ayokunle Olumuyiwa Omobowale

9 Graduates in the Informal Sector of Southwestern Nigeria 169
Adepeju Olubukola Odunlami, Ephraim Ifediri Nwokporo and Olayinka Akanle

10 Gender, Education and Informal Employment in Togo 198
Dossè Mawussi Djahini-Afawoubo

11 Gig Economy: the Experience of Nigerian Digital Freelancers 217
Adeola O. Opesade

12 Decent Work, Informality and Pandemic: Empirical Insights from Ghana 250
Alex Anlesinya and Joseph Gerald Tetteh Nyanyofio

13 Health Insurance and the Challenges of Public Response to Pandemics in Burkina Faso: Exploring the Role of the Informal Economy 273
Natéwindé Sawadogo

Index 293

Figures and Tables

Figures

2.1 Word cloud representation of responses on Introduction to *Keke* riding 34
2.2 Word cloud representation of responses on *Keke* purchase/payment strategy 35
2.3 Word cloud representation of responses on *Keke* operation (1) 36
2.4 Word cloud representation of responses on *Keke* operation (2) 37
2.5 Word cloud representation of responses on business duration 37
2.6 Word cloud representation of responses on the home front (1) 38
2.7 Word cloud representation of responses on the home front (2) 39
2.8 Word cloud representation of responses on challenges (1) 40
2.9 Word cloud representation of responses on challenges (2) 42
5.1 Special knives due for reshelling 89
5.2 Different drums and bowls 90
5.3 Grinder for grinding coconut meat 90
5.4 Adogan, pots, and basket 91
5.5 Raw material preparation 92
5.6 Milk extraction 92
5.7 Oil extraction 92
6.1 Border market in Seme border 111
6.2 Free movement of people and goods at Seme border post 113
6.3 Free movement at a border post in Ilara Border Community in Nigeria 114
6.4 The researcher at Seme Border Post 117
6.5 Ilara Border Post in Republic of Benin 123
11.1 Word cloud representation of responses on awareness 224
11.2 Word cloud representation of responses on motivation 226
11.3 Word cloud representation of responses on positive experiences 228
11.4 Word cloud representation of responses on negative experiences 231
11.5 Sentiment polarities of gig workers' attitudes 240
11.6 Word cloud representation of responses on improving digital gig 241
12.1 Data Abstraction and Data Structure of Decent Work in the Informal Sector amidst Covid-19 259
12.2 Integrated Theoretical Framework of Informal Decent Work 264

Tables

2.1 Sociodemographics of study respondents 29

5.1 The stages and by product in coconut oil preparation 92
9.1 Forms of Artisanal Work by Gender and State 177
9.2 Push Factors Influencing Involvement in Artisanal Work by Graduate Artisans 182
9.3 Pull Factors Influencing Involvement in Artisanal Work by Graduate Artisans 184
10.1 Correlation matrix of main explanatory variables 204
10.2 Descriptive statistics of main variables 205
10.3 Type of employment by level of education, gender, and place of residence 206
10.4 Main determinants of informal employment in Togo 208
10.5 Effect of different education levels on informal employment (marginal effects are reported) 211
11.1 Demographic Characteristics of Respondents 222
12.1 Profile of Research Participants 257

Notes on Contributors

Adebimpe Oluwabukade Adefila
is a PhD candidate at the Department of Sociology, University of Ibadan. She has a bachelor's in economics, a master's in sociology (development) and her doctoral research is on the palm oil industry in Southwestern Nigeria (sociology of development). Adebimpe has a special interest in the economic sociology of the informal sector, gender relations in the workplace and the globalisation process (email: bimpefila@gmail.com).

Bernard Adeniyan
is a First Class Bachelor Honours Degree graduate of Sociology from the University of Ibadan. He also received his Masters's degree in the same discipline from the University of Lagos and an MBA from Obafemi Awolowo University Ile Ife. Dr. Bernard obtained his doctorate in Sociology, with specialisation in development, from the University of Ibadan. He was a grant attendee at the postgraduate summer school of the Center for African Studies, University of Basel, Switzerland. Dr Bernard also has over 15 years of experience in corporate and commercial banking (email: adeniyanben@gmail.com).

Mojisola Adeyemo
holds a M. A. in Gender Studies. She is presently a doctoral student in the Gender Studies Programme, Institute of African Studies, University of Ibadan, Ibadan, Nigeria. Her research interest surrounds gender and urban mobility studies (email : ademoj63@gmail.com).

Seun Ajoseh
is a PhD student in the Department of Sociology Criminology and Law at the University of Florida. He holds bachelor's and master's degrees in Sociology from Lagos State University. Previously, he was a graduate assistant in the department of Sociology, Lagos State university. His research interests include medical sociology – maternal healthcare, alternative medicine, migration, Race, and well-being. He uses qualitative, quantitative, and computational social science methods to answer his research questions. He is a fellow of the Summer Institute of Computational Social Science and has presented papers at International Conferences. He is a member of the Southern Sociological Society and the Florida Society for Social Sciences (email: Seunajoseh@ufl.edu).

Olayinka Akanle
PhD, is a lecturer in the Department of Sociology, Faculty of Social Sciences, University of Ibadan, Nigeria and a Research Associate in the Department of Sociology, Faculty of Humanities, University of Johannesburg, South Africa. He is a World Social Science Fellow (WSSF) of The International Social Science Council (ISSC), Paris, France and was a Postdoctoral Fellow at the South African Research Chair Initiative (SARChI) in Social Policy, College of Graduate Studies, University of South Africa (UNISA), South Africa. He is a scholar and an expert on International Migration and Diaspora Studies, Sociology of Development, Social Theory, Social Policy and Child, Youth, Aging Gender, and Family Studies in Post-Colonial Africa (email : yakanle@yahoo.com, olayinkaakanle75@gmail.com, o.akanle@ui.edu.ng).

Alex Anlesinya
(PhD, University of Ghana) is a multiple award-winning researcher, experienced lecturer/management trainer with extensive consulting experience. He is Lecturer in HRM and Organisational Behaviour at De Montfort University, United Kingdom, and Associate Editor of Review of Business Management (RBGN). He has consulted for several institutions in Ghana. Alex received Best Paper Awards from several prestigious organisations including Emerald Publishing Limited; Wiley; Sage/FIIB Business Review; and was also valedictorian. Alex researches at the intersection of work, human resources and sustainability, specifically, talent management, sustainable HRM, decent work, CSR strategy, and grand societal challenges. He has published severally in high impact journals and presented in top international conferences (email: alex.anlesinya@dmu.ac.uk).

Dauda Aderemi Busari
holds a PhD degree in Sociology from The University of Ibadan, Nigeria and he is also a Senior Lecturer in the Department. Dr. Busari was a Post-Doctoral Research Fellow in the Population and Research Training Unit of the North West University (Mafikeng, Campus), South Africa. He has worked on social, and consumer research in a consultancy capacity, with a focus on strategic assessment of customer needs and attitudes to different products using a broad range of methods. His research interests, include Sociology of Development/ Development Studies, Rural Sociology, Social Theory, Sociology of Religion, Migration, Gender, and the Sociology of the Family. He is an associate member of the Nigeria Institute of Marketing Research (NIMRA). He has published in international and national outlets (email: dabusari@gmail.com)

Dossè Mawussi Djahini-Afawoubo
holds a PhD in Economics at the University of Lomé, Togo. His main areas of interest are the analysis of multidimensional poverty and inequality, the analysis of efficiency, the informal economy, and the distributional effects of public spending on basic services. He has published several articles on these issues. He teaches macroeconomics at the University of Lomé, Togo (Email: ddjahini-afawoubo@univ-lome.tg / dossedjahini@gmail.com)

Olugbenga Samuel Falase
holds a PhD in sociology from the University of Ibadan. He is a recipient of the Social Science Research Council (SSRC) Doctoral Fellowships (2014, 2016, 2017 and 2020) respectively, and Lift Above Poverty Organisation (LAPO) Doctoral Research Support Grant, 2015. He is a specialist in development and rural sociology and the sociology of forests. He is a lecturer at the Department of Sociology, Lead City University, Ibadan, Nigeria. He is also an International Partner and Participant in the International Network on Women on the Move COST Action (CA19112) 2020–2022 https://www.cost.eu/cost-action/women-on-the-move (email: flash4real@yahoo.co.uk).

Ephraim Nwokporo
is a master's degree student of Sociology of Development at the Department of Sociology, Faculty of the Social Sciences, University of Ibadan, Nigeria. He is currently a Research and Teaching Assistant at Lagos Business School, Pan-Atlantic University. He is a member of the International Sociological Association (ISA) and the Nigerian Anthropological and Sociological Practitioners Association (NASA) and a Research Fellow at the Institut Français de Recherche en Afrique au Nigeria (IFRA-Nigeria).

Joseph Gerald Tetteh Nyanyofio
(PhD, University of Ghana) is Lecturer in Public Administration & Policy, Strategic Management, and Governance in the Faculty of Management at the University of Professional Studies, Accra (UPSA). He served as Secretary and Organising Secretary to the UPSA branch of the University Teachers' Association of Ghana, an academic board member of UPSA, and Coordinator for Management Programmes at the School of Graduate Studies. He is a member of the Ghana Institute of Directors. His research interest spans across governance, policy analysis and development. He was part of the brain behind the establishment of UPSA's annual International Conference on Business Management and Entrepreneurial Development (email: joseph.nyanyofio@upsamail.edu.gh)

I.O. Odejimi
is a lecturer in the Department of Sociology, University of Uyo with special interest in Child development and Mental health. Her research interests include Sociology of medicine, development and health, social health, rape and mental health, as well as psychology. Her current research interest is in the rape and its effect on the mental health of teenage girls (email: jimibkay@gmail.com)

Olubukola Adepeju Odunlami
holds a degree in Sociology from the Department of Sociology, Faculty of the Social Sciences, University of Ibadan, Nigeria.

Molatokunbo Olutayo
holds a PhD in Political Science from the University of Ibadan. She is a Senior Research Fellow at the Institute of African Studies, University of Ibadan. She currently teaches in and coordinates the Gender Studies programme of the institute. Her research and teaching interest surrounds gender and development studies and Political economy and a facilitator in the Pedagogical Leadership in Africa (PedaL). Having undertaken various research, Olutayo's work speaks to transformation in contemporary gender discourse. She has published in reputable journals including African Notes, Comparative Sociology, Journal of Sociology, Social Science and Humanities Open, Elsevier Journals and African Development (email: kunbo@yahoo.ca; ma.olutayo@ui.edu.ng).

Ayokunle Olumuyiwa Omobowale
(PhD) is Professor of Sociology at the University of Ibadan. Dr Omobowale studies development in context. He has won the University of Ibadan Postgraduate School Award for scholarly publication, 2007, Institut Français de Recherche en Afrique Research Fellowship 2009, American Council of Learned Societies-African Humanities Program Post-Doctoral Fellowship 2010 and African Studies Association (USA) Presidential Award 2014. Dr Omobowale was also Visiting Scholar at the Centre for African Studies, Rutgers University, New Jersey, USA in November 2014. His works have appeared in peer-reviewed journals and edited volumes locally and internationally. He served on the Board of Editors of International Encyclopaedia of Revolution and Protest (2009) and he is the author of The Tokunbo Phenomenon and the Second-hand Economy in Nigeria (2013). Dr Omobowale is Editor of Ibadan Journal of Sociology and he is also an International Partner and Participant in the International Network on Women on the Move COST Action (CA19112) 2020–2022 https://www.cost.eu/cost-action/women-on-the-move (email: ao.omobowale@gmail.com).

Mofeyisara Oluwatoyin Omobowale
holds a PhD in anthropology. Her doctoral research was on space, sexuality and power at Bodija Market, Ibadan, Nigeria She is a recipient of the American Council of Learned Societies-African Humanities Program (ACLS-AHP) Doctoral Fellowship 2012, the Cadbury Fellowship (Department of Anthropology and African Studies, Birmingham University) 2014 and ACLS-AHP Post-Doctoral Fellowship 2016. Her interests lie in medical anthropology, cultural studies, sexuality issues and maternal, child and adolescent studies. Mofeyisara is Research Fellow/Lecturer at the Institute of Child Health, College of Medicine, University of Ibadan, Nigeria. Dr Mofeyisara Omobowale is a co-investigator on Global Grand Challenges (Round 23) project on Immunisation Strategies for Working Mothers 2019–2021 https://gcgh.grandchallenges.org/grant/immunisation-strategies-working-mothers (email: feyisarat@yahoo.com, feyisarat@gmail.com).

Adeola O. Opesade
(PhD) is a Senior Reader at the Department of Data and Information Science, Faculty of Multidisciplinary Studies, University of Ibadan, Nigeria. She had her first degree in Electronic and Electrical Engineering, her first Master's degree in Industrial and Production Engineering, her second Master's degree and her PhD in Information Science. Her research interests include Cyber Security, Machine Learning, Text Data Mining, Quantitative Methods and Emerging Technologies. She has her publications in highly referred journals and conference proceedings (email: morecrown@gmail.com).

Olufikayo Kunle Oyelade
is a trained teacher, independent researcher, and Methodist Church Nigerian ordained clergy member. He obtained a Bachelor and Master's degrees in Religious Studies. Realizing the scholarly depth of Sociology in explaining the social dimensions of religion, he obtained another Master's and doctoral degrees in Sociology with special bias for Development Sociology and Sociology Religion in 2011 and 2018 respectively, from the University of Ibadan. He won ISA PhD Students' Laboratory Fellowship, 2015. He reviews for a number of reputable local and international journals. His research interest includes Gender, Social Ethics, Health and Social Care, Sociology of Religion, and Development Sociology. (email: oyeladeok@yahoo.com).

O. S. Raji
(PhD) teaches in the Department of Sociology, Lagos State University, Nigeria. He received both B.Sc. & M.Sc. degrees in Sociology and Anthropology from Obafemi Awolowo University, Ile-Ife, and holds a Doctorate degree (PhD)

in Medical Sociology (with special focus on Sociology of Health and Well-being) from the University of Ibadan, Nigeria. His research interests include Public and Community Health, Migration and Diversity, Social Exclusion and Discrimination, as well as Development and Governance. His current research is in the health conditions of emerging/minority communities. Dr. Raji, who is a recipient of AfHEA grant (2014); Brown University International Advanced Research Institutes (BIARI grant, 2015); DSA grant (2020) has also published in foreign and local reputable outlets (email: sakiru.raji@lasu.edu.ng).

Natéwindé Sawadogo
(PhD) is an Assistant Professor of sociology at the University of Thomas SANKARA in Burkina Faso (and also affiliated with the Africa Multiple Cluster Centre, University of Joseph Ki-Zerbo, Burkina Faso. He is currently the Deputy Coordinator of the Centre of Excellence for Studies, Training and Research on Social Risks Management, funded by the World Bank (email: natewinde.sawadogo@yahoo.fr).

Introduction

Ayokunle Olumuyiwa Omobowale

The informal sector is a major lifeline for the African economy. It provides employment for about 70 percent and 62 percent of sub-Saharan Africans and North Africans respectively. Despite colonialism and modernization of the African economic system, the informal economy has proven resilient in the face of diverse post-independence challenges irrespective of the changes it has experienced over the years. The structure of the informal economic system is a critical factor that has played a vital role in its dynamism and resilience. The informal sector has remained relevant to economic survival, politics and governance, political participation, public health and health management, and security and policing among other issues. Hence, the informal system cannot be ignored, not just because of the huge population of actors in the system, but because of its contribution to the stability, growth, and progress of the continent. This edited volume particularly examines diverse issues and areas of the informal sector to reveal the critical importance of the sector to the African economy. Though understudied, the vibrancy of the sector at providing employment, livelihood and survival for the teeming population of unskilled, semi-skilled and skilled people who otherwise may be jobless makes the informal sector an important area of the economy whose structure, strength and resilience despite challenges, should be understood, and where necessary, aided with policy and funds. It would be misleading and non-factual to keep the informal sector in the backwaters of the economy. A sector of the economy that engages over 60% of the population and contributes to GDP, is not backwater, irrespective of the crudity of its methods and structure. The informal sector is; a mainstay of the African economy that contributes immensely to survival for a vast population of Africans, who otherwise, would be broken and forgotten in economic doldrums.

Despite the dearth of statistical data on the informal sector across African countries, literature affirm that the sector makes immense contributions to GDP and labour across sub-Saharan and North Africa (see for example, Nguimkeu and Okou 2021, Kiaga and Leung 2020, Guven 2019). The informal sector contributes up to 40% of the GDP in Africa. The GDP statistics and population in the informal sector, however, vary across countries with South Africa at (18% GDP, 20% of labour), Morocco (30% GDP, 80% of labour), Kenya (33% GDP, 80% of labour), Egypt (50% GDP, 63% of labour), Nigeria (over 64% GDP, 65% of labour) and Zimbabwe (67% GDP, over 84% of labour). In Africa, the informal

 | DOI:10.1163/9789004692657_002

sector is intricately connected to the formal sector because many of its segments serve as critical lines of supply and distribution for the goods produced by the formal public and private sectors. Transport workers are critical for the movement of finished products to retail centres. The commercial transport sector formerly regarded as an exclusive preserve of the menfolk now increasingly welcomes women as transport operators. The informal market serves as a major retail centre for finished products, and the market is so structured that it retails to the financial capability of the buyer across socio-economic lines. Low-end ICT artisans also serve as important accessories and maintenance artisans for many users of ICT/GSM products and an increasing population of ICT-savvy Africans take part in the unregulated digital economy. Also, the auto-mechanics trade is gradually being transformed by modern technologies such as auto scanners and graduates are increasingly moving into the informal sector as active participants and service providers. The informal sector stays strategic to the economy of Africa as an employer of labour and GDP contributor that cannot be ignored.

Africa's informal sector is no doubt challenged in diverse ways. The informal sector is unregulated by state agencies, its activities are subject to charisma and whims of its leaders, irrespective of the protest channels that may be available to members. The informal sector is untaxed, yet, members pay charges and dues to associational coffers, with little or no accountability by leaders (Omobowale and Fayiga 2017). Traders are hardly able to access business support and funding from banks and are thus vulnerable to exploitative usury loan givers at the expense of financial punitive measures and emotional and physical assaults by loaners for repayment default (Adeniyan 2017, Omobowale 2011). Also, automobile and ICT repair artisans claim absolute expertise on any faulty vehicle and ICT gadget presented. The artisan stays non-liable for further damage caused to vehicles and gadgets. The customer would have to bear the cost of further repair or replacement irrespective of protestations. Hence, the informal sector is not all *uhuru,* without challenges. This volume does not attempt to paint a picture of a perfect informal sector. Nothing is ever perfect in any case. Mankind continuously and continually attempts to improve situations across sectors as their worth to societal progress are appreciated.

This edited volume, proposed to be published in the Brill Series: *Studies in the Political Economy of Global Labour and Work* present empirical case studies on various aspects of the informal sector in Nigeria, Burkina Faso, Ghana, Togo and one comparative study of Nigeria and Kenya. These are only four countries out of the 54 nations in North and sub-Saharan Africa yet, the structure and content of the informal economies of these countries are reminiscent of informal economies across the continent. The volume has 13 chapters. Molatokun Olutayo and Mojisola Adeyemo's chapter on women's involvement in commercial tricycle transportation (*keke*, Nigeria, and *boda*

boda, Kenya) reveals a major shift in gender barriers that kept the transportation business as men's preserve. Easy entry and exit of the trade with assurance of daily income make tricycle transportation attractive. Women tricycle operators are economically empowered to *support* themselves and family and gain some degree of independence. The chapter discusses the reasons why women engage in commercial tricycling, and challenges they meet and describes the structure of the trade in Nigeria and Kenya. The authors note that despite the challenges of the trade, women have devised means of survival in the business while negotiating and competing with male counterparts in the predominantly male profession that remains influenced by patriarchal normative elements. Dauda Busari's chapter on female commercial three-wheel tricycle (popularly called Keke Marwa in local parlance) operators corroborates the research of Olutayo and Adeyemo that women are increasingly moving into the male-dominated tricycle transport business. Women particularly opt for commercial tricycling to satisfy breadwinning roles that they increasingly take up on the home front. The chapter affirms that women tricycle operators are encouraged by the appreciation they receive from the public. They are celebrated as brave and virtuous women who are ready to take up hitherto men's roles for economic emancipation and care of their children.

Furthermore, Mofeyisara Oluwatoyin Omobowale and Olugbenga Samuel Falase's chapter on emancipated adolescents' involvement in unsolicited vehicle windscreen cleaning in the traffic; provide a unique insight into the workings of an uncoordinated collection of young boys cleaning windscreens at traffic stops on major roads. These boys appear once there are traffic stops to clean windscreens and thereafter plead for money for unsolicited service done. Some compensate the boys, many others do not. However, the research reveals that the practice is a structured trade with some older men at the background who assign the boys to locations and collect fractions of money made as operational charges. The adolescents are admitted into the trade by social networks, and they make daily income of ₦1000($2.4) to ₦7500($18.2). Many of the adolescents are below the age of 18, are exploited by underground patrons and exposed to road hazards. Olufikayo kunle Oyelade's chapter examined business networking among auto-artisans. Auto-artisans include working class skilled workers such as mechanics, auto-electricians, braking system repairers, automobile painters and panel beaters among others. Mechanics are the dominant group among the lot. However, the auto-artisans work with normative value for cooperation in competition (see also Omobowale and Omobowale 2019). Some of the problems they encounter include low skill, scarce and expensive spare parts, and advanced electronic technology in post-2010 vehicles among others.

Adebimpe Oluwabukade Adefila and Ayokunle Olumuyiwa Omobowale's chapter examined the local processes in the processing of coconut oil, marketing strategies and the challenges associated with the industry. The chapter examines the local technology used and the stages in the processing of coconut oil. Some producers and middlemen sellers have introduced fancy labelling and online adverts to market their products and attract consumers. Coconut processing is labour-intensive because the technology of production is poor. The producers and traders cope with challenges through social networking and traders' associations that provide financial and social support. Furthermore, O.S. Raji's chapter on trading activities and health preferences of border residents along the Nigeria-Benin Border corridor submits that the border area is a convergence of internationality and locality. Petrol, groceries and textiles are the most commonly traded products in border markets. The border markets are major centres of goods smuggling between Nigeria and Benin. Communities along both sides of the border do not see themselves divided by international boundaries. They perceive themselves as one united by same language and customs. Hence, they do not perceive the goods they move across borders as contraband, nor their activities as smugglings against legal statutes. The numerous unofficial and unmanned routes along the border corridor provide channels of movements for the traders and they access traditional medicine as therapeutic option due to the dearth of effective modern healthcare in border areas. The chapter of S.M Ajoseh, S.O. Raji and I.O. Odejimi on medicinal herb traders noted that the trade is structured along familial relations. Certain families that have been able to keep knowledge and practice of traditional medicine along generational lines are involved in the trade. This is not to suggest that entry into the trade is closed. Traditional medicine traders admit apprentices usually through referrers. Traders collect and buy medicinal roots and herbs from diverse locations across Southern and Northern Nigeria. The roots and herbs are naturally dried for preservation. Buyers are mostly traditional medicine practitioners and some clerics. The processes of medicinal herb trade are basic, yet it remains a thriving venture, irrespective of the competitive challenges that modernized herbal medicine practice and marketing increasingly pose to the trade. Credit system and capital are major challenges of the informal sector Bernard Adeniyan and Ayokunle Olumuyiwa Omobowale's chapter examines the indigenous usury system in Ibadan Nigeria. Unable to access credit from banking institutions, traders depend on money lenders with prohibitive interest rates. The system is exploitative of the lendee, yet the lendee-trader rationally views the loan and lender as critical lifeline without which business support and survival would be impossible. The traders are inexplicably entangled in unbalanced and exploitative relationships that favour the lender, with little or no help from formal institutions.

Olayinka Akanle, Olubukola Odunlami and Ephraim Ifediri Nwokporo empirically discussed the involvement of Nigerian graduates in the informal sector. The chapter documented the vocations where graduates involved as the following: Aluminum fabrication, appliances repairs, auto-mechanic, block making, bricklaying, cloth weaving. decoration, events planning, catering and confectionaries, chef, hairdressing, woodwork (carpentry) and painting among others. The push-pull factors included inability to gain formal employment, poor wages and the need for a second source of income and the need to continue family tradition. The jobs are strenuous due to lack of equipment, yet, they are driven by the need to satisfy survival goals, which artisanship trade readily provide outside tertiary degrees graduates have. A similar chapter on Togo by Dossè Mawussi Djahini-Afawoubo affirmed that while university education reduces the challenges associated with employment in the informal sector, female graduates are likely to be engaged in the informal sector than their male counterparts. Adeola Opesade wrote on the experience of Nigerian freelancers in the Gig economy. The ICT and the gig economy have transformed access and participation in the global cyber transactional space. The global cyber transactional space has erased geographical boundaries in competitive edges in the gig economy. Many unemployed graduates and computer-savvy individuals find reprieve in the gig economy by supplying freelance services such as content and creative writing, software engineering, voice-over artistry, website development, poetry, graphic design, and business development consultancy among others. The gig economy provides jobs and needed income, yet the freelancers complained of contract failures and the refusal of clients to pay for jobs done. Freelancers want a regulation of the gig economy to be protected.

Furthermore, COVID-19 came as a ravaging pandemic in December 2019 with a devastating economic impact on the informal sector (Omobowale, Oyelade, Omobowale and Falase 2020, Omobowale, Falase, Oyelade and Omobowale 2020, Omobowale, Bamgboye, Akinyode, Falase, et al 2021). Writing on Ghana, Alex Anlesinya and Gerald Joseph Nii Tetteh Nyanyofio submitted that the COVID-19 pandemic affected descent work among informal workers. The pandemic particularly compromised income, work fulfilment and health, safety and wellbeing. Natéwindé Sawadogo affirmed the positive contribution of community-based health insurance (*mutuelles de santé*) in health management among low-income informal workers in Burkina Faso. The pandemic unfortunately affected social support among low-income workers adversely affecting contributions to community-based health insurance and health management.

The informal sector is a versatile segment of the African economy. It provides employment and reprieve to semi-skilled, skilled and professionals who otherwise, would be left out of the employment bracket. In short, it puts food on the table, alleviates poverty and keeps the working class economically afloat despite the vicissitudes of liberal economic principles that African countries have been subjected to since the 1980s. This edited volume does not claim the informal sector makes stupendous wealth for most of its participants; it at least makes survival possible for many of its actors across skills and capability lines.

References

Adeniyan, Bernard Olusegun (2017) *Indigenous Usury System and Informal Microfinance in Ibadan, Nigeria* A Ph.D. Thesis in the Department of Sociology, University of Ibadan, Nigeria.

Guven, M. (2019). *Extending Pension Coverage to the Informal Sector in Africa. Social Protection and Jobs* Discussion Paper, No. 1933. World Bank, Washington, DC. © World Bank. https://openknowledge.worldbank.org/handle/10986/32179 License: CC BY 3.0 IGO.

Kiaga, A. and Leung, V (2020) *The Transition from the Informal to the Formal Economy in Africa.* International Labour Organisation, Global Employment Policy Review, Background Paper No 2. Accessed 2 March 2022 from https://www.ilo.org/wcmsp5/groups/public/---ed_emp/documents/publication/wcms_792078.pdf.

Nguimkeu, P., & Okou, C. (2021). Leveraging digital technologies to boost productivity in the informal sector in Sub-Saharan Africa. *Review of Policy Research*, 38(6), 707–731.

Omobowale, A.O. (2011) Social Capital and Ajo System Among Working Class Traders in Ibadan, Nigeria. *WorkingUSA: The Journal of Labor and Society* 14 (3): 333–346.

Omobowale, A.O. and O.O. Fayiga (2017) Commercial Motor Drivers, Transport Unions and Electoral Violence in Ibadan, Nigeria. *Development and Society* 46 (2): 591–614.

Omobowale, M. O., Bamgboye, E. A., Akinyode, A., Falase, O. S., Ladipo, T. O., Salami, O., & Adebiyi, A. O. (2021). Contextual interpretation of COVID-19 pandemic among public space users in Ibadan Metropolis, Oyo State, Nigeria: An ethnographic review. *Plos One*, 16(11), https://doi.org/10.1371/journal.pone.0259631.

Omobowale, M.O. and A.O. Omobowale (2019) "Oju and Inu: Solidarity in the Informal Market Space in Ibadan, Nigeria" *Journal of Black Studies* 50 (4): 401–420.

CHAPTER 1

Women's Involvement in Keke and Boda Boda Transport Business in Nigeria and Kenya

Molatokunbo A. S. Olutayo and Mojisola A. Adeyemo

1 Introduction

Globally, urban mobility is vital in blending the different sectors of the economy, as it contributes to both rural and urban development which, in a way, helps achieve targets embedded in the Sustainable Development Goals. The urban mobility systems in developed societies are operated in a form of mixed modality which include both public and private transport options (Loorbach et al., 2021). This is also the case in most developing societies, especially Africa, where both modalities are now operated as means of movement. Urban mobility is patterned after technological development, through which over the years different forms of transportation have emerged (Miskolczi et al., 2017). In addition, the evolution of new forms of urban mobility is informed by a growing demand for transportation services as well as urbanization. Therefore, meeting the ever-increasing movements of people and goods will help improve their lives and livelihood in an integrated way that ensures that all individual needs are met (Becker et al., 2020). The evolution of newer modes of transportation and expansion of the transportation system is embedded in the informal economy as the formal economy has failed to meet the unending mobility needs of the people.

The informal economy consists of diverse enterprises in which workers engage, in the various sectors and or institutions that are covered or insufficiently covered by formal setting. (Tonuchi et al., 2020). In the last three decades (especially in the 1990s), the informal sector has taken over some activities and the financial performance in different outfits of the society, such as telecommunication, power, postal services, airlines, transportation, amongst others which originally were under the purview of Public Enterprises (Krukru, 2016). Women have also increasingly participated in different activities in the informal sector, though at a minimal rate as compared to men and not without its own challenges. Thus, it is gendered such that, there is a sort of unequal level of involvement and participation of men and women especially in the transportation sector which is the focus of the study.

 | DOI:10.1163/9789004692657_003

Gender is a social construct that describes the roles, responsibilities, attitudes, behaviours and expectations of women, girls, men, and boys. It also describes the socially constructed roles and responsibilities of women and men in a particular culture or society (Gillis and Jacob, 2017). Gender can also be refered to as the performance, characteristics and roles that are socially attributed to women, men, girls, and boys in certain historical, cultural and socio- economic contexts which is beyond their biological differences. These explanations also contribute to defining responsibilities, opportunities and barriers between men and women. These expected gender roles are not innate but learned in each society, which in turn define what activities or tasks are meant for a particular sex.

Men and women in most cultures are participants within the system of commerce, production of service in their various societies. In some developed societies where there are no strict gender roles, both men and women engage in as many professions as they would want to, though in most cases, women need to combine these roles with their family roles at home. These roles are most times consistent with their own culture's gender definitions, in as much as they do not impinge upon women's responsibilities at home (Evans, 2015). The thrust of this paper, however, is on the participation of women as drivers of the three-wheeler also referred to as *Keke napep* in Nigeria and the motorcycle known as *boda boda* in Kenya transport industries.

2 Emerging Trends in Urban Mobility in the Informal Sector: a Global View

The transportation sector has always been male-dominated and in most cases, male-oriented, as men are seen to engage more in the transportation business. In addition, the travel needs and patterns of men and women have been generalized and largely one-sided, not putting into consideration how it impacts on men and women differently (Godfrey and Bertini, 2019). Though a lot of women make use of different means of public transport to move around for different purposes daily, they rarely navigate the transportation space as a profession. However, with the economic crises faced by many African countries, coupled with the failure of the various governments to reach the essentialities of the populace, the economic condition of most countries became unbearable such that so many people were unemployed and are still unemployed or losing their jobs daily in the formal economy and had to find alternative means of survival. It thus became necessary for those affected to find an alternative means to survive in the informal economy.

The informal economy has minimal government control in their activities, while workers consist of self- employed firm owners. International Labour Organisation (2007) defines the informal economy or sector as all activities that are not covered by any formal arrangement. It can alsobe refered to as the unregulated, non-formal portion of the market economy that produce goods and services for sale as well as other remunerated services, cutting across the different sectors of the economy. The transportation sector of African societies is also largely controlled by the informal economy. The transport system can be referred to as a service that involves more passenger who are not going to the same destination together and it is always available for use by the public at large.

Though transportation service in all its various forms was handled both by the government and majorly in the informal economy, in recent times the form of transportation in most African societies has changed dramatically (Kumar, 2011). The transportation sector is concerned with the moving of persons and goods from one place to another, thus mobility, in this case, is a product of society which includes the way means of transportation emerge as population and demands increase to make ends meet. In addition, with modernisation, there has been a global change in urban mobility particularly in most African countries (Oyesiku et al., 2020).

The world of transport is changing rapidly because of development globally, as mobility is on the increase, changing how people are moving across villages, towns, and cities and across the globe for various reasons, goods are also being moved all over the world. Transportation tends to build markets, link people and connect local communities to the world; thus, helping foster development (Global Mobility Report, 2022). In most developed counties, more means of road transportation emerge as societies develop. There are trams, buses, trains and in recent times, electronic buses. Developing countries are not left out in the expansion of transportation, because of the pressing needs of the increasing urban passenger, newer forms of transportation such as tricycles and motorcycles in many cities in Africa as an alternative in the means of transport were introduced into the transport sector (The World Bank, 2015).

In addition, various forms of informal, privately-operated public transport such as second-hand minibuses, taxis and most recently, commercial motorcycles took over the roads (Moyo and Olowosegun, 2021). Though most governments put bus companies and trains in place to address mobility, it did not really help. Thus, the informal economy expanded, with newer forms of transportation emerging. Motorcycles came up to replace the unreliable public transport services. They are privately operated by small-scale services and owned by individuals variably referred to as 'para transit' (Nwaogbe et al.,

2013). The informal sector is characterized by little or no government regulations or intervention, whilst the demand and supply forces determine fares and are fixed by the union. It is often gendered and gives room for women to engage in their activities (Peters, 2013).

In Doula, Cameroun, according to Koining (2006), due to the high rate of unemployment and unending transportation problem, a lot of unemployed youths opted to use motorcycles as taxis for business known as the *bend skin* (Wankie, 2021). Public transport in Kampala, Uganda was initially taxis, but this inadequately met the needs and high demands of the people. The increased number of cars on the road and subsequent traffic jams made motorcycles a necessity (Porter, 2014). In Ouagadougou and Bamako, privately owned motorcycles were common in moving peoples from areas of residence to a convenient place where they can get a taxi or bus, however in recent times, motorcycle services have taken over the nooks and crannies of most areas.

In Nigeria, *Okada,* and the three-wheelers or *keke napep* as it is popularly referred to, are the main mode of transportation and the most common form of informal transport system in all areas except where they are banned by authorities (Ojukwu et al., 2020). These means of transportation gained relevance in the societies and are used by different categories of passengers especially when they are in a hurry to avoid delay because of hold up, or when they need to, they can maneuver inaccessible routes and their ways in between cars since they are able to negotiate roads that are unreachable for vehicles. As a result of unemployment, the transportation business now does have more women navigating a profession which was initially male-dominated, unlike in the public transport sector where the male dominated in this sector, the profession is now gendered. This leads us to the discourse on gender roles in the transportation services of three-wheelers in Nigeria and *boda boda* in Kenya.

3 Gender Roles in the Transportation Services

Scholars such as Evans (2015) also observed that some occupations are becoming less segregated by sex as collaborated by labour market data. For instance, in copper belt, there has been an increase in the percentage of women over men who are employed in both professional and technical occupations over the years in Zambia. To Barnet and Hyde (2001), women's labour force participation has also been observed to be on the increase since World War II in different professions. Gran (2017) posits that globally, women dominate some professions such as the agricultural labour force. In African societies, the majority of the agricultural products come from small farmers, most of whom are women. This is also the case in other professions always tagged as a male domain, which include (among others) engineering, consultancy, and construction. Men and women in most Nigerian societies do engage in both formal and informal economic activities, but more women are found in the informal labour force.

The conveyance of humans and goods from one place to another according to Lei et al. (2019), has been an indispensable activity and it is as old as the history of mankind (Ademiluyi and Solanke, 1989). Transportation systems of all kinds have played and are still playing very important roles in moving people and goods around towns and cities all over the world (Oyesiku, 2016). However, despite all means of movement, the problem is still how to move the many people around. The emergence of motorcycle mode as urban public transportation is occasioned by the rapid population growth with rapidly expanding cities, astronomical increase in the price of vehicles, and rapid disappearance of public vehicles from urban roads among other factors, all representing a phase in addressing the needs of those living in urban areas. Urban residents have been utilizing buses, taxis and motorcycles, buses, and taxis for moving around. Due to the increase over time of the population in Nigeria and Kenya, these means of transportation has not been able to serve the teeming population. This has led to the emergence of another means of transportation called tricycle. A tricycle as would be further described is a three-wheeler which like other means of transportation are being driven mostly by men (Oyesiku, 2016).

Women have been involved in this new means of transportation as commercial drivers unlike other means, which are mainly driven by the men folks (Rise Notes, 2017). Walsh (2007) in her study explained that the transportation profession is now expanding such that more women are seen to participate actively in this terrain that is traditionally dominated by men in both developed and developing societies. She further explained that this was not the case in time past as there were female workers in the transportation services. However, recently, numerous opportunities for women to engage in the labour force, has in a way made them expand their frontiers to being drivers of buses, managers of trains as well as pilots and three-wheeler drivers and motorcycles (Kaisen, 2019).

4 Contextualising Women in Three-Wheeler and *Boda Boda* as a New Mode of Transportation in Nigeria and Kenya

Transportation services were operated by both the government and the informal economy actors. The government oversaw the rail transport, airlines, as well as buses. However, with economic recession where most of the government or public owned enterprises were closing, a lot of workers were laid off, which also resulted in increase in unemployment. In addition, many of the government services were privatized such that the government lost total ownership and control over its coordination and revenue, such vehicles included buses and trains. In Ibadan at that time, we had the Trans City Transport Corporation (TCTC). By this, the Informal Public Transport (IPT), comprising of privately owned and operated vehicles came to stay (Cervero, 2006).

The tricycle, also referred to as three-wheeler, is a new means of transportation in Nigeria (Ipingbemi and Adebayo, 2016). It was introduced into the transportation service in 1996 by a former military administrator in Lagos State, Buba Maruwa. The tricycle was at that time named after him as *keke Maruwa.* This tricycle became more popular in 2001 during the Olusegun Obasanjo administration when the federal government replaced the Poverty Alleviation programme (PAP) with the National Poverty Eradication Programme (NAPEP) (IMF, 2019). This programme is a government agency that oversees the activities of the different institutions in charge of poverty reduction. With NAPEP, tricycles were distributed to unemployed youths all over the nation, thus the name *Keke Napep* emerged (Nwanne, 2016).

Though there are diverse brands of tricycle (Keke Napep) in Nigeria, however, TVS and Bajaj are the popular brands mostly because TVS dealers offers the drivers free servicing, free engine oil and oil filter (Abichuela, 2016). The commercial drivers interviewed revealed that this brand of tricycle is user-friendly and fuel efficient. It is also important to state that initially it was an all-male affair in the owning and driving of the three-wheelers, but about five years ago, women decided to venture into this male-dominated transport business for so many reasons that will be revealed in the findings.

5 Historicizing *Boda Boda* in Kenya along Gender Lines

Motorcycles as a means of transporting persons and goods play a major role in Kenya today. This means of transportation emerged as a substitute mode of transport, and are many in rural and semi urban areas, these are areas highly populated by the low- and middle-income earners. It also serves other persons living or working in areas where other means of transportation are not readily available. It is a fast means of moving people around and can get to areas that are not easily accessible.

Motorcycle transport services in Kenya emerged from Uganda in the 1960s as *boda boda.* It originated from the cross-border trade and other activities at the border region of Uganda. The initial means of moving people and goods about in Uganda was the bicycles initially used as a means of movement especially in lowlands as a taxi service hired to move persons and goods from the border situated in Eastern Uganda, precisely Busia country of Tororo district to their destinations (Mutiso and Behrens, 2011). The bicycles have cushions fixed on the rear seat to make it convenient for passengers to sit. It is pertinent to note that these bicycles were overtaken by light motorcycle services in the 1990s. Motorcycles thronged Kenyan's roads extending over both the cities and villages (Duchene, 2011). The *boda boda* business took root in this country in a significant manner. This is the case as motorcycles became readily affordable for all.

This mode of transportation became popular after the duty levied on imported motorcycles below 250cc was legalized to create employment for young people (Nyachieu, 2013). This is because of many factors including the failing or failed public transport system, poor road network, as well as rapid urbanization (Uteng, 2011). This gave way to a sort of increase in the demand for more transport systems, thus expanding the use of various modes of transport. Interestingly, after the tax waiver, these *boda boda* expanded to both urban and rural areas, Kisumu, a town in the Western region of Kenya environ, well known for its long history and overwhelming number of *boda boda* motorcycles.

In Kenya, the *boda boda* bicycle and motorcycle taxi, which provide a lease type of transport services for passengers and goods, serve as noticeable temporary business activity especially for accessing work activities. Kenya experienced immense growth in the transport sector as regards to the *boda boda* which there is a record increase from 37,599 to 140,215 annual registrations between 2005 and 2011 with the youths dominating the industry because of unemployment (Nyachieu, 2013), and have been increasing over the years and the industry expanding. This is mainly because it is the most affordable and convenient (Kumar and Barrett, 2008).

There are different forms of motorcycle found in the different counties in Kenya. These are: the Open motorcycle, a motorcycle that is still in its original form and has not been modified, thus come in the original state; the second is the covered motorcycle, which is a modified state as it is covered with an umbrella; the third is the trailer motorcycle, which comes with three wheels, and finally the passenger motorcycle, this also has three wheels and popularly referred to as *tuks-tuks*.

6 The Place of Women in the *Boda Boda* Business

The *boda boda* space is also male dominated with very few women participating in the transport activities. Women in Kenya have very minimal access and courage to participate or engage in the transportation sector. This is informed by the norms and beliefs of the different culture or ethnic groups in this country (Uteng, 2011). The structure of most African societies is patriarchal in nature, that is, male-centered, male-oriented and male-dominated in nature, therefore certain gender roles or profession are for men probably because of its nature and risks involved. Women are therefore mostly discriminated against when it comes to participating at any level in the transport services, although they contribute to transforming mobility.

7 Methodology

The ethnographic and descriptive research designs were adopted in the study, while the qualitative method of data collection was adopted, utilising In-depth and Key informant interviews techniques to elicit information on the subject matter. In-depth interviews were conducted with ten female and six male *Keke Napep* drivers from Ibadan, Nigeria, six females and four males in Kenya, based on their full participation in the *keke napep* and *boda boda* businesses respectively. Key informant interviews were conducted with three male and female executives each in the *keke napep* transport services. Respondents were purposively selected from Ojoo, Mokola and gate in Ibadan, Nigeria and Nyandarua, Kisimu, Laikipia counties in Kenya because these are places where more women participating in the selected transport services are found. In addition, non-participant observation also formed the basis of data collection, the researchers on many occasions took a ride as a passenger to make observations.

8 Major Findings

Findings from this study are discussed in line with the set-out objectives of the study.

8.1 *Why Women Venture into Three-Wheeler Transport Business in Nigeria*

According to the female three-wheeler drivers, most of them ventured into the three-wheeler transport business for various reasons. These include, among others, because of the death of their spouse who happened to be the breadwinner of the family, unemployment which has made it difficult to make ends meet, and the need to be gainfully employed to support both immediate and extended families. Those whose spouses are of late find it difficult to cope with the various burdens of a provider especially where there is no assistance from the husband's family. Paying for children's school fees, food, clothing, and offsetting house rent bills becomes difficult. Another important reason why women venture into the three-wheeler business is bankruptcy, as some of them started businesses and ran into financial crisis due to inability to recover money owed them by their customers.

The economic situation in Nigeria is unstable such that only a minimal number of people get appointment in the formal economy. The government can no longer provide employment for the teeming graduates being turned out every year by various higher institutions in the country. Hence, we even have graduates venturing into various transport business in Nigeria, from being in motorcycle business to taxi driving business, Bolt and even three-wheeler transport business. Some of these female three-wheeler drivers are single parents who must be both father and mother to their children. In Nigeria, there is no welfare package for children, so such women are the sole provider for their children. The responsibility of paying school fees, clothing, feeding and even paying house rents lies solely on them.

8.2 *Various Challenges Encountered in the Three-Wheeler Transport Business*

Findings showed that there are bound to be diverse challenges in this three-wheeler business because it is a male-dominated business. Nigeria, being a patriarchal society where males are used to dominating, women have to negotiate to overcome the various challenges that may come their way. According to a female three-wheeler driver at Bus Stop Gate area of Ibadan, which happened to be one of their joints, the female three-wheeler drivers have been experiencing untold oppression from the male three-wheeler executives and the National Union of Road Transport workers (NURTW) executives. According to her, these executives extort money from the women drivers at every point, which means a female three-wheeler driver pays seven hundred naira (₦700.00) to these male executives everyday apart from the union dues, which the women found to be too much.

In addition, the females experience unending obstacles from these male executives who are also in the business. These men prevent the female drivers from having their own union because they would not want them to be independent of the men. Also, since they are mostly financially independent, which has been a major challenge. Most women drivers cannot afford to purchase a three-wheeler which costs between nine hundred thousand to a million naira (₦900,000.00–1 million).

According to an interviewee, who is a single mother and a graduate,

> all efforts made by the manufacturers of the TVS brand of the three-wheeler) to link the women with a particular micro finance bank to give financial aid to the women in form of loans were thwarted by the male executives of the road transport and that of three-wheeler who wanted the women to buy the three-wheeler directly from them.

She further explained that:

> This is the reason why most female three-wheeler drivers obtain them on hire purchase, which expects the women to turn in eighteen thousand naira (₦18, 000.00) per week to the owner of the three-wheeler as delivery money. If they can turn in the amount (₦18, 000.00) faithfully every week by one year four months they would have completed the payment and the three-wheeler becomes theirs. But most of them find it difficult to meet up with the payment due to the various ways the male executives' unions extort money from them.

8.3 *Risks on the Job*

Though there is no profession without its own challenges, the different professions do have peculiar challenges because of the structure and nature of the profession. Major themes that emerged from the findings in Nigeria are issues of harassment. There has not been any report of sexual harassment among the female commercial three-wheeler drivers in Ibadan Oyo State Nigeria. But a different form of harassment was reported by the women.

According to her:

> One of them was severely beaten at Oje bus stop in Ibadan Oyo State, by a tout who demanded money from her, the tout was eventually apprehended and taken to police custody.

This kind of incident is bound to happen, especially when the male gender feels threatened that the females are making it in this form of profession mostly believed to be male-dominated.

Another female commercial driver reported that her three- wheeler was vandalized and the wind shield broken by a commercial motor cyclist. These commercial motor cyclists see the female three-wheeler drivers as threats and rivals because they are so many now and their presence affects their business.

One female three-wheeler said these commercial cyclists asked them to back off because commercial transportation is not for females. This incident happened at Ogunpa in Ibadan Oyo State. The commercial motorcyclists can carry only one passenger, while a three-wheeler can carry up to four passengers, so in every bus stop, a three-wheeler has the upper hand in picking passengers than a motorcycle. And because women are weaker and vulnerable, they are easy prey for these commercial motorcyclists. The female three-wheeler drivers also experience harassment from female policewomen who used the opportunity of being in the force to extort women by demanding for money from them at every bus stop.

Despite these challenges, the women are not ready to give up this profession. They have been able to, with patience, negotiate with these male commercial motorcycle riders because they see the three-wheeler transportation as very lucrative. Several suggestions have been made to encourage more women to participate in the transport business. This study suggests that government should put an end to gender inequality as this will curb the excessive use of power by the union executives oppressing the female tricycle drivers and make provision for government loans available to women, so that they will be able to purchase the tricycle directly rather than obtaining it through hire purchase.

8.4 *Why* Boda Boda *Business? and Experiences Shared*

The women are discriminated against, but most of the women in the business are determined because they joined to make a living, and to break through the sexist barrier under the pretense of norms by engaging in the profession. This is peculiar with women in Laikipia and Nyandarua counties, located in central Kenya. The motorcycles are readily affordable, and the mode of payment is also gender friendly.

One of the interviewees, who is 28 years, has been in the business for over six years, she joined the profession in 2014, and at that time there was only one woman from her county, Laikipia, in the business. She had to go into that profession because, being a single mother with three children, it was not easy to make ends meet and fend for her children with the little job she was engaged in. The driving force that pushed her to engage in this profession was because the manual job she was doing did not bring food to the table for herself and children. She must work to educate her children and meet other needs. She was determined to navigate into this space because she is of the opinion that there is no work for a specific gender. Though she faces a lot of discrimination because of prejudice and bias on her gender, this has motivated her to move on. These findings can be alluded to that of Duchene (2011) and Peters (2013) who were of the view that the norms of the society tend to limit women' s access to the transport business.

She further explained that there was discouragement on all fronts both from men and women. The women folk saw her doing something seen as a taboo, they looked down at her and said bad things about her, but this kept her determined. The men on the other hand did not have enough confidence on her ability to ride, they declined riding with her.

Another female driver who is a bit older in age (35 years) is a university graduate of four years without a formal job (B.Sc. Geography), in Kisumu, had to opt for this profession because of problems in her marriage which resulted in her husband abandoning her for other women, leaving her with her ailing mother and two children to take care of. When no formal job was forthcoming, she had to take up something. She has been in the *boda boda* business for 7 years and she can say she is successful because she now owns three other *boda boda*. The major challenge she faced over the years is that at times her passengers do run off without paying.

Many women faced discouragement from fellow women who see them to be wayward for venturing into a profession the society perceive to be a male one. They address them as not being submissive to the expected roles the society has assigned them. The older women also warn them to desist from the profession as it might cause infertility.

In addition, most of them mentioned the problem of multi-tasking, as it is difficult balancing expected family roles with the tedious and demanding nature of the profession. As a result, at times, they miss the early morning rush to enable them to take care of the children and their husbands before they set out to school and work respectively. They will also have to tidy the house and prepare food for the family to get something to eat when back before they can eventually set out for the day, and by this time the rush hour would be over. Also, later in the evening when workers are rushing back home, they have to be at home for the children. Those with husbands alluded to the fact that their husbands will not allow them to work late. As a result, the men in this same profession do not have spouses restricting them from working so they work full time and most times overtime as well.

One of the interviewees, who is a married woman, expressed her experience with her husband. According to her:

> The major problem is my husband, he is always picking up quarrels with me, accusing me that I am going out with other men, at times it leads to him beating me that I feel pains on my body the following day that I may not be able to work for days.

8.5 *Challenges*

The major challenge mentioned by the Kenyan interviewees is that of sexual harassment. According to the 28-year-old interviewee:

> Male customers see me as prostitute, probably because I am very young. Some of them touch my breast or squeeze my buttocks when on the highway. For safety's sake, I will just not complain since I know that the passenger will soon alight. This is not because I am enjoying it, but it is very risky to stop abruptly on the highway as it might lead to accident.

Women, because of the biological appearance as well as the way the society perceive them as a sex object, are the most vulnerable in the society. This finding correlates with the view of Ceccato (2017) who expressly argued that the female sex are victims of all kinds when in transit either as the riders or drivers because of their biological make up.

Others mentioned the fact that some male and even female passengers do not pay as they just get down and leave without paying and when I demand for my money, they shout at me that

> how dare I venture into a male profession

Another major challenge is the high rate of accidents especially with male motorbike riders. This is mainly because these men drink a lot of alcohol and at times they drive at very high speed. Though it is very rare that women get involved in accidents because we are very careful, at times the men due to their reckless driving tend to hit us. Wankie et al. (2021) also reported similar case in a study carried out in Bamenda, Cameroun. In this study, they highlighted causes of crashes on the road by motorbikes. One major cause identified is the influence of alcohol.

In addition, some males do not have confidence in them when driving: "… they are full of complaints and shouting that I must not fall them down. Some would out rightly decline that I should go, that they are waiting for a more mature male driver to pick them up."

9 Conclusion

In conclusion, findings from the study have shown that the transporting services, which is a means of moving people and goods in South-Western Nigeria and in the selected counties in Kenya, is a male-dominated space when it comes to practicing the profession where men see the women as not capable of maneuvering their ways into this profession. Though women are involved in these means of transportation they are nonetheless perceived to be too strong for their liking. This is an eye opener for other women to engage in the driving profession since the formal economy cannot provide employment for those that need it.

Bibliography

Abichuela M.V. 2016. "Motorized Tricycle Transportation Business Caranduanes" *International Journal of recent Research in commerce Economics and Management* (IJRRCEM) 3(4):132–136.

Ademiluyi, I., and Solanke, M., 1989. Problems and challenges of motorcycle mode of urban public passenger transport in Nigeria: www.globaacademicgroup.com.in.

Barnet R.C. and Hyde J.S. 2001 "Women, men, work and family and expansionist theory" *The American Psychologist.* October 56 (10): 781–796. Doi: 10,1037//000066x.56.10.781.

Becker, H., Becker, F., Abe, R., Bekhor, S., Belgiawan, P. F., Compostella, J., and Hensher, D. A. (2020). Impact of vehicle automation and electric propulsion on production costs for mobility services worldwide. *Transportation Research Part A: Policy and Practice,* 138, 105–126. https://doi.org/10.1016/j.tra.2020.04.021.

Cervero, R. 2006. Informal Transport in the Developing World. Nairobi: Habitat.

Duchene, C. (2011).' Gender and Transport'. *International Transport Forum Discussion Papers* 11 April DOI: 10.1787/2223439X.

Evans, A., 2015 'Women Can Do What Men Can Do. The Causes and Consequences of Growing Flexibility in Gender Divisions of Labour in Kitwe, Zambia.' *Journal of Southern African Studies* 40(5):981–998.

Gillis, M., and Jacobs, A., 2017. Introduction to Women and Gender Studies: An Interdisciplinary Approach. Oxford: Oxford University Press.

Global Mobility Report, 2022. Tracking Sector Performance. Washington DC, License: Creative Commons Attribution CC BY 3.0.

Godfrey, J., and Bertini, R., 2019. "Attracting and Retaining Women in the Transportation Industry" *Mineta Transportation Institute Publications.*

Gran, 2017 'The role of women in the work force. The Open University, globalvolunteers .org.

International Labour Office, 2007. The Informal Economy. *Committee on Employment and Social Policy,* ILO, Geneva.

International Monetary Fund, 2019. 'IMF 2019 Article IV Report for Nigeria. Selected issues 'IMF' *Country Report* 19/93 Washington DC.

Ipingbemi O. and Adebayo A. 2016. "Tricycle as a mode of public transportation in Ibadan metropolis. Nigeria. *Ife Research Publications in Geography* Vol. 14, 2016.

Kiasen, S., 2019. 'What explains uneven female labour participation levels and trends in developing countries? *World Bank Research Observer* 34(2): 161–197.

Koning, P., 2006. 'Solving transportation problems in African cities: Innovative responses by the youth in Douala, Cameroon'. *Africa Today*, 53: 35–50.

Krukru, 2016. Public Enterprises in Nigeria. A Critical Evaluation of the Performance. Term Paper. Grin Verlag.

Kumar, A., 2011. Understanding the role of Motor Cycles in African cities. A Political Economy perspective. Washington DC World Bank.

Kumar, A., and Barrett, F., 2008. Stuck in traffic: Urban transport in Africa. African Infrastructure Country Diagnostic Washington, D.C., *The World Bank, AICD, Background Paper.*

Lei, L. S. Desai and R. van Neman. 2019. 'The impact of transportation infrastructure in women's employment in India'. *Feminist Economics* 25(4):96–125.

Loorbach, D., Schwaren, T., Doody, B., Arnfalk, P., Langeland, O., and Farstad, B., 2021. Transition Governance for Just, Sustainable Urban Mobility: An Experiential Approach from Rotterdam, the Netherlands. *Journal of Urban Mobility*, 1 2021(10009).

Miskolczi, M., Foldes, D., Munkacsy, A., and Jaszberenyi, M., 2021 'Urban Mobility Scenarios until the 2030s' *Sustainable Cities and Society* 72:1–11 https://doi.org/10.1016/j.scs.2021.103029.

Moyo, D., and Olowosegun, A., 2021 Resilience of Informal Public Transport and Urban Land Governance in Ibadan in R. Home (Ed.) Land Issues for Urban Governance in Sub- Saharan Africa. Springer.

Mutiso, W. and Behrens, R. 2011. "Boda Boda" Bicycle Taxis and Their Role in Urban Transport Systems: Case Studies of Kisumu and Nakura Kenya. http://repository.up.ac.za/handle/2263/17308.

Nwanne, C., 2016.' Keke Economy dwindles as Mini Bus riles' *The Guardian Sunday Magazine*, 17 January.

Nwaogbe, O., Ibe, C., and Ukaegbu, S., 2013. Quality of the pan transit service (tricycle) and its operations in Aba, Nigeria: An analysis of customers' opinions. *Journal of Transport and Supply Chain Management* 2(2): 262–276.

Nyachieu, M. 2013. 'Creating Employment through Transport, the Youth and Motorcycle (Boda-Boda) in Kitengala, Kajiado County, Kenya.' *Organizational Psychology and Educational Studies* 2(4): 154–157.

Ojukwu, C., Okemuo, A., Madu, C., Caesar, C and Moris, A. 2020. 'Pulmonary functions of commercial tricyclists Keke Napep riders in Enugu state'. *African Health Science*, 20(2):798–805. June.

Oyesiku, O., Somuyiwa, A., and Oduwole, A., 2020 Analysis of Transport and Logistics Education Regulations and Economic Development. *Transportation Research Procedia* 48 (1):2462–2487.

Oyesiku, O.K., 2016.' Analysis of mobility patterns and challenges of transportation needs of the elderly in a fast-growing city in Nigeria' *Advances in Social Sciences Research Journal*, 3(1):141–151.

Peters, D., (2013). Gender and Sustainable Urban Mobility. Nairobi: Global Report on Human Settlements. https://unhabitat.org/wpcontent/uploads/2013/06/GRHS.2013 .ThematiC.

Porter, G. (2014) Transport Services and Their Impact on Poverty and Growth in Rural Sub-Saharan Africa: A Review of Recent Research and Future Research Needs. *Transport Reviews*, 34:1, 25–45, DOI: 10.1080/01441647.2013.865148.

Rise Notes, 2012–2017. The Role of Women in National Development. https:/www.risenotes.cpom.Essays.

The World Bank. 2015. Understanding Poverty Transport brief urban transport. The World Bank.

Tonuchi, J., Peters, I.,Olofunso, A., and Mimiko, O. 2020. How large is the size of Nigeria's Informal Economy? A mimic Approach. *International Journal of Economics, Commerce and Management* 8 (7): 204–228.

Uteng, T., 2011. Gender and Mobility in the Developing World. Washington, D.C.: World Bank.

Walsh, M., 2007 'Gender in the history of transportation services: A historiographical perspective '*Business History Review* 81, 545–562.

Wankie, C., AL- Delaimy, W., Stockman, J., Shaffer, R., and Hill, L., 2021. Prevalence of Crashes and associated factors among Commercial Motorcycle Riders in Bamenda, Cameroon.*Journal of Transport and Health* 20:0 March. Elsevier.

CHAPTER 2

Female Commercial Three-Wheel Tricycle (*Kèké Marwa*) Riders in the Ibadan Metropolis, Nigeria

Dauda Aderemi Busari

1 Introduction

Women's advancement and progression in career trajectory are often limited by a deliberate imposition of formal exclusion, the creation of informal barriers, glass ceilings, and discrimination practices, especially in patriarchy-dominated continents like Africa. This trend, however, seems to be giving way to a situation where the narrative about women and their involvement in the context of organizations and creating a culture of inclusion in specific roles hitherto dominated by men is changing. For example, the public transportation sector globally has been acknowledged to be traditionally dominated by men, even though women are the largest users of public transport as evident in the case of a three-wheel tricycle popularly known as *Keke Marwa* in Nigeria (Turnbull, 2013). Many scholarly works have also argued that the transport sector is controlled, upheld, and sustained by perhaps men since it is a vocation considered to be physically draining (see for example Jandeska and Kraimer, 2005) thus making it a 'no-go area' for women.

However, in what can be described as a shift in the paradigm, a surge in the number of women who are participating in the transport sector has seen a radical departure in a sector that is seemingly keen on meeting up with gender diversity and inclusiveness in all sectors of the economy as pronounced by the Sustainable Development Goals (SDG). According to ILO (2019b), only 20% of females are represented in the global transport workforce, information that was substantiated by Harvard Business Review, which argued that despite the 20% female engineering graduates, only 40% of them find their way into the transport profession as many of them quit due to numerous challenges thus, making the industry a male-dominated profession. Similarly, there are different modes of transportation ranging from road transport, rail transport, sea transport, and air transport but, it is not surprising to see gender discrepancies in the transport sector as women represent a small portion of the public transport operators which is contingent on the stereotypical mobility culture that has existed for decades which states that, 'the wheels belong to men' (Turnbull,

 | DOI:10.1163/9789004692657_004

2013). However, the purchasing power of many households dwindling, and the capacity to purchase daily and essential goods becoming difficult, leading to the loss in value of family income and stagnated remunerations due to an increase in inflation and poverty especially among the middle and low-income earners, many families are devising alternative source of income for sustenance and dependence.

Rapid urbanization in Africa has increased the mobility needs of the people, which the state constantly fails to meet due to poor planning. And oftentimes women are underrepresented in the transportation sector, due to their low economic status, which restricts them from far-distance travel, unlike men. Their economic empowerment and contribution are always undermined particularly in the discourse of development in the society. However, literature on mobility needs has argued that there is an infiltration of women into traditionally male-dominated occupations recently. Gender mainstreaming has become necessary for the success of public transportation in every human society. Decades ago, despite women's effective contribution in another aspect of life, the commercial transportation business was solely reserved for men but more recently, such narrative has begun to change around the world as the transport sector is experiencing a rapid increase in female operators. Although, many of these women have complained about the issue of safety, violence, and abuse against women in transit, and sexual harassment among others the advocacy for women's inclusion in the industry to ensure their experiences are properly catered for, especially at the decision-making table. However, aside from the issue of safety and the like, a major factor that necessitated women's infiltration into the transport sector is the poor economy.

In Nigeria, women are typically seen in a subservient and subordinated position economically, politically, socially, and culturally. Their increased economic participation is confined to the buying and selling of goods. In the workforce, women are seen in semi-skilled and unskilled low-paying and less strength demanding jobs. The Gender Gap Report (2012) argued there is persistent marginalization of women in every sector of Nigeria which has a dangerous consequence for her economy. Despite occupying about 48% of the country's population, women are less empowered compared to their male counterparts in all works of life including the transportation sector (AFDB, 2015). Gender stereotyping has been a major factor of gender inequality, particularly in the transport sector as it creates a negative consequence for women by questioning their ability to penetrate male-dominated jobs or navigate their way to leadership positions (Heilman and Parks-Stamm, 2007). Nevertheless, despite the increased marginalization being experienced in the workforce and cultural perception of women as weaker vessels even in the transport sector, some women have dared the long-standing traditional work perception. The advent of globalization and urbanization around the world has compelled changing patterns particularly in cultural norms in different households across the globe as women began to take up responsibilities that were initially reserved for men due to men's constant loss of jobs and inability to fend for the family. The transformations that followed globalization and urbanization challenged cultural norms which made women poor and illuminated the importance of women's participation in the political and economic sphere.

Considering the inflation in Nigeria caused by the economic downturn and the aftermath of the COVID-19 pandemic; families are faced with various financial difficulties as men who were the breadwinners constantly lose their jobs thus, relinquishing the breadwinning duty to the women whose income could barely feed themselves (Hallmark news, 2019). According to Business Hallmark (2019), women took up the Keke Marwa business against all odds as a means of survival through harsh economic conditions. Considering the population surge due to urbanization in different parts of the world, accidents caused by motorcycles, and endless waits for buses or cars among others; tricycles became a necessary evil to help drive the mobility of the enormous population in most urban centres (Mukhtar, Waziri, Abudulsalam, and Dankani, 2015; Obioma, Nwaogbe, and Ukaegbu, 2012). Also, the perilous state of the economy has left many unemployed individuals to find solace in the occupation. Rapid urbanization in different parts of the world is accompanied by spiral population growth hence the increasing rate of public transport demand necessitated various modes of the transportation system and transport infrastructures to ease the burden off the citizens. Urbanization remains a significant driver of transformation across the globe in the history of human evolution. The increasing rate of penetrating the cores of human society engendered different challenges that need urgent and proactive attention. Therefore, urban mobility remains a major challenge in the discourse of urbanization in many parts of the world particularly in developing nations, Nigeria inclusive. It is plagued with several challenges such as congestion, accidents, parking space, air pollution, transit crime, and most importantly, a defective development issue (Badejo, 2011) cited in Solanke (2013). However, an attempt to proffer a solution has included the introduction of different modes of transportation such as public mass transit, motorcycles, and then now the famous tricycle popularly called "Keke Marwa" in Nigeria. Keke Marwa became an intersection between four-wheelers ever since its introduction. Though the use of tricycles is not synonymous with Nigeria as a country like India, China, Indonesia, Bangkok, and Bangladesh among others also saw the need to adopt the Keke transport.

Literature has also established that any country attempting development is required to break down barriers limiting the smooth mobility of its citizens. In Nigeria, although, low participation of women in transport is gradually reversing as Nigerian women are confronting the masculinization of vocations in the informal sector of the economy, breaking barriers, and challenging the patriarchal male-ordered domination while recovering space for themselves in vocations conventionally dominated by the men. Women are no longer intimidated by men's physical power or challenged by men's brawns in the informal employment sector. The female Keke Marwa riders are challenging men's dominance in the commercial public transportation space in Nigeria. The status quo that has seen a male-dominated commercial transportation sector has seen men occupy the sector either as trunk drivers, bus drivers, tricyclics, motorcyclists, and tricyclics, etc. In recent times, however, an upsurge of women who are taking on the vocations hitherto subjugated by men. Thus, the assumption that the tricycle vocation (popularly called *Keke Marwa* in local parlance) is restricted only to males is gradually waning with the emergence of many women as operators (riders). Hence, political leaders, public officials, stakeholders, and private sectors must ensure full compliance with the gender equality policy as transportation in any society is linked to economic development. It is against this background that this study examined.

Based on the aforementioned, it is evident that the full participation of both genders in achieving national development cannot be overemphasized. Thus, it is imperative to understand the economic status of Nigerian women within the global context bearing in mind the existing gender gap within the workforce. Historically, women have been overly marginalized when it comes to seeking and tapping into social and economic opportunities in their immediate environment based on several barriers. Affirming this view, Lawal, and Ojo (2006) opined that the social marginalization of women in society has existed for decades because of the patriarchal nature that dominates all spheres of human society. Hence, this patriarchal nature has rived women's liberation across societies thus, leading to advocacy for gender equality at all levels. One of such is the 1985 advocacy known as the Convention on Elimination of all forms of Discrimination against Women (CEDAW) (Agbalajobi and Oluwalogbon, 2019). This convention aimed at fostering equality between both men and women at all levels including social, cultural, economic, and political spheres by ensuring the state prohibits all forms of discrimination (CEDAW, 1985 cited in Agbalajobi and Oluwalogbon, 2019).

2 Three Wheels Tricycle (Keke Marwa) in Nigeria

Keke Marwa became is an intersectional and acceptable alternative mode of transportation in developing countries to help curtail the urban transport challenges posing a threat to the socio-economic development in the society. Keke Marwa as the case may be was adopted as an integral mode of public transportation in different parts of the world and specifically in Nigeria. Keke transportation began in the era of government personnel known as General Buba Marwa (Rtd), a former Lagos state governor between 1996 and 1999 hence its name "Keke Marwa" (Mgbemena, 2013). However, it became prominent nationally due to the National Poverty Eradication Programme (NAPEP) by former President Obasanjo's administration as it was used to empower economically incapacitated citizens and served as a medium of poverty alleviation in the society. The NAPEP poverty alleviation scheme launched and distributed about 2000 tricycles as the commercial mode of transportation to help minimize or eradicate the issue of thugs or area boys while also fulfilling citizens' mobility needs in Nigerian society. Since the inception of Keke Marwa, it has become a dominating mode of transportation in many cities, connecting residents with their daily social and economic activities and most sought after by many road users due to its sense of safety than motorbikes. Aside from its common use in terms of commercial means of mobility, Keke Marwa serves as a political and clientelism tool in Nigeria's political sphere, particularly as a bid to drive economic growth within the context of job creation and poverty alleviation (Mgbemena, 2013). The adoption of Keke Marwa skyrocketed due to government policy to ensure the security of the lives and property of her people. Many governors in major cities where motorbikes were rampant had at one time placed a ban on motorbikes as a commercial means of transportation due to allegations leveled against the operators of collaborating with criminals to perpetrate crimes. Such a policy had a consequence for many Okada riders as many of them became jobless and thus fell into poverty and misery.

The poverty rate in Nigeria is exorbitantly high and politically disconcerting looking at the enormous human and mineral resources that the country possessed. Although, political leaders in different eras (military and democracy) have made poverty eradication a focal policy of their administration based on its crucial component towards achieving sustainable development (Aibieyi and Dirisu, 2010). Thus, the National Poverty Eradication Programme (NAPEP) joined the host of existing poverty eradication programs in Nigeria as a response to the scourge of poverty. The NAPEP has a multi-approach to dealing with poverty that involves the empowerment of the citizens hence the acceptance of Keke's mode of transportation. However, just like most poverty schemes, NAPEP did not live up to expectations as many Nigerians continue to fall into poverty and depression.

3 Method

This study adopted the exploratory cross-sectional research design and was conducted between June 6th and July 30th, 2021, among female three-wheeler tricycle (Keke Marwa) riders in Ibadan North Local Government Area of Oyo State. The Ibadan North Local Government (LGA) was purposively selected because of the high number of women plying different routes with the Keke Marwa in the Local Government. The Ibadan North LGA comprises 12 wards, with a landmass of 420 km2, and a population of 856,988 as of the 2006 Census (oyostate.gov.ng). The local government plays host to the University of Ibadan, and many other key government establishments. The paper employed a qualitative method of inquiry; the approach enabled the comprehension of the experiences of female riders and the other stakeholders in the transport space. Respondents in the study were randomly selected based on availability and their consent to participate in the study. In-din-depth interviews (IDI) were conducted with Keke Marwa riders at Gate, Agbowo, and the University of Ibadan Bus Stops, and Key Informant Interviews (KII) with Park managers at the selected Bus Stops. The data for the study were collected using twelve (18) In-Depth Interviews among female operators (16) and two park Managers', using the purposive and the snowball sampling approaches. Qualitative research data were transcribed and analyzed using NVIVO qualitative software. The NVIVO, a qualitative software tool, enables a systematic approach to the classification of events, objects, places, people, and actions, that share similar discrete groupings (Berg, 2001). The identified respondents were duly informed that participation was voluntary, their willingness to participate in the study was obtained and they were told that the information supplied would be strictly confidential. They were also assured that the findings of the study were used for academic purposes only. Several potential respondents were reluctant to participate in this study. Thus, it must be pointed out that the sample size is not representative of the exact figures of female Keke Marwa riders in the Ibadan North Local Government Area.

3.1 *Socio-Demographics of Respondents*

When the subject matter of the public transportation business in Nigeria is been discussed, men usually come to mind. However, a few women are defying this conventionality to eke out a living in this male-dominated sector. Keke

Marwa business like other means of transportation in Nigeria is coordinated through the activities of a union dominated by men that holds several meetings and involves payment of several levies by the operators in the transport sector to the union. The business requires that any operator in the business must be versed in street smartness and be fierce to stand up to the representative of the union who intimidates or coarse them to pay union dues. This is the main factor why the number of women found in the transportation business is a handful. This study investigates the inroad of female riders in the Keke Marwa business and was conducted in Ibadan North Local Government of Oyo state. Two tricycle parks were purposively selected for the study. These are the University of Ibadan (UI) Park and Agodi Gate Park. The respondents were randomly selected for this study. Most of the respondents in this study are between the ages of 35 and 56 years, with park managers being younger than the female riders. Sixteen of the respondents are married, one is divorced, and

TABLE 2.1 Sociodemographic characteristics of study respondents

S/N	Age	Religion	Educational qualification	Marital status
Female Rider 1	50	Christian	NCE	Married
Female Rider 2	50	Christian	Secondary School Cert.	Married
Female Rider 3	50	Christian	NCE	Married
Female Rider 4	49	Muslim	Pry Six	Married
Female Rider 5	40	Christian	Secondary School Cert.	Married
Female Rider 6	–	Muslim	School Cert.	Married
Female Rider 7	50	Christian	Pry Six	Married
Female Rider 8	37	Christian	NCE	Married
Female Rider 9	56	Muslim	NCE	Married
Female Rider 10	52	Muslim	Secondary School Cert.	Married
Female Rider 11	43	Christian	Secondary School Cert.	Married
Female Rider 12	49	Muslim	Pry Six	Married
Female Rider 13	40	Christian	School Cert.	Married
Female Rider 14	38	Muslim	School Cert.	Separated
Female Rider 15	42	Christian	Pry Six	Married
Female Rider 16	33	Christian	School Cert.	Divorced
Park Manager 1	45	Christian	School Cert.	Married
Park Manager 2	35	Muslim	School Cert.	Married

one is separated. All the respondents were educated with a minimum of a primary six-education level. One of the park managers has a First Degree (B.Sc.).

4 Entry into the Business

The tricycle (Keke Marwa) is an expensive venture. Entry into the business involves ownership of some substantial capital to buy the tricycle aside from learning about the trade by an old hand. Female Keke Marwa riders are thus confronted with the daunting realities that shaped their worldview. Most of the female three-wheeler operators run on the hire-purchase scheme. This means the female riders make weekly or daily 'deliveries' to the owners of the three-wheeler machine. A new tricycle costs about N750,000,00–N850,000 (depending on the brand). Under the hire-purchase system, the female operator is expected to pay N2,500 daily or N20,000 weekly. The riders use the tricycles for a period and then take full possession of the tricycle after all the remittances have been paid to the owner on the terms of the agreement with the supplier. Aside from the cost of the procurement of the tricycle, the operators make payments of between N30,000 and N50,000 as registration fees at the park to the chairman of the route they plied. Daily operators pay N1,600 to the union cover after which they are issued a ticket by the park managers.

> "… to start this business requires a lot of money … the funds are not readily available so most of the time when you want to start the business and you don't have the wherewithal to start, you approach the hire-purchase. Some people borrow money to start a business and return the money every week or daily.
>
> Female rider/53 years/NCE/Married/July 2021

Another female rider has this to say:

> When I started riding on this route, I initially was under someone who guided me on the nitty-gritty of the operations for almost 4 months. Started with short routes and later commenced longer routes with my *oga* and when I wanted to start on my own, I was introduced to the hire-purchase scheme operator whom I am currently paying to weekly.
>
> Female rider/37 years/NCE/Married/June 2021

The Nigerian economic downturn led most of the women into the *Keke Marwa* riding business and many ventured into the business to complement other businesses while some others joined after trying out a few other businesses. Some others have their own business alongside the transport business. One of the women who had become the breadwinner of the family since the demise of her husband explained that she was doing the tricycle business in addition to selling foodstuff. This was to ensure that all the family needs were covered and to pull income from various means. Two of the women stated that they also teach in schools, which is seen as a morning job after which they resume the transport business in the afternoon. Thus, driven by the need to eke out a living and the need to make ends meet, there has been an increase in women/ ladies taking on vocations that are traditionally believed to be in the purview of men's control. Female Keke Marwa riders have in this light discarded the idea of male domination in that sector.

> What is there is that I do teach, so when I close from that place, I have to come and start this one in the afternoon
>
> Female rider/50 years/NCE/Married/July 2021

In the words of another respondent

> So, it was like four years back when I lost my husband and was selling foodstuff. You know I have kids, pay for school fees, pay for house rent, everything you understand, filling in the gas, I realised that I need to look for another thing to join the business.
>
> Female rider/37 years/NCE/Widowed/July 2021

Women joined the transport business for economic reasons to improve the economic situation of their families and to take care of their children's school fees and other miscellaneous expenses at home. To this woman, the business is better than all the ones she has engaged in the past. Not only does it pay her children's school fees, but she is also able to feed and pay her house rent from the proceeds of the business.

> It was when everything was tight, and I saw that I was not earning much from the tailoring business that I decided to take on this job. My boss who is also a female introduced me to it, she taught me the work. Since I joined, I have been able to contribute appreciably to the family income.

> I once paid my children's school fees and often bought and ed food for the household from my profit.
>
> Female rider/40 years/School Certificate. /Married/July 2021

This business is attested to be very lucrative as the women can support family finances, take responsibility for their care and that of their children, and even fund the education of their children as well. As one of the respondents stated, she has through this business been able to successfully train one of her children to the tertiary level.

> We thank God, it helps, at least, my former keke, used it to train two children at the university. One graduated this last year, and it helps.
>
> Female rider/50 years/NCE/Married/July 2021

The lucrative nature of the business has been responsible for the influx of people, male, and female, old and young, to make ends meet and be able to attain financial freedom. Proceeds from the business have been able to help some of them pay off debts and provide for the needs of the family.

> Ahh … , it is supportive because I can't give an account of what the keke is doing. It helps in many ways because if it is not helpful, you will not see people in it. It is helping very well, it is good. Very happy because since I started doing it, I am no longer owing the debt. Before I owed … you will not see me along that road again because nothing to pay. But now, after doing the daily work, I must go to the market and branch to buy whatever I need and pay the remaining money I owe.
>
> Female rider/50 years/NCE/Married/July 2021

However, the women also reported that the transport business is very stressful and requires hard work. But they also recognized the responsibilities required to take care of the family and this keeps them going even when they are tired. One of the respondents stated that working for a full day as a tricycle rider could make her sleep for two full days, but she doesn't have the luxury because the children must be educated and eat, and this requires money.

> They don't know the reason we started this work because it is not female work. Transport work is a hard job, it is not easy at all. As I am, if I lay on the bed, I might sleep continually for two days because I need sleep, but I don't have the time to sleep. It is just based on the hustle to find something to eat. Children are in school, and they will ask for money.
>
> Female rider/49 years/Pry. Six/Married/July 2021

This rider goes on to say, considering the stress of the job reports that there is an exit plan, and she would only go back to it as a part-time job after exiting. While it is a lucrative job, she would prefer to open her shop and buy goods. And so, while still doing this business she is saving up for that plan.

> Ah, I don't like it, o. If I pay up the installment and get enough money to buy my goods, I will go back to the shop. But I might be doing it occasionally, so I won't spend the goods money. So, let's say twice a week, I can do it. I can save with it, then stock the house with food, and then go back to my shop.
>
> Female rider/49 years/Pry. Six/Married/July 2021

Supporting this viewpoint another interviewee stated that the tricycle transport business should only be done for a short time, especially by women. It is, however, a good business for gathering funds to start another business.

> It is very stressful, seriously. It is not an occupation a lady can do for long. One should do it for a little time, achieve, and go back to one's former work … That is what I am saying, it is stressful work, and it is not work you can do for long. It is just for you to start a business.
>
> Female rider/School cert./Married/July 2021

4.1 *Introduction to the Business*

While some were trained by those close to them whom they had relationships with previously, others were able to seize the opportunity of getting connected through someone they know who knows someone who could enable their entry into the business.

> So, where I was living, my landlord's son is a tailor and there is a guy who used to look for a man who would be driving a tricycle. So, one day, I was now wondering can I do this thing? So, I was like let me ask this tailor man, anything that he said, so when I met the man, I explained that this man that used to come to your house, can I talk to him. He said yes and he asked about what. I told him that I was interested in this job, then I asked if I could do it. He said I can try. So, I met the man, I explained to him, and he said nothing bad, I can do it. I was living at Agbowo, so I was the first lady there, people who know me do call me the first lady. So, it was the man who trained me how to drive it so since then, I have managed with it.
>
> Female rider/37 years/NCE/Married/July 2021

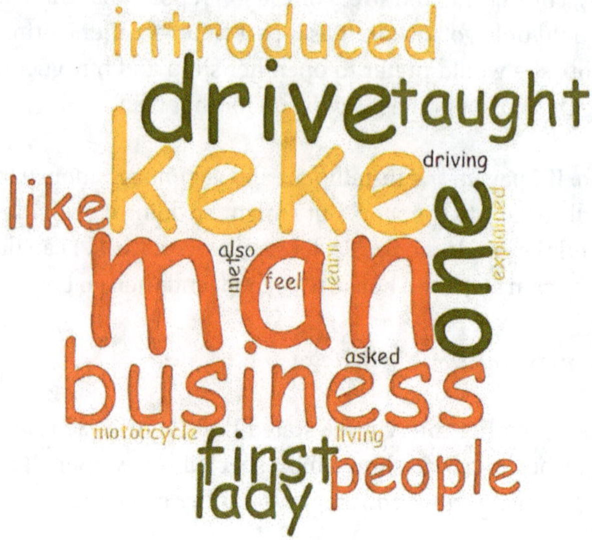

FIGURE 2.1 Word cloud representation of responses on Introduction to *Keke* riding
SOURCE: AUTHOR

Another interviewee, however, attributed her introduction into the business as an inspiration from God. However, they all had to go through the process of learning how to ride the tricycle from someone who had been in the business.

> Nobody introduced me to it, the spirit of God directed me. Since all these businesses have been doing didn't yield positively, what else can I do? The one that I am doing that I was supplying seaman to people to retailers at Ogunpa, then some people were coming from Olodo to sell it to them at a lower price, so they didn't allow me to sell very well, so I had to leave it for them then I went to learn Keke. Ahh, if I didn't learn it, I can't drive it. That was the last business I did before I started driving *Keke*.
>
> Female rider/50 years/School cert./Married/July 2021

The one person who reported not going through the learning process explained that she has previously learned how to ride a motorcycle:

> What happened is that I was riding a motorcycle before, so when I stopped, I opted for *keke*. They taught me how to drive a motorcycle, but no one taught me how to ride a tricycle.
>
> Female rider/50 years/Pry. Six/Married/July 2021

4.2 *Procurement of Tricycle*

Most of the women got their tricycles through instalment payments. At the time of these interviewees, most of them were still paying weekly or monthly to the company that gave it out to them. One of the riders responded that they did not have the capacity to start up the business with their own tricycle, so they had to get it based on instalments.

> Inside this place, there is no capacity to bring our own in until …
>
> Female rider/37 years/NCE/Married/July 2021

One of the women who now rode her own tricycle attested that she got the first one from a company and used to make weekly payments to the company. But after an accident involving the tricycle, she lost the right to it and her husband helped in acquiring a used one for her to continue the business.

> I collected the first one. So, when I collected the first one from our leading company. So, when I got into an accident with it, they collected it from me. So, I stopped doing the work. Because at that time, when I do with their own, I go to deliver, I pay weekly. After I stopped working with them, my husband had to look for money in their meeting to get this fairly used one for me.
>
> Female rider/50 years/NCE/Married/July 2021

Although they had several similarities, the interviewees had different resumption and closing times that they were able to decide based on the peculiarity of other things they had to do and the responsibilities back at home. The start

FIGURE 2.2 Word cloud representation of responses on *Keke* purchase/payment strategy
SOURCE: AUTHOR

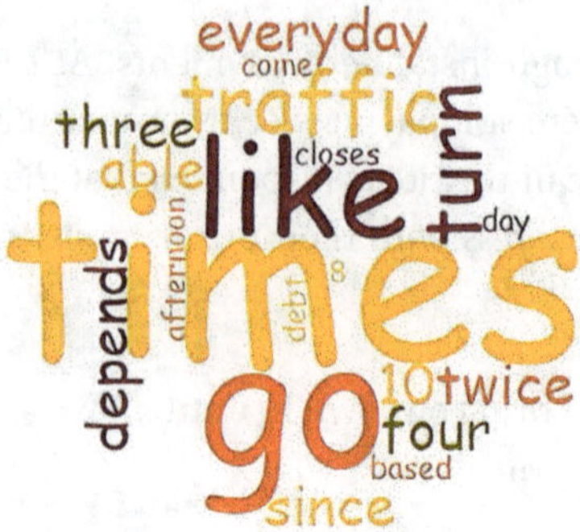

FIGURE 2.3
Word cloud representation of responses on *Keke* operation (1)
SOURCE: AUTHOR

time for most of the respondents was 8:00 am, although one of them resumed as early as 6:30 am as well. They averaged at least 5 to 8 rounds per day. This is determined by the resumption time, and traffic along their routes.

> That is what we are talking about, traffic. We are in the festive period, so we can take turns like that. But, if there is no traffic, at least, I will go five times a day. But, with this traffic, I've not gone for more than twice since morning.
>
> Female rider/49 years/Pry. Six/Married/July 2021

While some would go up to 10 times per day, depending on the day and how quickly they are able to load at each turn, some also go as low as 2 to 3 times a day and go home.

> It is based on turn, once I go like two to three times, that is enough for me. Since I can pay my debt.
>
> Female rider/50 years/Pry. Six/Married/July 2021

By 6:00 pm, female tricycle riders are getting ready to head back home with most of them reporting that they leave the park by 7:00 pm. Workdays for these women also vary based on their responsibilities back at home. While some work from Monday to Sunday, some reported that they don't work on Sundays or start their trips late on Saturday because of the chores they must complete at home.

> I don't have actual time because on Saturdays I must cook and prepare home and put it in order before coming out. For today, if I don't have anywhere to go , I close around six.
>
> Female rider/50 years/NCE/Married/July 2021

FIGURE 2.4
Word cloud representation of responses on *Keke* operation (2)
SOURCE: AUTHOR

FIGURE 2.5
Word cloud representation of responses on business duration
SOURCE: AUTHOR

4.3 *Duration in Business*

The female tricycle drivers interviewed have been in this business for periods ranging from 4 months to 8 years and were introduced to it by various means.

> What happened is that I was riding a motorcycle before, so when I stopped, I opted for keke. They taught me how to drive a motorcycle, but no one taught me how to ride a tricycle.
>
> Female rider/50 years/Pry. Six/Married/July 2021

4.4 *Balancing Home with Business*

From the responses of the interviewees, women with little children would find it difficult to balance business with the care of their young children. But for most of the interviewees, their children were already old enough to take care of themselves.

> When my children are old already, there is no problem. But, if one's child is still very young, there won't be time for such a child especially when you collect installments, ahh it will be difficult because one will have to work 24/7. There is no sitting down.
>
> Female rider/50 years/School cert./Married/July 2021

FIGURE 2.6
Word cloud representation of responses on the home front (1)
SOURCE: AUTHOR

For some of them, their children also provided the comfort of taking up some responsibilities at home like food preparation. This takes off some chores from the women especially when they come back after the day's work.

> My children are grown-ups, so I do not have a problem. If I get home, I will eat *ehn ehn* so, they will cook, and I will eat.
>
> Female rider/50 years/NCE/Married/July 2021

Female riders had various levels of support. One of them said her husband got her a used tricycle, she stated that this is the only support she received from him and thereafter she became responsible for several expenses in the family such as the children's education.

> As my husband has gotten this one for me, he is not supporting me in anything again because he said that since he has given me, he is paying for it. So, I am catering for my children both the ones in school and those in baby classes.
>
> Female rider/50 years/NCE/Married/July 2021

Some women, however, have no support from anyone within their family but must source for help themselves. One of the riders who complained about lack of support explained that because the business meets only daily needs, she risks going hungry if she does not go to work. Some days, she also faces the problem of the tricycle developing funds which requires expenses.

> For me, I don't get any at all. It's just like Jesus left me alone. If I don't work, I won't eat. Most times, when I am too weak, they push my keke for me. When you stay at home for a day, you will be hungry because it is a

FIGURE 2.7
Word cloud representation of responses on the home front (2)
SOURCE: AUTHOR

> daily need. Sometimes, the tire might have a fault, so we'd buy fuel or oil. So, the problem is per day.
>
> Female rider/50 years/Pry. Six/Married/July 2021

4.5 *Challenges Faced in Tricycle Business*

Apart from the challenges of maintaining the tricycle, women also face different challenges while conducting their business. This includes the expectation of park boys to receive payments even after they have gotten the required ticket from the park.

> Ehn, noting much, all those tout boys, collect *owo ita* (daily route dues). They are the only problem we have. Sometimes, they will force you to give them after collecting ticket #200, we will still be sharing #50.
>
> Female rider/50 years/NCE/Married/July 2021

Another interviewee also complained bitterly about the behaviour of policemen who also expect them to hand out money to them along their route. She opined that they should not be required to pay especially because they are women.

> There are lots of challenges we are facing. We are facing the policemen, their problem is too much, especially we women, they are not supposed to be asking for money. They don't know the reason we started this work because it is not female work.
>
> Female rider/49 years/Pry. Six/Married/July 2021

There is also the challenge of being ridiculed by passengers who try to ridicule or insult them while they conduct their business.

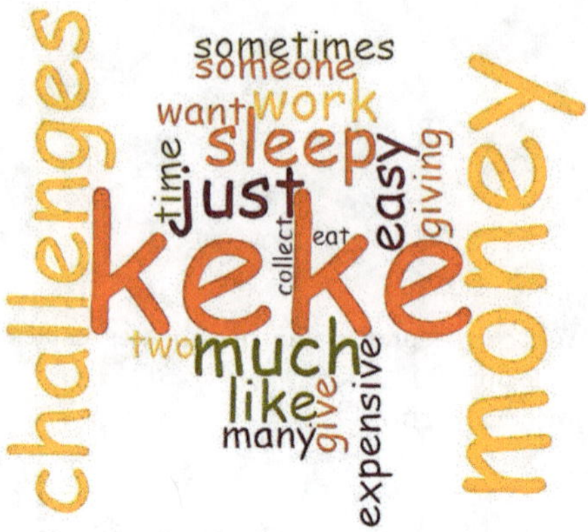

FIGURE 2.8
Word cloud representation of responses on challenges (1)
SOURCE: AUTHOR

> There are so many challenges. Maybe your mate or someone who is not up to your age should take to you with insult. Challenges are just many.
> Female rider/40 years/School cert./Married/July 2021

Yet another aspect of this challenge female riders face is the cost or affordability of the tricycle. The increase in the price of the tricycle and the cost of the parts prolongs the installment payment time. Because they must make the payments, they also must calculate how much is really theirs, and this results in the push to keep going on trips to make substantial gains each day. There is also the issue of the fault the tricycle develops because of its use making it difficult to buy.

> What happened is that Keke is too expensive. The parts are expensive too. They should be giving us 1.3 million or 1.2 million, it is too much. They are selling it for N980,000. it is not compared to when we used to buy it for 430,000 or 500,000. *keke* is expensive to the extent that they deliver money … it is not like we are not earning, but once you collect *keke* now and earn double the money daily, you must divide the money into two and keep it. So that when the *keke* would ask for it. By the time we paid back the money, *keke* would have been giving issues. That is why we can't say we want to buy it. Sometimes, we might not pay the debt finish before we sell it to collect another one. Those are the problems we have on *keke*.
> Female rider/50 years/Pry. Six/Married/July 2021

Sleep deprivation is also another challenge female riders face as they must push ahead to ensure they meet the target and pay back what they owe.

> No challenges except there is no time to, you know we close late in the evening, and we must wake early tomorrow morning. Sometimes sleep may be worrying us, to just go and park somewhere and rest for like 30 minutes, you won't be able to sleep long because of the money you want to make.
>
> Female rider/37 years/NCE/Married/July 2021

Although it is seen as a male-dominated occupation, women have been given room and accepted by their male counterparts in the tricycle business. As some of the interviewees reported, they enjoy support from male riders in different ways. For example, one of the women stated that:

> They are caring and they are cooperative because many times when the Keke breaks down along the roadside, they will have to park their own and come and help us. They are even happy. They are happy that we are doing it. They do respect us.
>
> Female rider/50 years/NCE/Married/July 2021

However, when they meet with male riders from other parks, they might not enjoy the care and acceptance shown by riders from their garage. As this interviewee explains, some set of riders have even been known to be rough drivers and because women are often riding gently, they might have some clashes on the road.

> Our relationship is okay, but we are in the same garage, and we are familiar with one another; we take it easy with ourselves on the road. But those we are not familiar with, those with dreadlocks, those who have injured someone in the keke. Well, it might be because we drive it gently. But they come out from different corners.
>
> Female rider/49 years/Pry. Six/Married/July 2021

The park managers also report the good behavior of most of the female riders and attest to a cordial relationship among all riders irrespective of gender.

> Hmm, the females are doing well, they ride well and there is no difference between them and males riding. They behave the same and they do the same thing with their co-riders. We treat them accordingly. There is no partial
>
> Park Manager/35 years/School cert./Married/July 2021

One of the park managers expressed admiration for women who have come to join their trade. Instead of going into a socially unacceptable business like prostitution. While they might not be quick to grasp how to ride, they usually have the confidence that they can do it. This park manager believes that women coming to join the tricycle business is either due to the husband not having enough, her previous not bringing in enough, or when there is a rift between the woman and her husband.

> You know, may God help us. It can be seen in various ways. First, before you start to ride the *keke*, there is work she was doing. She was not earning much, or she had a misunderstanding with her husband, and she didn't want to be in prostitution, so that is. So, once she sees a female riding *keke*, then she builds her confidence too and she does not want to be lazy or people feel like she is lazy, once you teach her, it might be difficult at first, but she will get used to it. What I see is that female riders, do not have a husband at home, I can't answer. And there are some that their husbands do not have enough, or they have misunderstandings.
>
> Park Manager/35 years/School cert./Married/July 2021

While he doesn't support women doing the business, as the park manager he ensures that they are treated right and gives support to those working in the park especially when they are being held for doing wrong. This is influenced by the perception that these women were making a sacrifice to do business to feed their children. However, the government and lawmakers through their representatives don't show this concern as one of the women had also earlier stated.

FIGURE 2.9
Word cloud representation of responses on challenges (2).
SOURCE: AUTHOR

> I don't support it oo. It can be seen in different ways. If it is to feed her children most of them are adults, we really don't have young ladies. You understand. So, because there is no work, that is it. When they are wrong in this garage, we stay by them till it is settled. No woman is working, and the policemen stop them, I will stay with them once I see them. If it is okay for women to drive *keke*, please leave her and let her go, I will beg. But, our government or lawmakers, when they see them do the wrong things, will ask them to park. You know, after seeing that they are women, instead of pitying her, they will make things difficult.
>
> Park Manager/35 years/School cert./Married/July 2021

5 Conclusion

Discourse along gender-related issues has assumed an important place in the work environment, globally. Gender, which explains the social, economic, and cultural factors associated with being a male or a female (Suda, 2002; Aina, 2012 and Boyi, 2013) is an important determinant of the divergent responsibilities at workplaces (Lawanson, 2003; UN-Habitat, 2003 and Aina, 2012) including informal the road transport sector. Gender is not entirely restricted to being male or female; it energises the relationships between them through the evaluation of roles and or responsibilities (Akindele, 2002). However, being a male or a female has become an essential social characterization of inequality (Akindele, 2002).

Public transportation in Nigeria and elsewhere is a male-dominated sector and the three -wheel tricycle popularly known as Keke Marwa is not left out. Like other modes of transportation, the sector is coordinated through a union and engages in nocturnal meetings, and involves payment of levies to the union officials and the local authorities. Initially, an all-male affair, Nigerian women faced with the reality of downtown in the economy have since joined in the Keke business to eke out a living for themselves and their families. The Nigeria economy like its global counterpart jotted by the novel COVID-19 pandemic has been plunged into a crisis and citizen's purchasing power has taken a massive decline, with an increase in food prices, inflation, and a rise in the unemployment rate. The World Poverty Clock (2021) has estimated that about forty-three (43%) of Nigeria's approximately 210 million people are living below the poverty line. In a bid to curtail the rising poverty, unemployment, and inflation the tricycle popularly called Keke Marwa has filled a huge gap in Nigeria's transport sector. The three-wheeler tricycles (Keke Marwa), popular in India and many Southeast Asian countries, as a method of transportation, were first introduced to the Lagos State populace by the former military administrator of Lagos State, Brigadier-General Buba Marwa. At the time of its introduction in Lagos, it was known as Keke Marwa.

The vocation of riding Keke Marwa for a living by female riders is a worthy endeavor but the challenges associated with the task can be daunting. Aside from having the responsibilities to convince family members and have the profitability of the venture they also must contend with the associated risks involved in the trade. Society has already assumed that the road transportation sector is for touts and never does well. Battling the challenges at the home front, especially in a patriarchic society can be demanding for the female riders' husband may go against his wife's involvement in such a trade because of the degrading insults that may be hauled at him by friends and relatives as one who Is not capable of taking care of his wife. Though many of the female Keke Marwa riders seem to be enjoying the support of friends and family, they are still contending with harassment from co-women who jeer and sneer at them. The perception of these women is that the female tricycle riders are touts who engage in illicit affairs, smoke, and drink like the male riders. The female Keke Marwa riders are also not exempted from harassment by men of the Nigeria Police Force, and transport union officials, as being a lady does not confer any benefit or privileges on the female riders.

The introduction of the three -wheel tricycles as a means of transportation has become an important means of alleviating poverty in Nigeria. The women who are involved in the trade have been supportive of their families from the proceeds of their vocation. Many of them have taken over the headship of their various households by contributing to the running of the home. The physical demand of the job notwithstanding, female Keke Marwa riders' involvement has demonstrated that a woman can fit into any male role if given the opportunity.

References

AFDB, 2015. Transport sector and economic governance reform program. Retrieved from http://www.afdb.org/en/projects-and-operations/.

Agbalajobi D.T. and Oluwalogbon L.A. (2019). "The Nigerian senate and the politics of non-passage of the gender equality bill". *African Journal of Political and Economic Relations*, vol. 3, pp. 17–23.

Aibieyi, S. and Dirisu, E.O. (2010). National Poverty Alleviation Programmes in Nigeria. Problems and Prospects. *A Journal of Contemporary Research.* Vol. 7. No. 2. Pp.www.ajol.info/index.php/lwati/issue/view/7526.

Akindele, R.I. 2002. A Pragmatic Investigation of Gender issues in Workers Motivation in Nigera. *The African Economic and Business Review*. Vol. 3, No. 1. Pp 41–59.

Badejo, B. (2011), *"Transportation, Removing the Clogs to Nigeria's Development"*, Anchorage Press and Publishers, Lagos, Nigeria. In Solanke, M.O. (2013), "Challenges of urban transportation in Nigeria", *International Journal of Development and Sustainability,* Vol. 2 No. 2, pp. 891–901.

Boyi, A.A. 2013. Gender Studies and Sustainable Development in Nigeria. *Journal of Educational and Social Research.* Vol 3 No 10 pp 31–35. MC SER Publishing. ISSN 2239–978x ISSN 2240–0524. Doi:10.5901/jesr.2013.v3n10p31.

Ceccato, V., 2009. "Safety in Transport Nodes: A Research Project". Presented in a seminar of Stockholm City Technical Office, Stockholm.

EDAW.(1985). Retrieved March 15th 2019 from United Nations http://www.un.org/womenwatch/daw/cedaw/.

Falola T (2018). "The ToyinFalola Reader on African Culture,Nationalism, Development and Epistemologies." Pan-African University Press, Austin, Texas.

Gauvin, L., Tizzoni, M., Piaggesi, S., Young, A., Adler, N., Verhulst, S., Ferres, L., and Cattuto, C., 2020. "Gender Gaps in Urban Mobility". Palgrave communications, Palgrave Macmillan, vol. 7(1), pp. 1–13.

Hallmarknews, 2019. Bitting Economy: More Women Take to Keke Driving. https://hallmarknews.com/bitting-economy-more-women-take-to-keke-driving/.

Heilman, M.E., and Parks-Stamm, E.J., 2007. "Gender Stereotypes in the workplace: Obstacles to Women's Career Progress", in: Wei-Shiuen Ng and Ashley, A (2020) The Gender Dimention of the Transport Workforce: International Transport Forum Discussion Paper. www.itf-oecd.org OECD Publishing, Paris.

ILO 2019b. Employment Distribution by Economic Activity (by sex)-ILO modeled estimates, annual. ILOSTAT Database. https://www.ilo.org.

Ipingbemi, O., and Adebayo, A., 2016. Tricycle as a Mode of Public Transportation in Ibadan Metropolis, Nigeria, *Ife Research publication in Geography,* vol. 14, pp. 74–95.

Jandeska, K.E and Kraimer, M.L., 2005. "Women's Perception of Organizational Culture, Work Attitudes, and Role-modelling Behaviours", Journal of Managerial Issues, vol. 17(4), pp. 461–478.

Kaufman M. (2003). "Addressing and Involving Men and Boys to PromoteGender Equality and End Gender Discrimination and Violence". Retrieved from http://www.michaelkaufman.com/wpcontent/uploads/2009/01/kaufman-the-aim-framework.pdf.

Lawal E.E, and Ojo R.C. (2006). "Politics of Gender Inequality in Nigeria". InE.O Ojo (Ed). Challenges of Sustainable Democracy in Nigeria (pp. 330–346). Ibadan: John Archers.

Mgbemena, J. (2013). Language, communication on wheels and national development: The inscriptions on tricycle (Keke) example. *International Journal of English and Literature, 4*(10):529–537. doi:10.5897/IJEL2013.0498.

Mukhtar, A., Waziri, M., Abdulsalam, B., and Dankani, I.M, 2015. Assessment of Tricycle as a Tool of Poverty Alleviation in Maiduguri, Borno State, Northeast Nigeria. *IOSR Journal Of Humanities And Social Science (IOSR-JHSS) Volume 20, Issue 8, Ver. VI (Aug. 2015), PP 14–18 e-ISSN: 2279–0837, p-ISSN: 2279–0845. www.iosrjournals.org.*

Obioma, R., Nwaogbe, C.C.I., & Ukaegbu, S.I. (2012). Quality of the Para-transit Services (Tricycle) and its Operation in Aba, Nigeria: An Analysis of Customers Opinion. *Journal of Transport and Supply Chain Management, 6 (1),262–276.*

Polak, C., 2012. The Demand Determinants for Urban Public Transport Services: A Review of Literature. *Journal of Applied Sciences 12(12).*

Ruxton S (2004). "Gender Equality and Men: Learning from Practice".Oxfam, GB.

Turnbull, P., 2013. Promoting the employment of women in the transport sector - obstacles and policy options. International Labour Office(ILO), Geneva. Working Paper No. 298. Retrieved from http://www.ilo.org/wcmsp5/.

Suda, C. 2002. Gender Disparities in the Kenyan Labour Market: Implications for Poverty Reduction. *Nordic Journal of African Studies*. Vol 11 No 3. Pp 301–321.

UN-Habitat. 2003. A Conceptual Guide to "Gender" http://www.unhabitat.org/gov.

CHAPTER 3

The Traffic Space and the Context of Emancipated Adolescents' Involvement in Unsolicited Vehicle Windscreen-Cleaning in Ibadan, Nigeria

Mofeyisara Oluwatoyin Omobowale and Olugbenga Samuel Falase

1 Introduction

The street economy is still integral to everyday realities in Nigerian societies (Onodugo, et al, 2016; Iwuoha, 2020). The nature and context of the street economy in many cities like Ibadan reveal cultural, social, political, and economic dynamics (Sari, 2020; Lutta, Schoonjans and Lupala, 2021). The street economy in its different forms is embedded with varying cultural values, ethos, and norms that shape the sociocultural and spatial constructions and organizations of the actors involved (Idowu, et al., 2020). One of the prominent forms of street economic practices in Ibadan is the involvement of emancipated or semi-emancipated adolescents (and young adults) in the street economy in the form of unsolicited vehicle windscreen-cleaning in traffic on major urban roads (Ugwuadu, 2017). Due to structural, human, and environmental causes, many urban major roads in Nigeria are congested in traffic especially, early in the morning and during closing hours in the evening. The traffic space in Nigerian cities context provides an avenue for many downtrodden Nigerians involved in the street economy to engage motorists in traffic space for transactions of goods (and now with the emergence of unsolicited vehicle cleaning) and services (Raheem et al., 2015; Jolaoso and Onalaja, 2021). These unsolicited vehicular windscreen-cleaning services by adolescents on the street are initiated and conducted in exchange for gracious gratification. The traffic space symbolically transforms into a "money/livelihood-making" space for the adolescent on the street involved in unsolicited vehicle cleaning practices (Adelagun, 2019).

In the submission of Hansen, Little and Milgram (2014: 4): "… combined … socioeconomic and political inequality, divisions along lines of age and gender have socio-spatial exclusionary effects. Such processes are affecting young people, particularly adversely because everywhere in the Global South, they compose a very large segment of these growing urban populations". All forms of inequalities have fuelled the emergence of adolescents on the street, and the street and its embedded economic opportunities have

 | DOI:10.1163/9789004692657_005

become an integral part of urban life and survival for economically challenged adolescents, yet, the economic network of the street is not bounded by the street but by the rules and regulations that govern it (Ahmad, 2021). These may be formal or informal but also point to the unacceptability of the practice, especially when it involves adolescents under 18 years (Ihejieto, 2020). The traffic space in Nigeria provides an unsolicited vehicle windscreen-cleaning practice in exchange for gracious gratification among economically challenged adolescents. It is an organized venture in the street economy under the control of shadowy adults, with adolescents 'posted' to strategic traffic 'slow down' and 'stop' points to wipe windscreens with soapy mixtures and thereafter 'beg' for alms. Hence, the traffic symbolically assumes the space of money-making for economically challenged emancipated adolescents. These emancipated adolescents use the traffic space to (re)negotiate their sense of belonging in everyday life through interactions. The practice is informally structured and gate kept. There was a social network and remittance system that served as push and pull factors for adolescents involved in the practice which is partly equal to child labour in its broad sense. This study considered unsolicited windscreen-cleaning among adolescents in Ibadan as a form of child labour with both policy and health implications.

Child labour remains a global public health concern that burdens developing nations, particularly, Sub-Saharan African societies like Nigeria (Admassie, 2002; Abebe et al, 2011; UNICEF, 2021). Child labour refers to all forms of work carried out by children under the age of 18 years within and outside the home, paid and unpaid that inflict negative impacts on their physical, social, educational, and mental well-being (Michael et al. 2018; UNICEF 2021 and Enebe, et al., 2021). Child labour does not only affect educational development in adolescents but also has detrimental consequences on their health, and physical and social well-being (UNICEF, 2021). Child labour includes child prostitution, child trafficking, child street/traffic hawking, and involvement of children in armed conflicts (children's soldiers) and street working children (Admassie, 2002; Ihejieto, 2020).

Specifically, this study considers the children in employment as any individual below the age of 18 years. One such practice that involves children in employment is unsolicited vehicle windscreen-cleaning on Ibadan major urban roads. Unsolicited vehicle windscreen-cleaning is a form of street-savvy economy and street culture that is multifunctional with rules and regulations that enable and restrict access to livelihood among economically challenged adolescents of different ages, gender, religion, and backgrounds on the street of Ibadan. Hence, the traffic symbolically assumes the space of money-making for economically challenged emancipated adolescents. This research examines the social network of adolescents' involvement in unsolicited vehicle windscreen-cleaning, their daily income and remittances, and the associated risks and challenges in Ibadan, Nigeria.

2 Contextualising Traffic Space in Informal Economy

'Traffic space', in this paper, is contextualised to mean an interactional public place of vehicular traffic, known as 'go slow' or 'hold up' through which vulnerable adolescents interact and contest for space to make a living. The traffic, which is a feature of most Nigerian cities, has produced a platform through which livelihoods connect with space for survival. This process has craved for much deeper analysis of the importance of social space over public space (Fearson, 2004). In this regard, the discourse on 'space' is not only limited to the geographical milieu but unravels the significance of social space, which is of interest to social researchers. Space, in this context, is not considered in its present spatial forms or the galactic place in the external surroundings of the earth, but its transformation into social relations (Logan, 2012). Yet, space here is not a place that denotes location or distance, but place becomes space at a point where gatherings and interactions among people surface with clearly defined meanings and subjective interpretations (Gieryn, 2000). Thus, the traffic space is contextually detached from a mere 'go and slow' movement of vehicular assets and/or 'hold up' of vehicular traffic, to symbolically translate to an interactional place where the vulnerable adolescents gather and interact to engage in economic competitions under the guidance of some indiscernible space controllers.

The livelihood-acquired space provided within the traffic jam constitutes a means of livelihood for the urban poor. In this case, there are two interacting spaces, which are the physical/public space and the social space. While the physical/public space supplies the available place for social activities, the social space provides a platform for societal interactions and catalyzes social solidity (Pandelaki, Suprapti, Firmandhani, 2017). Also, Feldman and Tilly (1960) emphasise the interlocking of the physical space that entails the objective-economic activities and the social space that gives credence to sentimental-non-economic factors. It then shows that the spatial location of people, interactions, and their activities influence social formations, which need regulations through the enforcement of rules, institutional frameworks, and approvals. Hence, understanding the concept of social space is fundamental to the preservation of social order in the city.

As the traffic space looks, it is a closed structure. The fact that the space exists within the confines of the traffic system and is extensively used for livelihood means speaks more about who has the power to access such space (Milgram, 2011). In this sense, Bourdieu (2018) opines that no space exists without social hierarchies, while (Logan, 1978; cited in Logan, 2012) concludes that the power of inequality that exists in such space means that every space is socially constructed. Hence, the traffic space is controlled by the agency of people who monitor the entry to the traffic space. The acquisition of space in the traffic system is contested and negotiated for by vulnerable social actors. Adebayo and Akinyemi (2019) while discussing wheelbarrow livelihood for survival in Ibadan explain how poor people interact with their object (i.e., wheelbarrow) for space contestation and maintenance, which continues to challenge and restructure the urban landscape. This subject-object interaction is a social process through which livelihoods and space continue to be interlinked. Yet, the interlink further justifies the social relevance and construction of space as gendered space, contested space, and negotiated space (Hackenbroch, Baumgart and Kreibich, 2009), within which the context of livelihoods is determined. Consequently, components of livelihoods are not only economically based but include other complex non-economic factors to manifest.

The (re)production of livelihoods is intertwined with space (re)production (King, 2011). This creates more avenues for space contestations, and invariably, more profits for space managers in the form of profits of localization, rents, and profits of occupation (Bourdieu, 2018). The social struggles over space acquisition also depend on the strategies and capital that one owns to secure the best space. Thus, within existing livelihood opportunities and challenges, the acquisition of space depends on the exercise of power among the actors and agents. So, examining being 'urban', urbanisation process, and urbanism, produces a reflection on how the concept of the city is redefined with much emphasis on space. The significance that the context of space has provided by the reality of traffic space is reflected in the writing of Gieryn (2000) that social life is not fixed to any location or place but moves through points of power and social network. Therefore, an analysis of traffic space generates a piece of empirical information on everyday city arrangements, challenges, competitions, contestations, and negotiations among vulnerable actors in the urban landscape.

3 Methods

The study that informed this chapter was conducted in Ibadan, Nigeria. Ibadan is one of the largest cities in Nigeria and Africa. It is precisely the most populous city and the third largest city in Nigeria considering its population, after

Lagos and Kano. It is an ancient city with many unique traditional urban slums. The city is endowed with mega roads, there are many major roads of dual carriage across the city. Due to its peaceful nature and location of big markets like Bodija, Gbagi, and Aleshinloye in the city, many people across South-Western Nigeria, visit the city for both economic and social transactions in addition to dilapidated roads, causing incidence of traffic jams on major roads of the city.

The study design was exploratory. Qualitative methods of data collection were used to elicit data from the study population. Due to the nature of the study population, a small group of downtrodden young people, scattered across major roads in the city of Ibadan, in line with Bernard's (2006) explanations, formed the participants for the study and were sampled using purposive and snowball sampling techniques. In addition to observational methods that lasted for over 13 months, a total of 26 In-depth interviews (IDIs) were conducted with adolescents (10-18 years) and young adults (19-23 years who have done unsolicited windscreen cleaning since their adolescent years), involved in unsolicited vehicle windscreens cleaning on major roads of Ibadan and 6 key informants' interviews (KIIs) with those who stand in the place of significant others, since many of the adolescents and young people involved in the study were emancipated. Specifically, five major roads with perpetual traffic were purposively selected for the study, namely: Total Garden, Mokola, Sango, Ojoo, and Iwo-road in Ibadan. Informed consent and ascents were obtained verbally from all participants. The average age of the adolescents involved in vehicle windscreen-cleaning in Ibadan was approximately 15 years, while the youngest age was 8 years and the oldest young adult was 23 years. All participants were male and of the Yoruba ethnic group. Many of the youngest participants had spent over one year on the job and the oldest had spent 7 years on the job. The average age of the Key informants was 34 years, 2 were commercial drivers, 3 petty traders, and an artisan, who is a vulcanizer.

All study participants were allowed to decide on their involvement in the study. Observations were written down in a note, while all interviews recorded were transcribed and cleaned. All clean data were coded using descriptive coding to provide an inventory of topics for indexing and categorizing and value coding to capture participants' values, attitudes, and beliefs, representing his or her perspectives or worldview (Miles, et al. 2014). Data were later subjected to descriptive content analysis.

4 Findings and Discussion

4.1 *Social Network of Adolescents in Vehicle Windscreen-Cleaning*

Getting into the vehicle windscreen-cleaning business is not as easy as it looks. The business is not open, but closed and gate-kept, hence, its admission requires the approval of the 'superiors', who are seen as the bosses/leaders monitoring the happenings of the business. Admission into the business depends on the informal relationship and networks that have existed between the adolescents/young adults and the bosses/leaders that introduce them. A respondent made it known that:

> Anyone that wants to start the business must meet with the boss. Nobody can start the job without consulting the boss and that person will undergo some training. After the training, the person will be delivering for the leader/boss.
>
> Male/Mokola/18 years

These bosses, which may be area brothers are also the ones providing tools for the adolescents, which they use in cleaning vehicles as explained thus:

> There is nothing much, the brothers will call us, give us the instrument, and ask for whatever we need. They are just like our area brothers. Not that they are teaching us bad things.
>
> Male/Mokola/20 years.

Also, adolescents in the business form a group where personal ties and social bonds exist. This group is not a formal association but an informal in-group where they get to know each other and discuss matters relating to the business. One of the respondents noted that.

> We have a lot of groups in the business. Most of our peers are along the stadium road at Mokola where we gather especially at the close of the day and discuss.
>
> Male/Iwo Road/15 years

As the business is closed to newcomers, one needs to go through the bosses due to the connection that they have with the police or their influence in protecting those in the business. It was gathered that:

> In most cases, when one of us is arrested by the police, it is these bosses that will come and bail us out. They will relate with the police and settle them. These bosses will also protect us from the 'big boys', who may want to collect or extort money from us. So, if you don't have them, you will suffer if anything happens to you.
>
> Male/Sango/17 years

The response above depicts a form of social protection, which is necessary for the emancipated adolescents involved in windscreen-cleaning exercises. While it is agreed that they are vulnerable, their protection, however, depends on their cordial relationship with their bosses/superiors, who remain invisibly relevant to their socio-economic survival.

4.2 *Adolescents' Socio-Economic Statuses, Daily Income and Remittances*

The quest for survival and overcoming poverty is a major reason for the migration of many individuals to the city. Specifically, for vulnerable adolescents, the poor socio-economic status of parents, conditions at home, the current rate of unemployment in the country, and the inability to finish high school are some of the reasons for their involvement in windscreen-cleaning practice. A respondent explained that:

> I join my people in the street because of my condition. My father died when I was in school and most time, my mother used to travel. I am always alone at home. I stay in the house that my parents rented. I had to leave school when I was in Junior Secondary School 1 (JSS1). I could not continue because there was no money.
>
> Male/Mokola/21 years

Another adolescent who has a similar experience also stated that:

> I join the business. I do not want to steal because I am the only one. I do not stay with my parents. They stay in Oyo, but I am here in Ibadan.
>
> Male/Oojo/19 years

Besides the social and economic conditions and familial factors, some adolescents are also lured into the business by the so-called area big brothers who take advantage of their socio-economic conditions. A respondent said:

> Some of us joined the business through our brothers in the neighbourhood. Particularly, those that are like brothers to me introduce me to the job when they see me playing on the road or roaming about in the street because I am an orphan. I have lost my parents.
>
> Male/Sango/20 years

However, the income made in the business depends on adolescents' skills, patronage, and smartness. These three components are embedded in the zeal to rush towards washing a vehicle screen and how the washing is being carried out. As this is done, more money is expected to be made. Since the main aim of the business is to put money into the pockets of most adolescents, the majority are said to have an edge over the poverty line at the stipulated benchmark of $1.90 by the World Bank for developing countries. Most adolescents interviewed made a daily income ranging from ₦1000 ($2.4) to ₦ 7500 ($18.2). In a day, there is certainty that one will go home with some income as one of the interviewees noted:

> There is money in it. Sometimes one person can give you ₦1000 and when we collect it like that and sometimes one of us can make ₦ 7000 or ₦6000 and sometimes one may make ₦500 or nothing if God has written it.
>
> Male/Iwo Road/20 years

Depending on the number of adolescents that are competing for vehicle windscreen-screening, a minimum of ₦ 1500 ($3.6) could also be a take-home fee. Where many people are on the street working, you may go home with ₦ 1000 ($2.4) or ₦ 500 ($1.2) but when people are few, the chances of getting more fees, are high (Male/Sango/18–22 years). Similarly, a respondent explained the condition for the income received. The amount made per day depends on the nature of the traffic as he explains thus:

> If there is no go slow, I may not go home with less than ₦ 1000 ($2.4) or nothing, but if there is go slow, I may go with ₦ 2500 ($6.1).
>
> Male/Mokola/17 years

For another respondent that calculated his income monthly, he makes an average of ₦ 500 daily. He explained that:

> If I calculate my income in a month, I make nothing less than ₦10000 ($24.3) to ₦12000 ($29.2).
>
> Male/Sango/23 years

To think that the income received by any adolescent is fully owned by him depends on the availability and/or unavailability of the presence of the 'superiors'. The presence of superiors limits the amount that an adolescent takes home because he needs to pay his dues as a form of loyalty. While some respondents acknowledge that they have superiors, some explained that they have none and that whatever they make belongs to them. As a form of loyalty, one must pay his dues to his boss/leader that made him join the business. A respondent explains how he used to pay the area brother that introduced him to the business before he travels out of town.

> I used to pay the brother that made me join the business. He was the one who gave me the tools I was using, and I pay him after the day. I used to let him know how much I made, and I pay his dues. But now that he has moved to Lagos, I spend my money alone.
>
> Male/Mokola/19 years

Strategic places and areas to work are also dictated by the superiors, who, know the ins and outs of traffic areas. So, people under them are positioned in these areas to make money as one of the respondents affirms:

> We have superiors that tell us where to go. You must be good and must not steal. The superiors position us in the areas that will fetch us more money so that we can pay them. In the end, we give them (i.e., superiors) their dues. If you fail, you will be in trouble.
>
> Male/Sango/14 years

Loyalty is needed in the windscreen-cleaning exercise and the positioning of adolescents is premised on the responsibility of their superiors who are familiar with and have a good understanding of commonly noted traffic places that are supposed to produce more income in Ibadan. Although the amount remitted is not fixed but depends on what one makes per day, it is expected that an adolescent who is posted in a traffic-laden environment should be able to make above-average daily income compared to others, pay his dues, and save some income for himself. Yet, some of the adolescents involved in the business do not have bosses they report to.

4.3 *Associated Risks and Challenges Involved in Vehicle Windscreen-Cleaning*

One of the major emerging concerns about the involvement of young people in unsolicited windscreen-cleaning is the associated risks which include the health implications of the practice and some other related social/psychological challenges faced by the study populations. The practice as it appears is situated between alms begging and street work. The young people involved are neither alms beggars nor street hawkers, and yet they do some work, and their work is compensated by gratification, although no fixed charges. The state of the practice also incurs natural health and well-being implications.

The participants experienced health issues since their involvement in the practice. Many of them reported self-medication abuse, as reiterated by one of the participants:

> On this job, if one does not take care, one will be hill, but we use drugs every night. When I go to a chemist, s/he will sell the medicine to you. (Pharmaceutical drugs like analgesics, antibiotics, anti-malaria, and so on) We just tell him/her to help us get a drug for body pain and s/he will give us in different colours and once swallowed, you are good for the next day. We also make sure we take herbs every evening to renew the nerves.
>
> Male/Sango/17 years

The above response which was confirmed by others in some informal discussions revealed that the study populations are involved in constant abuse of pain-relieving medications and herbal remedies with potential grave consequences for health statuses and well-being.

Another participant noted that they are subjected to physical and psychological abuse by motorists. He explained thus:

> There are a lot of dangers in it, some people may decide to hit you or even hit you from behind unknowingly. Some of them may curse us when we ask for money from them.
>
> Male/Iwo Road/20 years

To see if he will be pitied by motorists, another participant shared his experience thus:

> Anytime I wash the windscreen of any car, I will kneel to beg for money. Each time I do this, I used to be ashamed. At times, when they see me kneeling, some of them will give me money, but not in all cases.
>
> Male/Ojoo/20 years

While also narrating the various challenges faced in windscreen-cleaning practices, a participant noted that:

> There was a time someone got us arrested because we were trying to wash his windscreen but later released us. Some will shout as we are approaching to wash their windscreens. And at times, some people that get hit by the car could not come to work for many days. One of the challenges that we also face is the way some of us are attacked by the 'boys'. At times, they

> will slap and beat you up for not giving them money or grab your testicles to collect money from you.
>
> Male/Sango/19 years

The result presented gives an in-depth understanding of the context of traffic space in the informal economy and adolescents' predicament as well as their coping mechanisms and challenges in the unsolicited vehicle-cleaning practices in Ibadan. The vehicle windscreen-cleaning practice is a form of business that adolescents use to fight back against poverty and engage the vicissitudes of life. The dominant factors that predispose adolescents to this practice are the death of parents, socioeconomic status of parents, unemployment rate, and other familial issues. As Bergman, Axberg and Hanson (2017) noted, the death of a parent could result in mental and psychosocial problems among already stressed children, while Ellis, Dowrick and Lloyd-Williams (2013) emphasised that the death of spouses could disrupt and discontinue the needs of children. Other adolescents, whose parents lack financial ability or those that experience family problems, lack proper social supports that they could have benefited from. While these various unpleasant conditions could have lured adolescents into illegal or unlawful deeds, engaging in vehicle windscreen-cleaning becomes a choice to combat poverty and make ends meet. As most of the respondents noted, the fear of becoming pickpocketers, handset snatchers, and robbers, contributed to the reasons for involving in windscreen-cleaning.

Adolescence describes the period of transition from childhood to adulthood. At this critical stage, children experience a lot of physical, psychological, and social development. Young adolescents (10–17 years) take up risky tasks and easily become vulnerable to peer pressure compared to older adolescents (18–24). As Christie and Viner (2005) noted, it is a stage that is described as a period of independence, and productivity, thus, making it possible for adolescents to have uninterrupted freedom to engage in any activities without any check (see also Falase and Ogunwale, 2020). Adedeji (2016) raised a concern about the devastating conditions of adolescents who roam the street of Ibadan without meaningful activities and ended up in juvenile rehabilitation centres for crimes and other misconducts. While some of these adolescents are involved in stealing and begging, others take up menial jobs that seem to be contributing nothing to development. Although Adedeji regarded washing a car's windscreen as a meaningless activity, findings however, show that the vehicle windscreen-cleaning is a job through which adolescents make a living and contribute to the functioning of the informal economy.

Significantly, regardless of how the vehicle windscreen-cleaning is being perceived and categorised, it is a form of social capital through which emancipated adolescents renegotiate their sense of belonging in everyday interactions and contribute to the functioning of the informal economy. The importance of the informal economy cannot be underestimated. The economy comprises a lot of informal workers and traders that face exploitation and receive little or no financial support from the government (Omobowale, 2019; Omobowale, et al., 2020). It adopts many people without formal certificates or training to display their skills and expertise. In Lagos, Neuwirth (2013) noted that 90 percent of the money realised from Lagos state as a contribution to Nigeria's GDP comes from the informal sectors. This is to argue that as little or no formal recognition that the informal economy receives, it is a channel that continues to pump money into the country's purse for national development. Consequently, the vehicle windscreen-cleaning job operates under the informal economy and constitutes a source of income for adolescents. With the World Bank's (2020) estimation that there is high poverty in Nigeria and over 50 percent of its population live below the poverty line of $1.90 per day, the income realised from the windscreen-cleaning job is enough for adolescents to feed themselves and subsist above the poverty line. Although washing windscreens does not guarantee an automatic payment, some car owners gift and pay out of kindness to support the economically challenged emancipated adolescents and not necessarily for the unwanted service rendered for them. But if nothing was given in return for the service, the adolescents beg for alms. However, whether adolescents are remunerated or not, findings show that adolescents made an average income between ₦ 1000 ($2.4) to ₦ 7500 ($18.2) daily if the competition is reduced, and an average income of ₦ 800 ($1.94) to ₦ 2500 ($6.08) if the competition is high. Monthly, there is the possibility of making an average of ₦ 10000 ($24.3) to ₦ 12000 ($29.2). Then, there are chances that adolescents with this range of income will be able to live comfortably, save some monies, pay their dues, and live above the international poverty line approved by the World Bank.

An avenue through which adolescents make sense of their socioeconomic conditions is through the traffic space. This space is gate-kept and controlled by shadowy adults that post and direct adolescents to strategic public areas to wash vehicle windscreens. It should also be known that these shadowy adults remain invisible to the public, yet they control the happenings within the traffic space. Having strategically placed adolescents where they will work, they sit, monitor, and expect returns to be delivered to them at the close of work. This invariably suggests that windscreen-cleaning exercise requires some techniques of mastering the areas that are always laden with traffic within the urban geographical terrain. Access to this traffic space to work is not free, but contested and negotiated, and depends on the relationship an adolescent has established with the superiors. In this case, the existing level of trust and personal ties and the daily interactions between adolescents and their superiors go a long way in securing a traffic space to work. The more the traffic jam, the more available chances of making more money and vice versa. For the new adolescents, the help and instructions of these shadowy adults and/or superiors, are needed to start and settle in the job.

Livelihood making in the street has not been without some challenges and risks, specifically, among the emancipated adolescents making a living in the traffic space. While unsolicited traffic windscreen-cleaning represents an informal economy that employs adolescents, the hazards and the oppression they experience cannot be underestimated. They were vulnerable to physical, sexual, and psychological abuse from 'superiors' and drivers. The participant engaged in dangerous self-medication and sometimes extend it to dangerous integrative medicine, mixing both high-rated alcoholic herbal products and pharmaceutical medicine and consumed simultaneously. Unknown to them, this act damages some valuable internal organs and results in non-communicable health problems later in life. Another health-related experience by the participants is traffic accidents. Many of them have been occasionally hit by 'hit and run' drivers in the process of washing windscreens, although no death was reported, serious injuries were variously described by many participants. A study conducted by Masuri, Isa and Tahir (2012) reports that young people that are on the street are highly involved in road accident cases and this may result in death or deformity of the body.

Also, the participants were vulnerable to conflict and bullying by older young people who have institutionalized themselves as leaders in the practice. These leaders are known to be the participants' superiors and mostly, their resting spot is located inside a nearby cemetery close to their working sites in Ibadan. The cemetery spot serves as their office, meeting spot, and resting place for wining and dining and where a lot of other resocialization activities like alcoholism, substance use, bullying, and dangerous self-medication take place. The health risk associated with living in a cemetery is numerous, including vulnerability to infectious diseases. Another dynamic of health risk associated with unsolicited vehicle windscreens is the infliction of psychological pain on adolescents by some divers raining curses and abuses on them when they attempt to wash their windscreens. In some cases, they were arrested by drivers who may find their services offensive, while they are subjected to sexual abuse from their superiors. The arrested ones that have a well-established relationship with their bosses get released on time because of their connections with law enforcement officers. At times, the participants are robbed and physically abused by the so-called 'big boys' that are mostly louts and thugs.

There is no gainsaying that the government has initiated several empowerment programmes for young people in Nigeria, aimed at improving their socioeconomic conditions in society. With this development, it is expected that all categories of young people are direct beneficiaries and inclusive of the programmes. It is also assumed that the success of these programmes will change the lives of many young people and lift them out of poverty. However, while these programmes exist on paper, majority of the adolescents have not benefitted immensely, either because they are unaware or are not properly enlightened. The assumption that these empowerment programmes include all youths in society is a misconception that makes scholars and policymakers believe that some adolescents like those involved in windscreen-cleaning do not encounter a definite distinct set of problems that make them unique compared to the rest of the population. Till now, the unemployment rate among adolescents and youths continues to increase. The ILO (2013) reports that 43.3% of the youth between the age 15–24 years, is either unemployed or underemployed, hence, the youth generation is at risk. While most of the adolescents recognized the fact that they are involved in windscreen-cleaning practices to alleviate poverty and to circumvent theft and illegal acts, they still aspire to benefit from any assistance that may emanate from the government to have a better life. The consequence of the network that has been created around the practice implies health danger to both adolescents and the public.

5 Conclusion

The windscreen-cleaning is an informal economic job that has contributed to the socio-economic survival of adolescents and their associated families. The daily proceeds from this job are used to cater for their needs and that of their loved ones, while also having some savings after remittance. Therefore, making a livelihood in the traffic space by economically challenged adolescents in exchange for gracious gratification should be seen as a response to the socio-economic challenges that this vulnerable population is facing. With different categorizations of dependent populations in society, these groups of adolescents represent a unique population that carries some distinct set of social problems entirely different from other groups. Since they are classified as the productive population capable to lift the country from its state of decadence to its peak of excellence, speedy attention and solutions are needed to resolve any form of socio-economic problems they face. Meanwhile, as these adolescents face the vicissitude of life on the street, contesting and negotiating for space, they are perceived as lazy, unproductive, criminals and street boys. Yet, they continue to strive for survival amidst the present socio-economic hardship. Hence, the traffic symbolically assumes the space of money-making for economically challenged emancipated adolescents. In attending to the needs of the windscreen-cleaning adolescents, their economic situations need to be treated with a matter of urgency.

References

Abebe, T. & Bessell, S. (2011). Dominant discourses, debates and silences on child labour in Africa and Asia. *Third world quarterly*, *32*(4), 765–786.

Adebayo, K. & Akinyemi, A. (2019). 'Wheelbarrow livelihoods', urban space and antinomies of survival in Ibadan, southwest Nigeria. *International Development Planning Review*, *41*(1), 23–42.

Adelagun O. (2019). Inside the Lives of Teenagers Running Mobile Car Wash Business in Lagos Traffic. *Premium Times*. https://www.premiumtimesng.com/news/headlines/328430-inside-the-lives-of-teenagers-running-mobile-car-wash-business-in-lagos-traffic.html.

Admassie, A. (2002). Explaining the high incidence of child labour in Sub–Saharan Africa. *African development review*, *14*(2), 251–275.

Ahmad, S. (2021). Chaos Amid Chaos: A Critical Debate for Street Vendors – Struggle and Adaptation Post COVID Era. In: *A New Social Street Economy: An Effect of the COVID-19 Pandemic*. Grima, S., Sirkeci, O. and Elbeyoğlu, K. (Ed.), 107, Emerald Publishing Limited, Bingley, pp. 147–153. https://doi.org/10.1108/S1569-375920210000107024.

Bergman, AS., Axberg, U. & Hanson, E. (2017). When a parent dies – a systematic review of the effects of support programs for parentally bereaved children and their caregivers. *BMC Palliat Care*, *16*(39), 1–15.

Bernard, H. R. (2006). Research Methods in Anthropology: *Qualitative and Quantitative Approaches*, 6th edition, Rowman & Littlefield.

Christie, D., & Viner, R. (2005). Adolescent development. *BMJ (Clinical research ed.)*, *330*(7486), 301–304.

Ellis, J., Dowrick, C., & Lloyd-Williams, M. (2013). The long-term impact of early parental death: lessons from a narrative study. *Journal of the Royal Society of Medicine*, *106*(2), 57–67.

Enebe, N. O., Enebe, J. T., Agunwa, C. C., Ossai, E. N., Ezeoke, U. E., Idoko, C. A., & Mbachu, C. O. (2021). Prevalence and predictors of child labour among junior public secondary school students in Enugu, Nigeria: a cross-sectional study. *BMC public health*, *21*(1), 1–12.

Falase, O.S. & Ogunwale, G.I. (2020). The Nigerian Youth and the Rhetoric of Globalisation. *Ibadan Journal of Sociology*, *11*(1), 93–110.

Fearson, D. (2004). Georg Simmel, The Sociology of Space. *CSISS Classics*. https://escholarship.org/uc/item/7s73860q.

Feldman, A.S. & Tilly, C. (1960). The Interaction of Social and Physical Space. *American Sociological Review*, 25(6), 877–884.

Gieryn, T.F. (2000). A Space for Place in Sociology. *Annual Review Sociology*, *26*, 463–496.

Hackenbroch, K. Baumgart, S. & Kreibich, V. (2009). The Spatiality of Livelihoods: Urban Public Space as an Asset for the Livelihoods of the Urban Poor in Dhaka, Bangladesh. *DIE ERDE 140*(1), 47–68.

Hansen, K. T., Little, W. E., Milgram, B. L., Babb, F. E., Bromley, R., & Clark, G. C. (2014). *Street economies in the urban Global South*. SAR Press.

Idowu, E. A., Nwhator, S. O., & Afolabi, A. O. (2020). Nigeria' s street children, epitome of oral health disparity and inequality. *The Pan African Medical Journal*, *36*, https://doi.org/10.11604/pamj.2020.36.77.20404.

Ihejieto, C. (2020). *Child labour, child education and poverty: a study of children on the street in Nigeria*. (Doctoral dissertation, University of Sunderland, United Kingdom). https://core.ac.uk/download/pdf/323306827.pdf.

ILO (2013). Global Employment Trends for Youth 2013: A Generation at Risk. International Labour Organization, Geneva. https://www.ilo.org/wcmsp5/groups/public/---dgreports/---dcomm/documents/publication/wcms_212423.pdf.

Iwuoha, V. C. (2020). Street-hawking in a Foreign Land: Social Dynamics of Migrant Petty Traders' Livelihoods in Nigeria. *Journal of Asian and African Studies*, *55*(8), 1209–1229.

Jolaoso, B., & Onolaja, O. A. (2021). Significance of Informal Trading Activities in The Emergence of Urban Spatial Vernacular: Case Study of Lagos Island, Nigeria. *Local Wisdom: Jurnal Ilmiah Kajian Kearifan Lokal*, *13*(1), 112–125.

King, B. (2011). Spatialising livelihoods: resource access and livelihood spaces in South Africa. *Transactions of the Institute of British Geographers*, *36*(2), 297–13.

Logan, J.R. (2012). Making a Place for Space: Spatial Thinking in Social Science. *Annual Review of Sociology*, *38*, 507–524.

Lutta, J., Schoonjans, Y., & Lupala, A. (2021). The Complexity of Social and Cultural Dynamics in Emerging of Collective Spaces in Unplanned Urbanisation: Learning from Mlalakuwa-Dar es Salaam. *Current Urban Studies*, *9*, 445–463.

Masuri, M.G., Md Isa, K.A. & Tahir, M.P.M. (2012). Children, Youth and Road Environment: Road Traffic Accident. *Procedia - Social and Behavioral Sciences*, *38*, 213–218.

Michael, O., Justina, O., & Olabode, D. (2018). Child labour and protection: An exploration of vulnerable children in Lagos state, Nigeria. *Humanities*, *6*(4), 171–179.

Miles, M. B., Huberman, A. M., & Saldana, J. (2014). Qualitative Data Analysis: A Methods Sourcebook. 3rd edition. SAGE Publications Ltd.

Milgram, B. L (2011). Reconfiguring Space, Mobilizing Livelihood: Street Vending, Legality, and Work in the Philippines. *Journal of Developing Societies*, *27*(3&4), 261–293.

Neuwirth, R. (2013). Life and Livelihood. *SAIS Review of International Affairs*, *33*(1), 65–71.

Omobowale, A.O, Oyelade, K.O., Omobowale, M.O. and Falase, O.S. (2020). Contextual reflections on COVID-19 and informal workers in Nigeria. *International Journal of Sociology and Social Policy*, *40*(9/10), 1041–1057.

Omobowale, M.O. (2019). Class, gender, sexuality, and leadership in bodija market, ibadan, Nigeria. *Journal of Anthropological Research*, *75*(2), 235–251.

Onodugo, V. A., Ezeadichie, N. H., Onwuneme, C. A., & Anosike, A. E. (2016). The dilemma of managing the challenges of street vending in public spaces: The case of Enugu City, Nigeria. *Cities*, *59*, 95–101.

Pandelaki, E. E., Suprapti, A., & Firmandhani, S. W. (2017, December). Typology of social space in Kauman Kampong Semarang. In *IOP Conference Series: Earth and Environmental Science*, *99*(1), 012011).

Raheem, S. B., Olawoore, W. A., Olagunju, D. P., & Adeokun, E. M. (2015). The cause, effect and possible solution to traffic congestion on Nigeria road (a case study of Basorun-Akobo road, Oyo state). *International Journal of Engineering Science Invention*, *4*(9), 10–14.

Sari, M. (2020). Rehabilitation of Children Working on the Street. In: *Global Street Economy and Micro Entrepreneurship*. Grima, S., Sirkeci, O. and Elbeyoğlu, K. (Ed.), 103, Emerald Publishing Limited, Bingley, pp. 97–99. https://doi.org/10.1108/S1569-375920200000103013.

Ugwuadu, M. E. (2017). *Experiences Of Street Children in Iwo Road of Ibadan, Nigeria*. (Doctoral dissertation, University of Ghana, Legon, Ghana. http://ugspace.ug.edu.gh/handle/123456789/23289.

UNICEF (2021). Child labour. https://data.unicef.org/topic/child-protection/child-labour/.

World Bank (2020). Poverty and equity brief: sub-saharan Africa: Nigeria April 2020. https://databank.worldbank.org/data/download/poverty/33EF03BB-9722-4AE2-ABC7-AA2972D68AFE/Global_POVEQ_NGA.pdf.

CHAPTER 4

Business Networking among Auto-artisans in Ibadan Mechanic Villages, Nigeria

Olufikayo Kunle Oyelade

1 Introduction

Artisans form a large percentage of the workforce in the informal sector of Nigeria's economy and the importance of their activities to economic growth cannot be overemphasized. This sector has been adjudged to have a huge potential to play a great role in reducing the unemployment rate and contribute to a fast recovery from the economic recession in which the country has presently found itself, due to over-concentration on the formal sector of the economy (Onwe, 2013). Contemporary Nigeria is marked by deplorable conditions of intra and intercity roads resulting in frequent automobile damages. A very large number of vehicles and motorcycles ply the roads, and unquestionably they need to be serviced from time to time for maintenance purposes. Petty repairs and temporary servicing are usually carried out by roadside auto-artisans of various areas of specialization such as mechanics, panel beaters, painters, and auto-electricians among others. Many times, this encourages trying and error on the auto-mobile system, especially when auto-artisans are ill-trained, unqualified and equipment deficient.

In many cities in contemporary Nigeria, auto-artisans devise a way of working in groups at any available vacant space to make auto-artisan business more comfortable for them (artisans) as well as their customers. The case of Ibadan is not different. History has it that mechanic villages in Ibadan started with the need of the artisans to be working together for effectiveness of their business. At any discovered vacant or unused large space, it takes a mechanic to take a bold step, clear the space and call it a workshop, before long another artisan would join him and from there, different artisans would continue to join until a community of auto-artisans is created. This vacant space could belong to individuals or even the government, and they are usually allowed to stay until the owner sees the need to use the property. Such spaces become unofficially designated to auto-artisans for business purposes, popularly referred to as mechanic villages or workshops. A city may have several such places in proportion of its population and automobile activities. They comprise artisans

 | DOI:10.1163/9789004692657_006

of various automobile related skills, and well-structured in such manners that they could be described as modern-day Auto-mechanic Centres. They form a fundamental part of informal sector and sustain the Nation's economy in no small measure, especially in providing jobs and automobile amenities for many Nigerians (Onwe, 2013). The massive population of the actors engaged in the sector and its contributions towards stability, growth and progress of several other sectors cannot be dismissed with a wave of hands. In fact, its relevance to economic survival of various auto-artisans with different areas of specialization within the Auto-mechanic informal system, and the public in general is worth noting. These artisans engage in social networking among themselves for commercial purposes and consequently, enhance their means of livelihood (Omobowale, 2008). The structure of this informal economic system signifies how critical it is, and a factor that has played vital roles at its drive and resilience. This research therefore investigates the business networking among Auto-artisans in Ibadan, Nigeria. It specifically examines the formation of Mechanic Villages in Ibadan, the structure of the selected Mechanic Villages, and the context of business networking among Auto-artisans in those selected mechanic villages in Ibadan. Preliminary findings reveal that the networking among the auto-artisans forms a major factor for sustainability of the centres and development among the people.

2 The Social Network of Artisanship Community

Artisans are skilled men who fashion artefacts with hands and tools in autonomous workshops without the aid of powered machinery. In other words, they are skilled craft workers who make or create things by hand and their activities are often characterized by low entry requirements in terms of capital and professional credentials, the small scale of operations, skills often acquired outside of formal education and labour-intensive. The activities of artisans include carpentry, hairdressing, fashion designing, plumbing, electrician, panel beating, auto-mechanics and a host of others. The contributions of artisanal activities to the growth of Nigeria economy cannot be overemphasized because they have positively influenced the growth of Nigeria economy (Omobowale, 2008; Onwe, 2013). They play an active role in the primary production and exchange of goods and services to millions of Nigerians and serve as great employers for those who by education or other requirements are unable to secure job in the organized or formal sector of the economy and promote entrepreneurial spirit in Nigerian society. The consequential effect of economic downturn on Nigerian automobile industries, especially as it affects production and costs of new vehicles and the inability of many Nigerians to acquire it has redirected the attention of many to the so called "Tokunbo" – second-hand new imported from other countries to Nigeria. Majority of these vehicles with the bad state of many roads cannot but require the services of auto-mobile artisans, to increase their level of durability and serve the owners (Omobowale, 2008). Hence, the auto-mobile artisans have no small roles to play in this matter.

In Nigeria, most especially Ibadan where land transport is in use, the use of automobile vehicles, either diesel or petrol driven is predominant. However, the vehicles cannot remain new forever, as the parts breakdown and wear out, and so they must be maintained. The presence of this guarantees their continuous functioning for a longer period and make the transportation continue and easy. In the opinion of World Health Organization (WHO), rapid importation and influx of used vehicles have caused a proliferation of numerous automobile mechanic workshops all over the country (WHO, 2006).

Social network theory is a theoretical concept used in the social sciences to examine relationships between individuals, groups and organizations or even entire societies. It is used to describe a social structure determined by such interactions (Borgatti and Halgin, 2011). The theory interprets relationships in terms of nodes and ties. Nodes refer to individuals within the networks while ties refer to the relationship between the actors. The power of the theory is embedded in its difference from traditional sociological studies, which undertake that the character of individual actors is what matters, whether they are friendly or unfriendly, smart, or dumb (Borgatti and Halgin, 2011). In this wise, the theory explains how people, individuals and groups or organizations interact with others inside their network or web. Auto-artisans in selected Mechanic villages in Ibadan seem enduring in their different but related businesses, for the reason of social network. The actors, consequent to their shared value of providing automobile facilities for the public as a means of living, create a community of Auto-mobile artisans, interact among themselves for commercial purposes, and have their means of livelihood enhanced. In this way, consciously or unconsciously the community of Auto-artisans are formed by the actors, networking is engaged for the reason of business, and consequently their means of livelihood is improved.

Social networking is very important because the entrepreneurs depend mostly on raw materials, information, technology, or knowledge to continuously develop their businesses and be acceptable to the public. Literature acknowledge that networking provides many benefits and aids business success. It increases profit from investment and access to growth, especially for newly established ventures and makes dynamic relationship to such establishments (Kinyanjui, 2016). The use of social network theory provides a good framework to explaining why a relevant social network should be engaged for business success. Although mechanic is a specialized skilled worker who repairs auto-mobiles (Kinyanjui, 2016). The work of a mechanic is simply the application of technical knowledge to solving daily needs of people in automobile maintenance and repairs. In Nigeria, most of the vehicle maintenance and repair jobs used to be by roadside mechanics until the emergence of designated open space at different locations in urban areas referred to as Mechanic villages. The importance of this role to the society notwithstanding, there is clear gap of divide between the learning of science and technology and actual practice of it in the society and in different organized setup like the mechanic villages, in Ibadan. This is because in actual practice, a mechanic needs to network with some other auto-artisans for effective service delivery. Auto-artisans refer to all workers who are involved in repairs and maintenance of automobile vehicles such as cars and motorcycle. These include, motor mechanic, motorcycles mechanic, panel work, auto painting, auto electricians, auto upholstery, battery repair, vulcanized work, wheel balancing and alignment works. *All these, with their interactions and social network become responsible for the servicing and maintenance of vehicles in Nigeria (Oyesiji, et al., 2021).*

In other words, considering the structure of Mechanic villages, it is evident that the Auto-artisans do network easily by the way they render their services to the populace in Nigeria at large, and Ibadan in particular.

3 Methodology

The vitality of exploratory research to any study among others is seen in the fact that it adds quality and insightful information to a study (Casula etal. 2020). and since the primary focus of this work is the formation, the structure, and the context of business networking among auto-artisans in Mechanic Villages in Ibadan, the research is exploratory. Qualitative data were collected from three selected modern mechanic villages in Ibadan and content analyzed. Ibadan, located in South-western Nigeria is the second largest city in the country, and the capital of Oyo state. Ibadan is a major city of informal traders and artisans, where mechanics and mechanic workshops contribute significantly to the socio-economic development of the city. The city also grew rapidly and developed manufacturing and service industries all that required effective transportation system to thrive continually. It is important to state that in contemporary Ibadan, road transportation is in use compared to other means of transportation, and the use of automobile vehicles, either diesel or petrol-driven is predominant. Hence, the need for skilled auto-mobile artisans cannot be over emphasised, and the focus of this research – the context of Business networking among Auto-Artisans in mechanic villages becomes significant. Forty-two (42) interviews were conducted in all; thirty-three (33) in-depth interviews (IDI); nine (33) with various artisans in each of the three selected modern mechanic villages, Samonda, Ijokodo and Bodija in Ibadan, and Nine (9) Key informant interviews (KII) with officers/village leaders among the Artisans across the three villages, and the contents were systematically analyzed. To ensure proper representation of all categories of artisans, at least One (1) and not more than three (3) of each category was interviewed for IDI while three (3) officers were interviewed in each of the selected mechanic villages for KII. The Artisans include, Mechanic, Auto-electrician popularly called Rewire, Panel-beater, Painter, Vulcanizer, Welder and Auto-furniture maker (popularly called Upholstery). Social network theory was adopted in explaining the crux of the research. Preliminary findings reveal that the networking among the auto-artisans forms a major factor for sustainability of the centers and development among the people. The map below shows the three (3) study locations; Bodija Ojurin, Samonda and Ijokodo in Ibadan.

It is important to mention that of all the three, Bodija Ojurin mechanic village is the earliest which was established in the late 1980s. The landed property then belonged to the Railway Corporation. However, as Bodija area developed, and some capitalists and Politicians claimed to have bought some portion of the land, there was the need for displacement and relocation of artisans, and that informed the formation of Samonda and Ijokodo as the affected artisans needed to look for where else to continue their work. Although, some artisans still occupy some portions of the Bodija Ojurin Mechanic Village as untitled tenants at the mercy of the Capitalists and Politician owners.

4 Major Findings

4.1 *The Structure of the Auto-artisans Village*

This section uncovers the structure of the modern mechanic village in Ibadan, it explains the origin of the mechanic village, categories of Artisans, artisans admitted into the village, and how artisans operate in the village; the leadership or officers of the village, management, rules, and regulations guiding activities in the village, security in the village, rift management between artisans and artisans and rift management between artisans and customers etc.

The formation of the auto artisan villages in Nigeria could be traced to the need for auto artisans' services in the face of urban development and eradication of environmental Pollution in Nigerian cities. This was explained an interviewee when he said:

> We were scattered all over the cities before, I mean people with different mechanic related jobs, but a time came when the government said that all of us should come together and be staying together, and you know it is good because it makes our job too to be more progressive. So, there are mechanic villages located in some places according to government decision, and you know when government gives order, we must obey. Although what they were saying then was that the way we were scattered, it does not make the town to be neat as they wanted.
>
> IDI/Mechanic/Ijokodo/August 2021

Another one explained:

> We were told that when people were becoming many in Ibadan and the government, hennn … the town planning people started moving people away from their shops that they were not supposed to be on the roadside, then the idea of mechanic villages came up.
>
> IDI/Rewire/Samonda/September 2021

The above suggests that the formation of contemporary mechanic villages against the citywide auto-mobile workshop practice in Ibadan was consequent to government policy related to urban planning and annihilation of environmental pollution. In explaining the idea of city-wide auto-mechanic workshop practice, workshops and centers are cited by individuals and different artisans all over the places in different cities, and it causes city-wide spill of used engine oil and consequently wider environmental pollution (Nwachukwu etal., 2012). Literature asserts that the hazard of environmental pollution through disposing used automobile oil on the ground in many developing countries is of immense concern to public health and ecology (Oloruntoba and Ogunbunmi, 2020). In mechanic workshops, there are deliberate or accidental discharges or releases of diesel, petrol, solvents, grease and lubricants on the land and atmosphere. Many of these petroleum products are organic chemicals that can be highly toxic and hazardous to soil and man (Oloruntoba and Ogunbunmi, 2020). Gupta and Gupta assert that the use of automobiles has also led to trace elements and heavy metals-contaminated soil, which have grave significances for organisms that dwell in the soil (Gupta and Gupta, 1998). Onibokun and Kumuyi on governance of waste management in Ibadan, remarked that the issues of great concern includes the city's unplanned growth since 1829, poorly managed solid waste and drainage systems, poor transportation facilities as well as environmental pollution (Onibokun and Kumuyi, 1919).

Another possible reason was the need to enhance the effectiveness of city transportation system. An interviewee said:

> All of us who do this type of work are very important if the transportation system will improve. There is no money in the circulation to buy new vehicles, it is *Tokunbo* from Europe and America, that people are buying, so they need us for those vehicles, and they can easily get us if we are together in a place like this. That is why I think government started this type of mechanic village, and it is not only in Ibadan, but also all over the country.
>
> IDI/Panel beater/Bodija/ October, 2021

In the above explanation, as population increases, there arose the need for more vehicles to ease transportation problem, and as the deteriorating economic situation would not allow for brand new vehicles, the second hand or used vehicles so called "Tokunbo" were being imported from Europe and America into Nigeria (Omobowale, 2008). If these vehicles would be properly maintained to be fit for Nigerian roads and relatively last long, they do not only require the services of auto-artisans of different skills, but also easy accessibility to such services. All this as a matter of fact in one way or the other confirms the need for contemporary auto-artisans' village.

With special reference to the Mechanic Village, Bodija Ojurin, it was discovered to be one of the major, established in Ibadan since the 1970s, and from there many others have seceded and moved as far as Osun, Ogun, and Lagos States, to establish there. This was explained in the words of an artisan:

> Irepodun Mechanic Village, Bodija Ojurin was established in the early 70s. It started with some mechanics which was later joined by other automobile artisans like panel beater, welder, painters, rewire, and upholstery among others. We have had people that started from here but later moved to other places in Ibadan and even to Osun, Ogun, Lagos etc. It started with some mechanics which was later joined by other automobile artisans like panel beaters, welder, painters, rewire, upholstery etc. We have had people that started from here but later moved to other places in Ibadan and even to Osun, Ogun, Lagos etc.
>
> KII/Secretary/Bodija Ojurin/December, 2021

Another said:

> I joined them here a very long time ago. People have left for different reasons, you know Ibadan is getting bigger every day, and not everybody in Ibadan can be coming to Bodija and again when we were told that Railway corporation has sold their land, some other people moved again to either establish somewhere else or join those who have established their already, like that of Ijokodo, Samonda, Sango and so on.
>
> KII/Secretary/Bodija Ojurin/December, 2021

The above clearly explains when, how and possibly why the Mechanic Village at Bodija Ojurin was established. It was established sometimes in the early 1970s by some Mechanics who delighted in working together as business colleagues. Their togetherness later attracted the attention and interest of some other artisans like panel beaters, welder, painters, rewire, upholstery etc who joined them. The formation and expansion of the mechanic villages from Bodija Ojurin has brought about formation of other villages, not only in Ibadan but also neighboring states in Southwestern Nigeria. It was further explained that the earliest group of people who moved from Bodija, because of discovery of the need for artisans in some other places as Bodija Ojurin became too distant to satisfy motorists who were far away, and other groups left when part of Bodija was sold by the government and the owners wanted to use their land.

The operation of the Village community and its leadership cannot be separated. In the words of an interviewee:

> We operate here as a community, Mechanic, Pannel beater, Painter, Rewire, Vulcanizer, "Agbede" all of us who work on a vehicle; we have our officers, like the Chairman, Secretary, Treasurer, and Community Police etc. they all have the role they play for the progress of the village. We elected them; they can only serve for four years, before we elect some other people. Our staying here in the mechanic village is 7.00am to 7.00pm, we all know, and who ever disobeys know there is penalty.
>
> IDI/Panel beater/Bodija/October 2021

Another interviewee explains:

> It is not as if we have a written constitution, but I can tell you that we are very organized, and the government knows about what we are doing. Before anybody can join us here, we must know where the person is

> coming from, we would have done our own investigations about him, and he must have a guarantor from among us. If he has just gotten freedom from his boss, we would know, and the way we work here, we work like a family, we want the progress of one another. We usually meet every month to talk about the progress of the mechanic village and people cooperate, they come, and everybody says his mind.
>
> KII/Chairman/Mechanic/Ijokodo/October/2021

Yet another said:

> If there is a misunderstanding among us, it is not difficult settle; that is part of the reason we have our officers, but we have always warned one another that we should avoid having problem with customers. You know if you fight with a customer, ten of them may leave you for another place. So, if anybody fights with customer, in fact we don't even do it here, and that is why you see this place full of vehicles it makes people to be patronizing us.
>
> KII – PRO/ Rewire/ Samonda/October, 2021

The Auto-artisans constitute an informal sector of the economy with shared value of making ends meet; they are of various automobile related skills, well-structured in such manners that they have community officers like the Chairman, secretary, and treasurer, community police, public relations officer, elected by members to administer the affairs of the mechanic village. Each officer could only occupy office for a specific duration of time, and admission of artisans into the village is not automatic, the process includes screening and investigating an intending community member, who must have a guarantor among the old community. The time to enter and leave the village is well slated and known by all members. There are also other rules and regulations by which the village is governed or administered. In the community, artisas for the interconnectivity of their different skills and shared value of making ends meet constitute themselves as an "auto artisan family" whereby relationship is built towards assisting one another, especially to attain success on the job. Community meetings are held regularly basically to discuss issues relating to the progress of the village. In this wise, beyond enforcement of rules and regulations, members are given equal opportunity to participate in democratic administration towards enhancement of sustainable development of the village. This explains the effectiveness of the auto-artisans village leadership in harnessing members, efforts towards community development and all these will certainly enhance peace and orderliness in the community, finding support in the words Ajayi and Otuya (2006) that Sustainable community development is most likely to happen when all actors participate and share their ideas, visions and responsibilities equally and democratically in steering and implementing their community or village development projects.

The leadership of the auto-artisan's village community has always taken the responsibility of settling rifts among members, in case there is any miss-understanding. However, every artisan is always cautious not to allow rifts between self and any customer; they consider it as a rule in the village that customers must not be fought with. The idea that customers are always right is thus consciously or unconsciously entrenched in the artisan-customers' relationship. Hence, customers are held in high esteem and in some ways, it enhances patronage from the larger community. In this wise, artisans learn to suppress their emotions and treat customers as respectfully to grow their individual businesses and the mechanic village.

4.2 *Business Networking among Auto-artisans*

This segment explains the business networking among the artisans in the modern day auto-mobile centers in Ibadan. It particularly discusses how artisans network for business engage referral services, how referrers are compensated, and profit-sharing formula are structured.

The term network and networking seem to have been overused in modern vocabulary. In sociological definition however, networks describe the way in which an individual in a social group is connected to other members of the group. It explains the way individuals are linked together in social relationships, which can be of various types; authority structure, family links, friendship links, links of an economic nature, and face-to-face communication (Burton, 2007). All these are not irrelevant to the relationships between auto-mobile artisans in mechanic villages in Ibadan. All members of the village community (artisans) for the reason of interconnectivity of their different areas of specialities, constitute themselves a family that can be referred to as 'Auto-mobile family', and for the reason of their shared value of making ends meet consciously or unconsciously engage business networking. In the words of an interviewee:

> You know, naturally we have some things in common. The types of work we do has brought us together, there is no one who does not need the other person if we must all make it in life.
>
> IDI/Coppersmith/Ijokodo/October 2021

Another said:

> … For example, I am a mechanic, when customers come to me to do something for them on their vehicle, and while working I see the need for

> rewire, I will only tell the customer and they will tell me to call rewire for them, or call the rewire that usually work for them in the village, so me I will be doing my own, and at the same time the rewire will be doing his own, it makes us even closer, and if it is what cannot be done in my work shop, when I finish my own, he will take the vehicle to his shop.
>
> IDI/Upholstery/Bodija/October, 2021

Yet, another reveals:

> I am the treasurer, with the nature of what each person learnt, mechanic o, rewire o, vulcaniser o, upholstery o, and so on. You don't usually say that you can't finish a work that your customer should go to another person. No! We must work together, even as mechanic to mechanic, if you are doing something on the car and you need someone to help you look at it, so that you can satisfy your customer ... because that is what we do, you don't have to think too much about money, because you can even learn from one another. People usually 'say no one is an island' It is here that that proverb is meaningful. The most important thing is to make our customers happy.
>
> KII – Treasurer /Upholstery/samonda/October 2021

Another interviewee declared:

> Although everybody needs money but when one finish spending the money, it is relationship that will remain. If it is a work that you are called to do like rewire or vulcanizer while the mechanic is working on a car, there would have been agreement with the owner on how much you will take, but if it is what for instance, the rewire called another rewire or mechanic call another mechanic to come and help him see to give advice on how to do it, money is never the problem.
>
> IDI/Mechanic/Ijokodo/October 2021

In the words of another interviewee:

> Well ... anyway, we are doing our best to satisfy our customers, that is why you see this place full of vehicles. They even bring their friends to this mechanic village.
>
> IDI/Spray Painter/samonda/October 2021

The above explains the idea of business networking among the artisans, referral services with compensation and profit-sharing. The artisans in their different vocations engage in social networking and interact with one another towards enhancement of their entrepreneurial ambition. They conceive the opinion that having different auto-mobile related skills necessitates networking, and in that without business networking, there would be lack in business success. Artisans with the consent of the owner engage network with one-another to work on the vehicle when such is necessary, such that referral service is done without any formality; fixing different problems by different artisans on the same vehicle at the same time while rendering referral service do generate interactions and make the automobile family bond to be stronger. The study further reveals that the referral service is usually engaged among artisans of different trades, and not among those of the same area of specialisation. Members of the community would rather support one another to achieve whatever set objective over a vehicle brought for repair, and when such is done the issue of sharing formula does not arise. However, in the case whereby the owner of the vehicle's consent is sought before or during referral, there must have been agreement on what and how individual artisan will be paid. It is important to mention that in all these, artisans among others engage a form of internal networking. Although internal networking as noted by McCallum et al. (2014), refers to networking opportunities within the organization, in this case it is within the mechanic village, more so that the artisans' automobile or mechanic village constitutes an organizational structure, whereby consciously or unconsciously, artisans' entrepreneurial capacity is being developed. All these find support with opinion that networking is highly necessary in entrepreneurial capacity development since networking aids learning, and that beyond learning, a business owner should be able to engage internal networking by interacting with others with the same type of business within the enterprises as well as external networking with other parties including individuals and existing firms (Ogunnaike and Kehinde, 2013).

Customer's satisfaction is not a mere matter to contemporary commercial and public service organisations; business and service organisations progress or retrogress based on the percentage of their customers they are able to keep; customers retention is thus a mark of customer's satisfaction and a key to business growth (Fečiková, 2004) The auto-artisans are aware of all these, the study reveals that the artisans put in their best possible to satisfy their customers, and with their orientation that customers are always right, the result is obvious in terms of patronage.

4.3 *The Business Survival Strategies among Auto-artisans*

This section focuses on business challenges faced by the artisans in the mechanic village and how in some ways, networking has aided solutions to such problems/challenges. The research uncovered that within the context of survival strategies among auto-artisans in Ibadan the aphorism "no man is an island" consciously or unconsciously plays out, as actors assists one-another in solving challenges that they face from time to time in business, not only to survive but also to progress in different their fields of vocation. Very important is the challenge of old and new day technology as well as how skillful each artisan is, in his area of specialization. It is a general knowledge that proficiency is key to success in every vocation, and that requires being current or kept abreast of day-to-day relevant information about the business especially in the face of technological development across the globe. However, auto-artisans in Ibadan, Southwestern Nigeria seem deficient in this area of their business. Many of them do not have what it takes to face the challenge of modern day auto mobile technology. This could be deduced in the statement of an interviewee when he said:

> The biggest problem is the type of modern vehicles that are outside today, there is a need for us to really know about them, so we need modern day machines to detect faults so that we can be satisfying our customers more. The way we solve the problem is by calling another person to come and look at it, and some of us have such machines already.
>
> KII - Chairman/Mechanic/Bodija/August, 2021

The inadequate knowledge of the artisans in relation to the modern-day technology seems to be a major problem, such that it becomes necessary for the actors to develop themselves to meet up with the challenges, procure modern day machines and equipment to diagnose faults on the vehicles. However, challenges of such are addressed by consultation with one-another. This is further explained by another artisan when he said:

> You know that we know this thing more than ourselves, and no one can say that he knows everything. You may be doing work in a vehicle, especially mechanical or electrical and you are unable to get it, what you will do is to call your colleagues to come and help you to look at it. By so doing, you too will know what you have not known before.
>
> IDI/Mechanic/Samonda/August 2021

Actors (auto-artisans) acknowledge the importance of networking in business, especially in tapping from one another's knowledge and experience on the job. In this wise, there are situations that consequent to day-to-day advancement in automobile technology, certain faults are not easily addressed in a vehicle, particularly electrical or mechanical fault, without an adequate knowledge or experience by the artisan involved; hence, it becomes necessary to consult with one another in addressing such matters if the problem must be solved to the satisfaction of the customer. By so doing, artisans learn on the job and have their knowledge or skill more developed. Hence, within the context of social networks the artisans boost their business productivity for sustainability.

The challenge in relation to auto-mobile spare parts was uncovered as one among others that artisans in mechanic villages in Ibadan face. Most of the spare parts that are available in the market for use are either "Tokunbo" (imported second hand). In the words of an interviewee:

> One of the problems is that of Spare parts, although it is a general problem. There is nothing original in the market again. Our customers also know that, but it makes one look like a liar, when you request to buy an original spare apart, but fake is sold to you, such that you fix the material and after how many weeks it becomes faulty again.

Yet another said:

> … even "Tokunbo" spare parts are far better than what they call original, and if you go to buy any spare part, it is better you let somebody help you to look at it, and not say that you know it. It is always by luck that you can get some spare parts that will be original … if you are not careful, you will buy fake as original. To crown it up, prices are not stable; you must call somebody who also will call another person before you are able to confirm the current price of the spare parts you need, if at all you will get it.
>
> IDI/ Battery Charger/Ijokodo/August 2021

Generally, original automobile spare parts are not available in the market and may in that business is being fraudulent in their activities, such that it affects the work of the artisans. They could most of the time get *Tokunbo* (used) which ironically seems better than what is referred to as new. There is always the need for second opinion at the point of deciding to buy spare parts, and to crown it up, the price of the items is not always stable. Hence, these are multiple problems surrounding the issue of automobile spare parts. However, the only aspect that could be solved through business network is the price, as calls must have to be called before the current price of the items could be established and given to the customers. All these are indications of economic downtown in the country as it affects informal sectors, especially the automobile informal sector. Ekannade reported that importation of used vehicle parts (Tokunbo Auto Spare parts) has been on the increase since 1983, when the government put in place austerity measures, which constrained the purchasing power of Nigerian citizens and encouraged trade liberalization. Ekannade, further explained that Nigerians; Igbo, in particular who had at that period migrated to America, Europe and Asia and had amassed wealth, pooled resources together, bought used vehicles, dismantled, and exported them the parts to Nigeria as completely knocked down parts (Ekanade, 2018).

Another major challenge that auto-artisans face is Political instability. Due to government change and policy, there is often relocation from one mechanic village to another. This affects their business because most of the lands they use as Mechanics village are government owned, and anytime they relocate, it brings some kind of retrogression. Apart from relocation, government officials visit the village from time to time, and anytime they do, they are bribed to be protected against undue threats. In the words of an interviewee:

> This land and in fact, all mechanic villages all over the country are allocated by the government, and you know government comes government goes, especially when new government is from another party different from the former one, they treat us as if we are also politicians.
>
> KII - Secretary/Ijokodo/Rewire/August 2021

Yet another stated:

> It is politics that the governments play in everything; they trouble us too much, especially when another government comes to the office from another party. They want to show power or maybe I should say those government people look for where they can make money. They just change policy anyhow. But with man no man … you know, and again what party that wins the election becomes our own party too, that is how we are solving that problem.
>
> KII - Chairman/ Samonda/ Pannel beatter/August 2021

The study here uncovers the interplay of partisan politics and auto-artisan informal sector. Politicians seem to have seen the informal sector as a powerful space to gain ground in electioneering and money making, which in some ways influence the policy or decision making on land use. The government allocates that land for the purpose of mechanic village and may decide to use the land for something else, without considering the socio-economic consequence of such decision, particularly on the artisans. Artisans therefore results to "man know man" that is networking, going through people they may have known in the corridors of power to talk to the government functionaries in their favour. However, some of the government officials see such situation as an avenue to amass wealth in terms of money from the public space, while the artisans also get involved in partisan politics with a view to protecting their auto-mobile business.

Socio-economic challenges are one among the major problems that humans face daily in all informal sectors of every developing country. This is not untrue of auto-artisan in mechanic villages in Ibadan. Another interviewee said:

> One thing is that it is not every time that one is buoyant, I mean when it comes to having money at hand, but we do raise ourselves, it may be borrowing or even giving depending on the situation, for instance why borrowing the money and when the money will be returned. Apart from the fact that we have monthly contributions among ourselves that we make, the person that needs money may talk to the person who is the owner of that contribution for that month, and if he too does not need money at that time, he will allow it. It is a matter of love and trust, and it has been helping us.
>
> KII-Secretary/ Pannel beater/ Samonda/ August 2021

Actors at times have financial challenges, and they have always assisted one another, either by giving or borrowing one another, depending on the situation, perhaps what the money would be used for, when and how the money would be refunded. In the mechanic village, the tool of *ajo* (thrift) is also used in solving financial problems; the actors among themselves arrange contributions of money to be collected by them in turns, one after the other as systematically arranged, all based on love and trust that they have for one another. In this wise, the artisans harness associational networking and social capital in form of Yoruba *Ajo* system to solve their financial problems towards business survival and sustainability. *Ajo* system in literature has been described as a provider of "needed succor for group members through material and nonmaterial assistance sourced from members' contributions and profits of investments of cooperative societies" (Omobowale, 2011; Abutudu, 2002). It is a type of social capital and network system which depends on bonds of friendship, kinship and trust to create and develop informal cooperative societies or systems (Omobowale, et al. 2016). Very important here is network system and the shared trust value among the Auto-mobile artisans which sustains cohesion and consequently business survival against their restraining socio-economic situation All these explain another major noteworthy business survival strategy adopted by the auto-artisans in Mechanic villages in Ibadan.

It is important to mention that there are challenges that auto-artisans in Mechanic villages Ibadan encounter and cope with or endure as they are beyond what business networking could aid for survival of the villages. They are the problems of epileptic power supply and non-availability of water, the challenge of inadequate physical space and Occupational health and safety challenges. All these are in one way or the other addressed but not necessarily with business networking as a survival strategy.

Epileptic electricity supply and non-availability of water among social amenities are other social challenges that are common in the mechanic villages. It is a general knowledge that water is a necessity for all human activities including the numerous automobile activities in Mechanic villages, regular electricity supply is another without which industries and businesses are not likely to thrive. Several automobile activities carried out by artisans of various areas of specialization require both water and regular supply of electricity, but these remain a twin challenge for the communities. As enumerated by several of the actors interviewed, for the electricity supply, they burn so much fuel in generator, to meet up with their need, while they must go to the wells or streams around to get water because they cannot dig a borehole without permission from the appropriate quarters. The appropriate quarters refer to the officials or government functionaries, who have been reported to be politicizing matters that have to do with automobile informal sector. Irregular supply of electricity and water as challenges is a general knowledge about many areas in Ibadan. Thus, it seems that the problems may have to remain with the automobile artisans until the situation of things are generally improved. The problem of physical space was also raised by some of the artisans, and it was in fact observed during the time of the interview that the space allocated as the mechanic villages where the research was carried out were full of vehicles, few were abandoned by their owners, perhaps for financial reasons or because their spare parts were not yet available, while others are still under repair. However, customers come and go, such that there is traffic in that some must wait for others to come in, because of space. In other words, as automobile businesses in the mechanic villages expand, and activities increase, the space allocated becomes smaller. Hence, despite all challenges that the artisans face, automobile businesses endure and that explains the import of business networking among auto-artisans in Mechanic villages in Ibadan, Southwestern Nigeria.

Occupational health and safety are very important for the effectiveness and efficiency of informal sector workers, and that does not exclude the Auto-artisans, it was discovered that in the mechanic villages, auto artisans are exposed to several hazards within their work environment: auto-mobile exhaust, solvents, oil spill etc. This is not different from the observation that Informal sector auto mechanics are exposed to so many hazards within their work environment (Brown, 1990). Brown, cited by Amfo-Otu and Agyemang

(2016) listed hazards such as asbestos, mineral oils, solvents, paint pigments, anticorrosive substances, and automobile exhaust. Amfo-Otu and Agyemang (2016) further mentioned that informal sector workers are opened to physical hazards like noise, vibration, messy environment, fire, dust, smoke, and inhalation of fume; Psychological hazards like stress and ergonomic hazard like poor posture among others. All these are not far from the experience of auto-artisans in mechanic villages in Ibadan, South-western Nigeria.

5 Summary and Conclusion

This study has brought to the fore a dimension of business networking among the artisans in the modern day Auto-mobile centers in Ibadan, Southwestern Nigeria. In summary, it has been revealed that Auto-artisan villages are integral to economic sustenance, environmental pollution reduction and social networking in Ibadan. Like most urban areas, Ibadan over time has had a population surge which warrants more auto mobiles use, thereby increasing demand for auto artisans. Auto-artisans constitute an informal sector domicile in mechanic villages. These mechanic villages are situated on government owned lands. They have a well-structured internal hierarchical system which ensures its sustenance. Auto-artisans specialize in different areas of auto mobile repair. Hence, they recommend other artisans when need arises (Networking) through informal referrals and compensation is usually by mutual understanding. Associational networking is also adopted to solve auto artisans' economic problems.

Although, auto-artisan's presence in mechanic villages and attendant networking predispositions through informal referrals has enhanced the solution to challenges relating to repairs of some old generation auto mobile, the advanced technology automobiles remain a challenge due to inadequate knowledge, non-availability modern equipment as well as spare parts. Again, political instability sometimes affects the location of the mechanic village. Epileptic electricity supply, non-availability of water and other basic social amenities in mechanic villages are also challenges deterring activities in Mechanic villages. The physical space available at times is inadequate due to congestion caused by faulty automobiles for which the artisans have not found spare parts.

Lastly, there is interplay of partisan politics and auto-artisan informal sector as politicians need the auto-mobile informal sector for elections; auto-mobile artisans need the politicians for suitable policies to ensure the sustenance of mechanic village location. The business networking, along with internal hierarchical organization and urbanization are the major factors embedded in survival of artisans as well as mechanic villages in Ibadan.

References

Abutudu, M. I. M. (2002.) Peasant organisations and grassroots empowerment in Nigeria: Limits and possibilities. In Peasants organisations and the democratic process in Africa, ed. M. B. Romdhane and S. Moyo, 184–218. Dakar: CODESIA.

Adewoyin, O. A, Hassan, A. T. and Aladesida, A. A. (2013). The Impacts of Automechanic Workshops on Soil and Groundwater in Ibadan Metropolis. African Journal of Environmental Science and Technology Vol. 7(9), pp. 891–898.

Ajayi, A. R. and N. Otuya (2006) Women's participation in self-help community development projects in Ndokwa agricultural zone of Delta State, Nigeria. Community Development Journal, 41 (2), 189–209.

Amfo-Otu, R. and Agyemang, J. K. (2016) Occupational Health Hazards and Safety Practices Among the Informal Sector Auto Mechanics. Applied Research Journal, 1(4): 59–69.

Anyadike N, Emeh, I. E. J, Ukah, F. O. (2012) "Entrepreneurship development and employment generation in Nigeria" Problems and prospects. Univ J Educ Gen Stud. 2012;1(4):88–102.

Asaju, A. S. 2002. The internal dynamics of peasant-based cooperatives and democratisation in Nigeria. In Peasants organisations and the democratic process in Africa, ed. M. B. Romdhane and S. Moyo, 52–75. Dakar: CODESIA.

Asogwa S. E. (1981) "A survey of working conditions in small-scale industries in Nigeria". J. Occup. Med.(1981). 23 (11):775–777.

Bishop, V., & Hoel, H. (2008) The Customer is Always Right? Journal of Consumer Culture, 8(3), 341–367. doi:10.1177/1469540508095303.

Borgatti, S. P., & Halgin, D. S. (2011) On Network Theory Organization Science, 22, (5), 1168–1181.

Brown, N. J. (1990). Health hazards manual for autobody shop workers. Ithaca, NY: Cornell University, Chemical Hazard Information, Retrieved from: Program. http://digitalcommons.ilr.cornell.edu/manuals/7 on 10/11/2021.

Burton, L.(2007) Social relationships in the local church. A comparison of networks in the rural and urban church. Journal of Beliefs & Values, Vol. 28, No. 1, April 2007, pp. 65–75 ISSN 1361–7672 DOI: 10.1080/13617670701251595.

Casula, M., Rangarajan, N. and Shields, P. (2020) *The potential of working hypotheses for deductive exploratory research.* Qual Quant (2020). https://doi.org/10.1007/s11135-020-01072-9.

Duchi, P (2005). "Planning for auto repair service industry in Zaria urban area, Kaduna State". An unpublished burp dissertation. Department of urban and regional planning. A.B.U. Zaria. 2005.

Edwards, T. (2000) Contradictions of Consumption. Milton Keynes: Open University Press.

Ekanade O. (2018) From an Invocation Space to a Commercial Emporium: The Evolutionary Dynamics of the Ladipo Auto Spare Parts Flea Market in Lagos, Nigeria – the 1950s to 20161 *Afrika Zamani*, No. 25, 2017, pp. 125–145.

Fečiková, I. (2004). "An index method for measurement of customer satisfaction. *The TQM Magazine* Vol. 16, No. 1, pp. 57–66. https://doi.org/10.1108/09544780410511498.

Gupta U. C and Gupta S. C. (1998) Trace element toxicity relationships to crop production and livestock and human health: implications for management. *Communications in Soil Science and Plant Analysis*, volume 29 : S1491–1522.

Khan, A. A, Inam S,,Idrees M, Dad Azra,Gul Khitab, Akbar H (2010) "Effect of automobile workshop on the health status of automechanics in NWFP Pakistan". Afr. J. Environ. Sci. Technol. (2010). 4(4):192–200.

Kinyanjui, M. N. (2016) Positioning Peasants, Artisans, and Traders: "The African Angle. Retrieved from http://www.worldpolicy.org/blog/2016/02/16/positioning-peasants-artisans-and-traders".

Macdonald, C. and Siriani, C. (eds) (1996) 'The Service Society and the Changing Experience of Work', in C. Macdonald and C. Siriani (eds) Working in the Service Society, pp. 1–28. Philadelphia, PA: Temple University Press.

Marshall, G. (1994) The concise Oxford dictionary of sociology (Oxford, Oxford University Press).

McCallum, S. Y, Forret, M. L and Wolff, H.-G. (2014) Internal and external networking behavior. Career Development International, 19(5), 595–*614*. doi:10.1108/cdi-08–2013-0101.

Moyo, S. 2002. Peasant organisations and rural civil society in Africa: An introduction. In Peasants organisations and the democratic process in Africa, ed. M. B. Romdhane and S. Moyo, 1–28.Dakar: CODESRIA.

Nwachukwu, M. A., Alinnor, J. and Feng, H. (2012). Review and assessment of Mechanic Village Potentials for Small Scale used Engine oil Recycling Business, African Journal of Environmental Science and Technology Vol. 6(12), pp. 464–475.

Ogunnaike, O.O. and Kehinde, O. J. (2013) Social Networking and Business Performance: The case of Selected Entrepreneurs in Ota, Nigeria. Journal of Business Administration and Management Sciences Research, 2 (5) pp. 116–122.

Oloruntoba, E. O. and Ogunbunmi, T. O. (2020) Impact of Informal Auto-Mobile Mechanic Workshops Activities on Groundwater Quality in Ibadan, *Nigeria Journal of Water Resource and Protection* Vol.12 No.7, (July 2020) DOI: 10.4236/jwarp.2020.127036.

Oluwagbemi, B. F (2007) Basic Occupational Health and Safety, Vertex Media Limited, Ibadan, Nigeria, 2nd Edition.

Omobowale, A.O. (2008) The *Tokunbo*: A Sociological Examination of the Imported Second Hand Automobiles Market in Nigeria in Tunc, T. E. and Babic, A. A. (eds.) *The Globetrotting Shopaholic: Consumer Spaces, Products, and their Cultural Places*

Newcastle upon Tyne: CambridgeScholars Publishing Pp. 183–191 (United Kingdom) ISBN 978-1-4438-0027-3.

Omobowale, A. O. (2011). Social Capital and Ajọ System Among Working Class Traders In Ibadan, Nigeria. *WorkingUSA, 14(3), 333–346.* doi:10.1111/j.1743-4580.2011.00344.x.

Omobowale, A. O, Ombowale, M. O., Olutayo, M. S. and Akinade, H. O. (2016) Harnessing Associational Networking and Social Capital For Development In West Africa. African *Journal for the Psychological studies of Social Issues,* Vol. 19, No. 3 https://ajpssi.org/index.php/ajpssi/article/view/195.

Omokhodion, F. O. (1999) Environmental hazards of automobile mechanics in Ibadan, Nigeria. West Afr. J. Med. 18 (1):69–72.

Onibokun, A and A. Faniran, (1995). Urban Research in Nigeria. New Edition, Ibadan: IFRA – Nigeria, ISBN: 9791092312188. DOI: htts://doi.org/10.4000/books.ifra.534.

Onibokun, A. and A. J. Kumuyi, (1999) "Ibadan, Nigeria (chapter 3)," In: A.G. Onibokun, Ed., Managing the Monster: Urban Waste and Governance in Africa, IDRC, pp 49–100.

Onwe, O. J. (2013) Role of the Informal Sector in Development of the Nigerian Economy": Output and Employment Approach. Journal of Economics and Development Studies, (2013).1(1), 60–74.

Orapin, S. (1996) People's participation in community development. TDRI Quarterly Review, 11 (3), 19–25.

Oyesiji, O. O et.al (2021) Assessment of Technical Innovation among Auto-Allied Artisans in Southwestern Nigeria. Journal of Management and Social Sciences. Vol. 6, Number 1 (June, 2021): 74–89.

Sambo M. N, Idris S. H, Shamang, A (2012). Determinants of Occupational Health Hazards among Roadside Automobile Mechanics in Zaria, North Western Nigeria. BOMJ. 9(1):5–9.

Stebbins, R. (2001). Exploratory Research in the Social Sciences. Thousand Oaks, CA: SAGE (ISBN 0-7619-2398-5).

Udonwa, N. E, Uko, E. K, Ikpeme B. M, Ibanga, I. A, Okon, B. O (2009).Exposure of petrol station attendants and auto mechanics to Premium Motor Spirits Fumes in Calabar, Nigeria. J. Environ. Public Health, 2009:1–5.

WHO (World Health Organization) (2006) Protecting Groundwater for Health. In: Schmoll, O. and Howard, G., Eds., Managing the Quality of Drinking-Water Sources, London: IWA Publishing, P. 678.

CHAPTER 5

Coconut Oil Processing, Marketing Network and Challenges in Badagry, Nigeria

Adebimpe Oluwabukade Adefila and Ayokunle Olumuyiwa Omobowale

1 Introduction

Coconut oil is among the class of indigenously produced oil with a wide consumer base in Nigeria and abroad, yet, produced largely manually and relatively simple technology. Nigeria's Minister for Agriculture and Rural Development in a 2021 presentation submitted that coconut oil production and marketing provide livelihood for more than 500,000 Nigerians, and Nigeria earned more than $150 million from coconut oil export in 2020, (representing 10 percent of foreign exchange earnings) with an estimate of $250 million for 2021 (see Emmanuel 2021). The Philippines, Indonesia, India, Vietnam and Mexico are the five largest producers of coconut oil and Nigeria ranks the 15th largest producer, globally. Nigeria is no doubt a major player in the coconut oil industry. Coconut oil is a natural oil that is obtained from the processing of coconut fruit. It can be processed through two major methods: the dried method which produces, the copra coconut oil and the aqueous method which produces virgin coconut oil (Shankar, Ahuja and Tracchio, 2013). The coconut tree is often described as a tree of life because all the components of the tree have huge benefits in cultures where the coconut tree is grown, nurtured and harvested for economic and livelihood ends (Chowdappa, Murlidharan and Rajesh 2017).

Coconut oil is a great natural resource to humanity, especially, due to its usefulness for industrial and domestic purposes. Due to its high content of lauric acid (a healthy saturated fat), it is useful for industrial purposes especially in the production of soaps, and it is also used domestically for cooking and as cosmetics (Suryani, Sariani, earnestly et al 2020). Coconut oil and market is a multibillion-dollar industry globally. The primary centres of production are Africa, Asia and South America. It serves as a major export and foreign exchange earner for countries and families in the Southern hemisphere. Coconut oil is rightly adjudged an economic resource of great importance; however, it is important to study its production chain. This study, therefore, examines processing, marketing and challenges of coconut oil in Nigeria.

 | DOI:10.1163/9789004692657_007

The coconut tree and production of coconut oil is quite common tropical coastal regions. On the one hand Wallace (2019) acknowledged the increasing popularity of coconut oil among consumers especially, in wealthy western nations because of its potentials as a source of vitamin E, polyphenols, fatty acids and lauric acids among other nutrients. Wallace (2019) notes that published essays confirm that coconut oil is beneficial in skin care, dental care and prevention of hair loss, while limited studies claim that coconut oil helps in the prevention and treatment of Alzheimer's disease, glycemic disorder and bone loss. Boateng, Ansong, Owusu and Steiner-Asiedu (2016) critique the negative perception of coconut and palm oil as unhealthy due to their high saturated fat content. They submitted that both coconut and palm oil have enormous nutritional and developmental benefits. On the other hand, Sankararaman and Sferra (2018) note that coconut oil is commonly frenzied in the USA and other Western countries as a 'super' food with tremendous health benefits to the heart, immunity, wound healing and memory retention among others (see p. 107). The authors contend this conclusion by disclosing that the high saturated fat of about 90 percent in coconut oil is potentially dangerous to health after prolonged consumption.

Irrespective of its health benefits or otherwise, coconut oil is certainly an economic resource of enormous importance especially in producing countries. In a study on the sustainability of the value chain of coconut in the Philippines, Acosta, Eugenio and Sales (2019) notes that coconut plants accounts for up to 30 percent of Filipino farmlands and that 3.5 million poor farmers are into coconut production while coconut oil accounting for 23 percent of the country's export and foreign exchange earner in 2015. Despite the strategic importance of the coconut oil industry to Filipino economy, Moreno, Kuwornu and Szabo (2020) submitted that it is plagued by declining productivity due to inability to meet global market demands as a result of ageing and aged coconut trees, poor yields, poor seedlings, poor soil nutrition, poor agricultural management and incessant felling of coconut trees. The research of Hebbar, Arivalagan, Manikantan et al. (2015) disclosed new technics at extracting sugar from coconut as an extension of value addition strategies and Rajendran (2002) described the vibrancy of the coconut economy in India, but the industry is challenged by poor tools, meddling by middle men and profit appropriation at the expense of the farmers, and poor storage facilities. A study on the copra and coconut oil markets in Mexico by Fortiz, Gómez-Gómez, Leos-Rodríguez et al. (2021) notes that domestically produced coconut oil is hardly competitive vis-a-vis those produced in industrial plants. The authors also submitted that Guerrero and Tabasco are the best producing states in Mexico, because they are the closest to industrial processing plants. The authors further acknowledge Mexican national policies that aid increased production of copra and coconut oil but warned that excess production without commensurate market demands would result in a sharp drop in prices and hurt profits. The literature reviewed above, and others consulted such as Peguero, Zapata, and Sandoval (2019), Infante-Amate, Luedtke, MacFadyen, Robins and Stevens (2019), Watkins (2015) and Hinder (2010) among others, confirm that coconut oil production enhances the livelihood of poor producers, though it might not elevate them significantly outside of the poverty trap, especially due to the challenges associated with substandard production tools and appropriation by middlemen. This research focuses on coconut oil production in Nigeria, and it examines coconut oil processing, marketing networks and challenges by probing (1) the machinery and stages of coconut production, (2) the marketing networks and adverts and (3) the challenges and coping strategies in the industry. This section presents the background and the next outlays the methodology. The third section discusses the machinery and the stages of coconut production, the fourth presents the marketing networks and adverts, the fifth discusses the challenges and coping strategies and finally, the sixth presents the conclusion.

2 Methodology

The research adopted an exploratory design and data were collected qualitatively. Exploratory design and qualitative method were appropriate because the research collected taken-for-granted processes that are involved in everyday production of coconut oil (Dominici, Boncinelli and Marone 2019, Carvalho, Scott and Jeffery 2005). Whereas, coconut oil is popularly produced in Nigeria and other West African countries, the research on it has largely been limited to its scientific nature, natural benefits, production volumes and consumption (see for example, Lima and Block 2019, Eyres, Eyres, Chisholm and Brown 2016, Cunningham 2011). The research lays emphasis on the production context of coconut. The research was carried out in Badagry, Lagos, Nigeria, as it is a major coconut production and marketing community in Nigeria (Ojo and Saibu 2018/2019). Data were collected through observation, key informant interviews and indepth interviews. The manual production processes and local instruments used were observed, eight KIIs were conducted with four executives of the producer's association and four major producers who are not executives. Also, 37 IDIs were conducted with 26 producers, seven traders and four production aides/workers. The data generated were contextually analysed.

3 Major Findings

3.1 *Labour, Machinery and the Stages of Coconut Oil Production*

The most crucial component of any production are the ingredients and equipment. Therefore, it is necessary to take off on the discussion of the production of coconut oil in Badagry by examining the materials and tools used for the production. Over 98% of the research participants affirm that they use different ingredients and instruments in the production of coconut oil. The instruments include: the hammer- for breaking the coconut because most of the coconut bought had been de-husked so they only need to remove the shell; the special knife created for removing the coconut from the shell; different sizes of bowls; drums; baskets; sieve or white cheese cloth; grinder or grater for grating the coconut meat; big stainless pot popularly referred to as *Adogan*; stoves or fire wood or gas cooker, and long spoon for stirring the coconut oil on fire as shown in Figure 5.1.

3.2 *Instruments Used in the Production Process of Coconut Oil*

For those whose method of production requires the use of extractors, the only instrument needed is the coconut meat that has been de-shelled and washed in the different bowls and then the extracting machine for the extraction of the oil from the milk. The production process of coconut oil in Badagry involves principally the use of labourers as few producers make use of machines. Few of the producers own grinding machines which is used to grate the coconut meat into small bits to extracts the milk. Therefore, this shows that despite technological innovation, coconut oil production involves more labour than machines. A major producer in Badagry pointed out that, "he cannot do the process of producing coconut oil himself despite the grinder he has, he would have to get labourers, male especially to carry out the tasking process of the production which reduces his profit'.

The production of coconut oil involves a systematic procedure with several different stages. These stages have beneficial proceeds to the economy as well as add value to the economy that produces it. The coconut fruit and materials that can be obtained from it are valuable; from the coconut shell to the coconut meat and the other by-products, coconut has therefore been described as the tree of life, due to the fact that all parts of the coconut palm can be used to satisfy human wants and needs (de- Silva, 2009; Uwubanmwen, Nwawe et al, 2011, Sankararaman and Sfera, 2018). The production of coconut oil starts from the stage of getting the coconut fruit, which seems to be a great deal of work

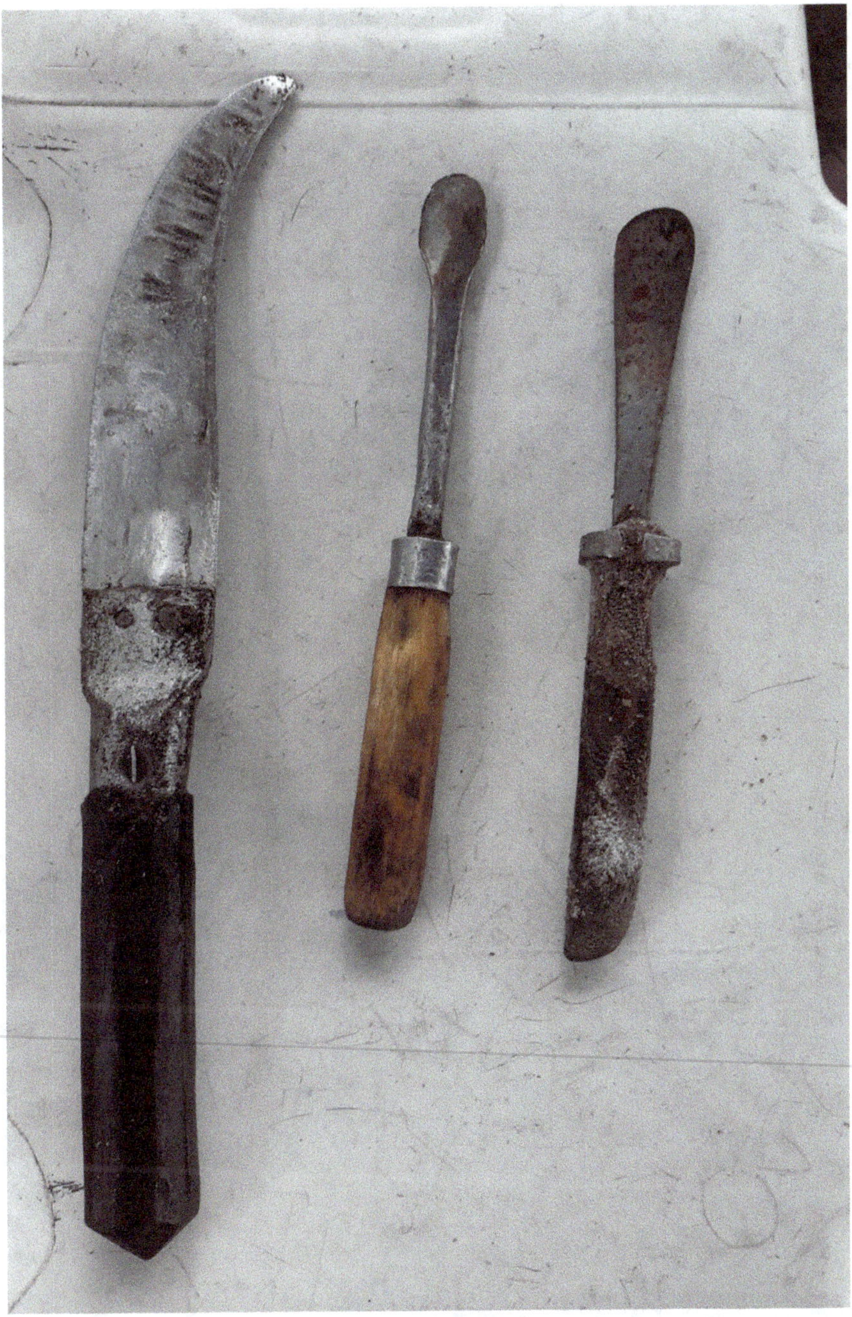

FIGURE 5.1 Special knives due for reshelling
SOURCE: AUTHOR

FIGURE 5.2 Different drums and bowls
SOURCE: AUTHOR

FIGURE 5.3 Grinder for grinding coconut meat
SOURCE: AUTHOR

FIGURE 5.4 Adogan, pots, and basket
SOURCE: AUTHOR

in Badagry due to the fact that the local coconuts are not sufficient to meet the demands of coconut oil producers in the country. Data from the fieldwork reveals that the coconut oil obtained from the local coconut is not as much as that obtained from coconut from Ghana. Coconut is imported from Ghana, Togo and all other neighboring countries that have coconuts in large quantity. The interviewees grouped the stages of production thus: purchasing the coconut, breaking the coconut, de-shelling, washing, grinding, extracting the coconut milk, cooking and extracting the coconut oil. A male producer, who has a primary career in civil service, expatiates on the process:

> The first category is the raw material preparation. That is getting the coconut, removing the husk, breaking the coconut, removing the coconut from shell also washing the coconut. The second stage is milk extraction is the process whereby the coconut is then crushed in the mill and then the milk is washed down from the shaft and then the milk is allowed to settle while the water stay under and the milk floats and the scooping of the milk from the water. The third category is oil extraction, you are doing cold pressed if it is cold pressed, the milk would be covered for a period of time somewhere till the oil comes out.
>
> KII/Male/Married/40–44/Egun/Civil Servant and Producer/Badagry Museum/30th May 2018

TABLE 5.1 The stages and by product in coconut oil preparation

Stages	Process involved	By-products	Pictures
Raw material preparation	Getting the coconut fruit. De-shelling. Washing of the coconut meat.	Coconut shell Coconut meat Coconut water	 FIGURE 5.5 Raw material preparation SOURCE: AUTHOR
Milk extraction	Grinding of the coconut meat Washing of the coconut shaft Coconut milk	Coconut shaft Coconut milk	 FIGURE 5.6 Milk extraction SOURCE: AUTHOR
Oil extraction	Coconut milk fermentation. Coconut milk cooking. Filtering of the coconut oil.	Coconut oil Coconut cake	 FIGURE 5.7 Oil extraction SOURCE: AUTHOR

SOURCE: AUTHOR, 2018

The different stages produce specific by-products which are useful to the economy. During the first stage, which is the raw material preparation, the by-product incurred includes the shell, the coconut water and coconut meat. The byproducts obtained from the second stage are coconut milk and the coconut milk shaft. At the last stage, the coconut oil shaft is obtained. All these by-products are of economic importance, and they are used for other production and functions.

4 Marketing Networks, Labelling and Online Adverts

Networking is essential in any market structure. The network deals with the connection between the actors of production which includes the producers, labourer distributors, and the consumers. According to Giddens (2008), networks are direct or indirect connections that link a person or a group with another person or groups. Contemporaneously, information and communication technology has transformed social networks and marketing ensuring a critical link for access to consumers and business survival.

Furthermore, Fafchamps (1999) noted that the networks that pre-exists in most Sub-Saharan African market is affiliated to linage, co-residence and the sharing of common religion and ethnicity which can be classified as a direct link. This can be defined as the indigenous system of networking, however, due to technological innovations, technology enhanced networking has been developed, although some producers still use interpersonal means of connections. This was found to be the norm in Badagry market, based on the case study that was done, the producers' community had great influence on the customer base of the producers. The community helps producers to locate customers and they also serve as retailers. In Aivoji community there is an association that was set up by the community for coconut oil producers so as to encourage the growth of the business in the community and also make the community known for coconut oil production. The largest producers in Badagry were found in Aivoji, where these producers had their production plants and machines that makes production easier and faster. One of them was largely supported by the Lagos State Coconut Development Agency (LASCODA), where she was given a brand-new grinding machine to make her business grow. Aside the LASCODA, the Aivoji Community producers also have a body that coordinates them. One of the executives of the association explained thus:

> The name of the association is Aivoji Coconut Oil Manufacturers Association. It is a form of cottage industry that produces the coconut oil. The

> association was set up mainly because coconut fruit are available in relatively large quantity within this environment and instead of just taking the fruit to the market in form of coconut seedlings or seeds, we decided to process it further so that the by-product could be used for our piggery husbandry and some other livestock we have in this environment.
>
> KII/Male/Married/50–54/Egun/Civil Servant and Producer/Aivoji, Badagry/26th June 2018

Another interviewee said:

> Here in my extended family, we network. I still have 3 to 4 other producers. At the moment my factory is going through some re-organisation and renovation. We are working to have our product approved by the NAFDAC approval so they would be visiting in June. The network has helped. We have been producing in other people's factory since my factory is not accessible. And at times when I have orders that are large and urgent, I get from others to support the supply.
>
> KII/Male/Married/40–44/Egun/Civil Servant and Producer/Badagry Museum/30th May 2018

As Giddens (2008), stated informal networks tend to develop the economy fast as the families and cultures that come together in an informal setting ensure that their loved ones move forward as they also do, which is evident in Aivoji Community.

Further, the association serves as financers for the producers in the community. The association is made up of financial supporters who loan out money for particular projects over a period of time, to make it easy for producers in the community. The association can be classified as a means of social capital network for the members. Economic advantages are made available for members. Non-members would not be opportune to such advantages. This network in the Aivoji community has helped the producers to be one of the largest producers of coconut oil in Badagry. An interviewee also pointed out the functions of the financial supports to the society saying:

> Coconut oil production is capital intensive. A perfect production requires a lot of money. So, the women need to have financial strength to fully equip the necessary things. That is where you see someone say, I would give 40 coconuts … someone can finance that and say I would buy the coconut. Then the manpower would be provided by the women,

> or someone can also provide the grinder ... Someone can also be financially involved by providing the bus that would be used to transport the coconut. So, it is a network chain that attracts 5 to 10 people for effective production.
>
> KII/Male/Married/50–54/Egun/Civil Servant and Producer/Aivoji, Badagry/26th June 2018

There is also a level of closeness and trust between the community and the producers. The financial supports given to the people are contributions done by the people of the community with the aim of reducing the level of poverty among producers and the producing community while also ensuring that their women in particular have access to some earnings to enhance empowerment and household earnings. Transfer of knowledge of production to the next generation is also ensured by the association. This ensures continuity of production process of coconut oil. The association monitors production trainings to ensure that tutors have adequate understanding of the production process and are able to transfer same to learners.

Every producer or manufacturer aim is to make profit; as such the role of consumers, retailers and distributors is an aspect that is taken into cognisance in the coconut oil value chain. In Badagry, producers of coconut oil are always in search of consumers that would purchase their products from them. Some of them take it to the market while others sell in their production plants while looking for customers through social media (internet) in order to cover a larger sphere of the consumers across geographic spaces within and outside Nigeria. This affirms the potential and real contributions of information technology innovations to the advancement of the informal industry (Ndangwa, 2007). This is implied in the words of an interviewee thus:

> Because of the little exposure one has had, we have been able to move with the modern trends of marketing. I just told you a customer called ... [and] has just sent money to me for coconut oil. I do not even know her name. That is to tell you the positive contribution of online adverts. I started with marketing around my neighborhood and thereafter, I used the social media platforms such as: Jiji, Jumia and Nairaland among others to market my products. Then I also took advantage of popular international social media platforms such as Facebook, Instagram and Twitter, which have really helped my business tremendously.
>
> KII/Male/Married/40–45/Egun/Civil Servant and Producer/Badagry Museum/30th May 2018

Also, another interviewee said that:

> In our own company we do a lot of advertisement, we have a website, we have a twitter page, we have a Facebook page, we have Instagram page, so we are very present on the social media. And also, we use bulk SMS for advertisement. We do a lot of adverts on Facebook, Nairaland, and all social forums for Nigerians. So, our customers meet us online. More than 90 percent of them meet us online while 5 percent are from referrals, where people that have used our products refer their friends or some other people, they know needs our products. So that is how we connect to our consumers.
>
> KII04/Male/Married/45–49/Egun/Businessman and Producer/ Badagry Market/5th June 2018

Some others just take theirs to the market and sell. Some of the market women attest to it that they do not produce, but they sell coconut oil in the markets.

> We package in different bottles, we sell from ₦ 50 ($0.16), ₦ 100 ($0.32), ₦ 200 ($0.65), ₦ 250 ($0.81) and even ₦ 1000 ($3.26) depending on how people have money. We do not produce it, here we only sell it here. We get it from Badagry and then sell in small quantities to people who want to buy and use it for themselves.
>
> IDI/Female/Married/55–60/Egun/Marketer/Agbara Market/22nd June 2018

Producers look for every means to sustain their customer and some customers who see that they enjoyed the product would also help them get other customers. The network in the market is therefore not easy to manage as there are other producers of coconut oil. To maintain the connection that has been created by the producers, they ensure that they meet their customers need and use the social media as a competitive advantage. Hence, Facebook, Twitter, Instagram and other news and marketing social media platforms such as Jiji, Nairaland and Jumia are readily utilised to advertise coconut oil and network with consumers.

Furthermore, according to Ruf, Kuaku, Salinier and Courbet (2010), Nigerian coconut sellers have a debtor-creditor relationship with the Ghanaian coconut planters where some of the buyers of coconut buy on credit and not pay on time. However, this is not the case between producers and the consumers of coconut oil in Badagry. The research revealed that whoever wants to buy coconut oil must come with his or her money, before the coconut oil is handed over to the individual. Conversely, old customers who have over time built an adequate relationship and trust with the producers sometimes pay up to two million naira (₦ 2,000,000 ($6,535) ahead to the producer's bank account and s/he will be confident enough to get his or her product.

There is also a close/communal relationship among producers in the area. They communicate and solve challenges collectively. Aside from the aforementioned, they also depend on one another to loan goods to ensure smooth production and sales. This is buttressed by a female producer on the relationship among coconut oil producers:

> I connect with other producers very well. For example, now those that I know very well if I do not have coconut oil, I would go to one of my associates that I know produces and does not adulterate it. If a customer needs coconut oil urgently, I would call them to ask if they have, and if they say they have, I will quickly go and meet them and collect it and give the customer.
>
> KII/Female/Married/40–44/Egun/Businesswoman and Producer/Agelasho, Badagry / 30th May 2018

Some other producers however do not relate nor depend on other producers but run their business on a solo mode. One of such producers re-echoes this in her statement:

> Ehn, some people do meeting, but I do not join them, I stand on my own. If they come to me, we talk oh, but *Ilara* (hatred) won't allow them, so I stand on my own
>
> KII/Female/Married/60–64/Egun/Producer/Aivoji, Badagry/30th May 2018

Even though they are aware of the presence and benefits of networking, reasons why they isolate themselves are not farfetched from fear of unhealthy competition and hatred. Some of the producers find it hard to network conveniently with other producers as they feel they are in competition and if there is an unnecessary closeness, they might end up stealing their customers and leave them to ruins in the long run.

Packaging of coconut oil for selling is not common in Nigeria, although few sellers are now branding their coconut oil in other to gain customers attentions and enhancing sales. According to Daramola, Bello and Okafor (2014) packaging is an important part of an organisation's reputation which plays a major role in attracting and communicating the product and frailty to the consumers. They further posit that branding and packaging enhances advertising, promotion and ultimately sales. As such, for the sale of coconut oil boom, branding and packaging are major factors to employ. Most of the producers do not, however, involved in branding and packaging brand, they package their goods and sell in bulk to direct middlemen who then brand and package before they selling to retailers and consumers. This is re-echoed in the statement of a male producer:

> After we have cooked the milk, we sieve it and pack it inside kegs of 25, 10, 5, 2, 1 liter and put it inside, the people who want to buy would come to me and tell me the number of liters they want to buy. If its 25liters, that is about ₦ 27, 000.00 ($88.2), a liter is ₦ 1, 600.00 ($5.2), … [and] 75cl is ₦ 1, 200.00 ($3.9). That how we sell it.
>
> KII/Male/Married/65–69/Egun/Businessman and Producer/Aivoji, Badagry/6thJune, 2018

Another interviewee said that:

> Presently, the method we are using does not have a specialised style of marketing. We use 25 liters or 10 liters or 5 liters depending on what the customers require. But in other places, some do the packaging by branding, labeling, putting the nutrient values, the contents and all those things. We have not gotten to that extent yet; it is those people that come and buy from us that do all those things. At our level, what we do in the packaging is selling at liters customers want to buy
>
> KII/Male/Married/50–54/Egun/Civil Servant and Producer/Aivoji, Badagry/26th June 2018

Aside from selling to customers at wholesales, at production points, some producers have stores in the markets where they sell to wholesalers, retailers and consumers customers at whole sales and retail. Customers come from several locations within and outside Lagos to purchase coconut oil from the producers in Badagry irrespective of packaging. Packaging and branding are not necessarily the primary determinant of purchase, especially among consumers who attribute beneficial qualities to coconut oil. Nevertheless, packaging and branding serve the secondary purpose of identification of branded sellers for competitive advantage specially to attract and retain middle and upper-class consumers who may attribute branding and packaging with content quality and class identification. This confirms the findings of Daramola, Bello and Okafor (2014) that branding and packaging have positive effects on the buying decisions and habits of consumers.

Hence, producers who package also use it to build their customer trust and confidence. A male producer who brands and packages coconut oil explained further that the branding was necessary for him to improve his customer trust creating a network of trust between the product and the consumers:

> This packaging is not different from your [branded and packaged] vegetable oil. Even these days we do tamper proof, that you will need to break the tamper proof and even the seal use it. Some are also corked so that as to really improve confidence in our customers
>
> KII/Male/Married/45–49/Egun/Civil Servant and Producer/Badagry Museum/30th May 2018

A female producer who has embraced packaging and branding explains:

> Production is one thing; packaging and the marketing is another aspect. And in this business, packaging is the one key we need … if you do not package your stuffs well, no matter how organic they are, people will still look down on them. So, we do the packaging well before we sell. So, we have our brand names on our bottles and ensure that they are well covered and corked so that our consumers would not feel they are not buying something worth the price.
>
> IDI/Female/Single/25–29/Delta/Businesswoman and producer/Ajara, Topa, Badagry/5 June 2018

Branding and packaging of coconut oil product has not only improved the customer confidence, especially among elite consumers, they have improved demand and sales. This gives credence to the position that, it is worthwhile for producers to embrace branding and packaging as part of the marketing strategy to compete favorably in the expanding coconut oil trade.

5 Challenges and Coping Strategies

This section discusses the different challenges faced in the production process of coconut oil and the coping strategies that are used by the actors. The challenges revolve around cost of production, health issues, customers networking and shortage of resources (materials, equipment and finance). For any business to survive there is need for funds that would ensure the continuity of the production process. Coconut oil production is a labour and capital-intensive business and as such requires a lot of funds and manpower. The production of coconut oil is capital intensive for producers who focus on the use of machines, while laborious for producers who manually produce. One of the male respondents stated that the cost of production is capital intensive while another stated that raising the funds for large production is challenging. Most of the producers of coconut oil in Badagry are not buoyant enough to raise capital for the project, hence, they depend on loans they can get from the government. In most cases, the loans are not forthcoming as there are several protocols that they need to break. To further compound their challenge, their low level of knowledge restricts capacity to go through with the collection of those loans. Therefore, they mostly produce in small quantity and wait for those who want to buy and then raise money for the next batch of production. Another challenge is the issue of the laborious work that they go through as one of the labourers at the post of duty mentioned the body pains, he had in comparison to the ₦1000 ($3.2) he would get after the day's job, which to him is not worth it as he would have to buy pain killers from the money. The participants in the study stated the challenges of breaking the coconut shell, as it does injure their hands due to the very sharp instrument that are used. Also, the rigorous process of de-shelling the coconut, gives the laborers body pains especially back pains due to bending or sitting for a long period of time.

Producers of coconut oil are often faced with shortage of resource needed to produce coconut oil. Coconut fruit is the main material required in the process of making coconut oil. However, the dwarf coconut specie that produces much coconut oil is scarce in Badagry. Producers, therefore, have to import coconut fruits from Ghana, Togo and other neighboring countries that have coconuts in large quantity (Ruf, Kwaku, Salinier and Courbet, 2010). As such coconut fruits are not readily available to meet the supply of demands of coconut oil producers' customers. During the research it was revealed that a major company that was established for coconut oil production had shifted to palm kernel production due to limited coconut which cannot meet the demands of the country. Another challenge for the producers is the management of the grinding machines. The grinding machine develops faults easily, which also affects the production of the coconut oil reducing productivity. According to one of the interviewees "... *when the grinder is faulty, it delays the whole process because the coconut meat if removed from the shell would go bad and reduces the freshness of the oil*'. Others mentioned the problem of adulterations where the coconut oil is mixed with other oil and sold at the price of pure oil. This affects the integrity of the producer, and it is mostly done during the production process. For example, the researcher during a visit to one of the production sites witnessed the producer adding vegetable oil to the coconut shaft on fire and also allowing it to cook for a while. The adulteration is possible due to the oxidative stability of the oil making it easy for the smell of the coconut oil to be dominant (Krishna, Bhatnagar et al., 2009).

Some of the interviewees mentioned the challenges of networking with their customers and even being able to meet their needs as changes in price of the raw material and/or changes in the weather affects the production process as some of their customers have limited capital to purchase the product. A male producer expatiates on this:

> Most times we had to stop production itself because we haven't sold the one, we had done and some people even buy on credit, so there is no way you would do business that you won't give some people on credit which would later spoil the business. So those are the challenges.
>
> KII/Male/Married/45–49/Egun/Businessman and Producer/Badagry Market/5 June 2018

A female producer also reported the struggles she faces with her customers, who complained about her pricing as she claims to sell the original coconut oil, which is more costly than the ones obtained in the market. Yet, another male producer also reported similar issues about new customers where he would have to convince about the originality of his product as related to the price.

There are different coping strategies which are based on individuals' knowledge. Although, different people have different methods of solving the problems that comes their way by building on the indigenous knowledge they have learnt over time or employing the new scientific knowledge. One of the male producers describes the best way they solve the different challenges that they face in the production process.

> To solve the challenge of raw material, there is an association of coconut suppliers that goes to Ghana, so they buy in large quantity, like 10 trailers 20 trailers, solving the problem of trans-border problem. In terms of adulteration, we make sure, like this plastic am using is customised for me I use tamper proof ... so what am saying is we take extra measure to protect our customers and to educate them that watch out for the container ... In terms of fund, some of us are looking elsewhere for funding because most of us doing this are small scale business and we don't have collaterals to collect high stock bank loans so what we do is we deviate funds from other things, as you can see, am a public servant. Our packaging has really helped us, you can imagine the like of Blemco and Shoprite can order from us, and we package for them.... I spend more time and

> money on packaging than production you can imagine for me to have gotten to the extent of having so right under bottle, my sticker is digital and direct image printing I don't use this kind of printing, its laminated and it helps us to win the war of adulteration and people's trust.
>
> KII/Male/Married/40–45/Egun/Civil Servant and Producer/ Badagry museum/30th May 2018

The creation of associations was one of the major tools used by the producers to solve the challenges faced, as they come together to point out solutions and also make rules as guide line in the production processes. Further the association serves as financers for the producers in the community. The association is made up of financial supporters who loan out money for a particular project over a period of time, to make it easy for producers in the community. The association can be classified as a means of social capital network for the members. Economic advantages are made available for members. Non-members would not be opportune to such advantages. This network in the Aivoji community has helped the producers to be one of the largest producers of coconut oil in Badagry.

6 Conclusion

Coconut oil production in Badagry is an age-long activity that has been passed down from generation to generation. The findings show that, the production process of coconut oil in Badagry is carried out using the old method which was passed down over the generations. However, the production process is therefore made easier with the creation of machines such as the grinding machine, extracting machine and the expellers which makes the production process efficient. Although the traditional method is vastly used in the production of coconut oil, most of the producers still use machines in the process of producing coconut oil. The different stages of coconut oil production have its economic value that helps improve the producers' economic standard and by extension, the society. The stages of coconut oil production can be broadly divided into raw material preparation, milk extraction and oil extraction.

There is a strong network amongst the producers of coconut oil in Badagry, where different communities have association of producers who come together to solve issues surrounding coconut oil production in their communities. Those within the same community network together by helping one another in the production process and also brainstorming to bring forth solutions to the challenges they face in the production process. Aivoji community in Badagry is a typical example where the people of the community come together to improve their production techniques and process. Producers also connect with their customers through different methods of packaging, branding and advertisement through social media so as to ensure the loyalty of consumers. Although some of the producers in Badagry do not brand and package their product as they are the manufacturers, their distributors such as the retailers, brand and package the product to further attract their consumer.

Producers are faced with different challenges during the production process. These challenges revolve around shortage of materials- resources, finance, equipment and health challenges. Consumers also encounter the issue of adulteration, where some producers would have mixed the coconut oil with the groundnut oil and sell at the price of virgin coconut oil which also affect the other producers who do not mix their product.

References

Acosta, L., Eugenio, E., & Sales, J. (2019). *Assessment of organic certification in the coconut oil value chain in the Philippines.* UNCTAD Project (DA-1617AI): Fostering the development of green exports through Voluntary Sustainability Standards, January 2019. Accessed 10 July 2021 from https://unctad.org/system/files/official-document/UNCTAD_Assessment_VSS_VCO_Philippines.pdf.

Boateng, L., Ansong, R., Owusu, W., & Steiner-Asiedu, M. (2016). Coconut oil and palm oil's role in nutrition, health and national development: A review. *Ghana Medical Journal*, 50(3), 189–196.

Carvalho, L., Scott, L., & Jeffery, R. (2005). An exploratory study into the use of qualitative research methods in descriptive process modelling. *Information and Software Technology*, 47(2), 113–127.

Chowdappa, P., Murlidharan, K., & Rajesh, M. (2017). MEETING REPORT: Rejuvenating coconut sector for improving livelihood security. *Current Science*, 112(12), 2359–2360.

Cunningham, E. (2011). Is there science to support claims for coconut oil? *Journal of the American Dietetic Association*, 111(5), 786.

Daramola, G., Bello, B. and Okafor, L. 2014. Branding and packaging: Promotion of Marketing of fast-moving consumer goods in Nestle Nigeria PLC. *International Journal of Business and Marketing Management* 2. (1), 1–7.

de Silva, J. M. 2009. Production and marketing of coconut in India. *Market Research and Planning Cell MRPC86.* 111–122.

Dominici, A., Boncinelli, F. and Marone, E. (2019), "Lifestyle entrepreneurs in winemaking: An exploratory qualitative analysis on the non-pecuniary benefits", *International*

Journal of Wine Business Research, 31 (3), 385–405. https://doi .org/10.1108/IJWBR -06-2018-0024.

Emmanuel, A. (2021) Nigeria generates $150m from coconut oil. *News Agency of Nigeria*, 7 April. Accessed 10 July 2021 from https://nannews.ng/nigeria-generates-150m -from-coconut-oil/.

Eyres, L., Eyres, M. F., Chisholm, A., & Brown, R. C. (2016). Coconut oil consumption and cardiovascular risk factors in humans. *Nutrition Reviews*, 74(4), 267–280.

Fafchamps, M. 1999. The role of business networks in market development in Sub-Saharan Africa. *Community and Market in Economic Development* 1–45.

Fortiz, E. R. L., Gómez-Gómez, A. A., Leos-Rodríguez, J. A., Omaña-Silvestre, J. M., & Lagunes-Fortiz, E. (2021). Analysis of Copra and Coconut Oil Markets in Mexico. *Agro Productividad*, 14(4), 11–20, https://doi.org/ 10.32854/agrop.v14i4.1806.

Giddens, A. 2018. *Sociology*. 5th Ed. USA: Polity Press.

Haider, M. (2010). Raw Material Sourcing and Firm Performance: Evidence from Manufacturing Firms in South-West Bangladesh. *The Bangladesh Development Studies*, 33(4), 51–61.

Hebbar, K., Arivalagan, M., Manikantan, M., Mathew, A., Thamban, C., Thomas, G., & Chowdappa, P. (2015). Coconut inflorescence sap and its value addition as sugar – collection techniques, yield, properties and market perspective. *Current Science*, 109(8), 1411–1417.

Infante-Amate, J., Luedtke, B., MacFadyen, J., Robins, J., & Stevens, K. (2019). Fats of the Land: New Histories of Agricultural Oils. *Agricultural History*, 93(3), 520–546.

Krishna, G. A., Bahatnagar, A. S., Kumar, P. K. and Chandrashekar P. 2009. Coconut oil: Chemistry, production and its application. A review. *Indian Coconut Journal* 1. 15–27.

Lima, R. D. S., & Block, J. M. (2019). Coconut oil: what do we really know about it so far?. *Food Quality and Safety*. 3 (2), 61–72, https://doi.org/10.1093/fqsafe/fyz004.

Moreno, M. L., Kuwornu, J. K., & Szabo, S. (2020). Overview and constraints of the coconut supply chain in the Philippines. *International Journal of Fruit Science*, 20(sup2), S524-S541.

Ndangwa Noyoo (2007). Indigenous Knowledge Systems and Their Relevance for Sustainable Development: A Case of Southern Africa. In book: Indigenous Knowledge Systems and Sustainable Development: Relevance for Africa (pp. 167–172). Cape Town.

Ojo, O. E., & Saibu, I. A. (2018/2019) Sacredness and Religious Functions of Traditional Markets in Lagos: The Case of Oju-Olobun and Agbalata-Badagry Markets. *Ifè Journal of History*, 9 (1), 77–101.

Peguero, F., Zapata, S., & Sandoval, L. (2019). Agricultural Production of Central America and the Caribbean: Challenges and Opportunities. *Choices*, 34(3), 1–10.

Rajendran, S. (2002) Coconut Economy and Neera Tapping. *Economic and Political Weekly*, 37 (43), 4361–4362.

Ruf, F. Kwaku, A., Salinier, J. and Courtbet, P. 2010. The Nigeria Giant Hunger for its Neigbours' Coconut. *Grain de sel* 51: 33–34.

Sankararaman, S., & Sferra, T. J. (2018). Are we going nuts on coconut oil? *Current Nutrition Reports*, 7(3), 107–115.

Shankar, P., Ahuja, S., & Tracchio, A. (2013). Coconut oil: a review. *Agro Food Industry Hi-Tech*, 24(5), 62–64.

Suryani S, Sariani S, Earnestly F, Marganof M, Rahmawati R, Sevindrajuta S, Mahlia TMI, Fudholi A. (2020) A Comparative Study of Virgin Coconut Oil, Coconut Oil and Palm Oil in Terms of Their Active Ingredients. *Processes*. 2020; 8(4):402. https://doi.org/10.3390/pr8040402.

Uwubanmwen, I. O., Nwawe, C. N., Okere, R. A., Dada, M. and Eseigbe, E. 2011. Harnessing the potential of coconut palm in the Nigerian economy. *World Journal of Agricultural Sciences* 6. 684–691.

Wallace, T. C. (2019). Health effects of coconut oil—A narrative review of current evidence. *Journal of the American College of Nutrition*, 38(2), 97–107.

Watkins, C. (2015). African Oil Palms, Colonial Socioecological Transformation and the Making of an Afro-Brazilian Landscape in Bahia, Brazil. *Environment and History*, 21(1), 13–42.

CHAPTER 6

Border Markets and Traders in Seme

The dynamics of Trading Activities, Health Preference and Its Implications for Border Residents in Nigeria and Republic of Benin

O. S. Raji

1 Introduction

Communities and their citizens' identities have been shaken by the division of boundaries in African regional land. As a result of this move, what is now Nigeria is bounded by four francophone countries, namely the Republic of Benin, the Republic of Chad, the Republic of Cameroun, and the Republic of Niger. These artificial borders between Nigeria and other nations span thousands of kilometres and this affects millions of people in a variety of human life endeavours (Asiwaju, 2019; Raji, 2020). Border communities, although separated by colonial powers, still, maintain strong socio-cultural and economic relations. As a result, most border communities, particularly in Africa, are porous, and this is particularly due to the artificiality of the demarcation and colonialization. Since these divided border communities were once a single community, the artificial demarcation and boundary allocations encourages both formal and informal cross-border movement and socio-economic activities around the border communities in Africa (Asiwaju and Barkindo, 2013). Traders from all over the world, for example, use border villages as a stopover, hiding, and transit point for their social and commercial activities, which has usually led to the establishment of markets around borders post in most African border communities.

Border markets differ from other markets in several ways. Border markets arose because of different border policies and developed due to the structural similarities and cultural affiliations. While other local and national markets draw their wealth from their neighbourhoods, border markets owe their existence to the presence of border differentials and thrive at the point of convergence of transnational networks. Whereas most markets evolve slowly, border markets experience sudden booms or declines due to variations in price differentials, exchange rates between currencies, taxes between countries, and bans of imports and exports (Dobler, 2019, Raji, 2020). Contrasting to other markets that primarily owe their existence to the size and qualifications of their labour pool, border markets are dependent on the business opportunities offered by

 | DOI:10.1163/9789004692657_008

their peripheral location and international network. That is, it is the situation in the border market and the inflow of people from all over the world that determine the existence of a border market.

Seme was never a market before the artificial demarcation and eventual colonization of Africa. Seme is a settlement, a part in Republic of Benin and the other part in Nigeria, a community that now shares a boundary with the Republic of Benin, at a distance not far from Badagry local government area of Lagos State, on the coastal road between Lagos and Cotonou. Seme is a part of the Badagry Division of Lagos State in Nigeria. Historically, Seme was not a market community before the independence of the two countries (Nigeria and the Republic of Benin). After the independence of the two countries, Seme as a community was divided into two, aside was made to belong to Nigeria and the other side in the Republic of Benin. This demarcation has contributed significantly to the economic development of the market in Seme border. The socio-cultural linkage between these communities divided into two facilitates cross-border movement and socio-economic activities resulting in a border market in most parts of Africa where such artificial division of communities took place (Raji, 2020).

It is on record that the partition and later colonization of Africa by the Europeans resulted in numerous tariff barriers within the West African sub-region, particularly between Francophone and English-speaking countries. It also reflected in the pattern of trade links established across Nigeria's and the Republic of Benin border territories after their existence. The border residents avidly participated in cross-border trading as a convenient method of subsistence. As a result, enormous markets brimming with traded items and people coming from the two countries and other parts of the world purchases and sales have sprouted up. Seme as a border community become a market, an international one for that matter, because of economic need. Many individuals were drawn to Seme town because of the large-scale business operations that are taking place there. Eventually, varieties of ethnic groups from both Nigeria and the Republic of Benin are virtually found along with the two countries' border areas.

More importantly, while the Nigerian government restrict the importation of certain goods, their neighbour country, the Republic of Benin, operate an Open Trade System (OTS) that allows all goods to come in and be sold in the Republic of Benin. Availability of all sorts of goods in Benin also encourages markets at their border with other countries.

Studies on cross-border issues (Adekunle, Sule, and Muturu, 2000; Asiwaju, 2014; Shaikh and Hatcher, 2015) have primarily focused on political and economic issues related to trade (Balami, 2015; Abass, 2018; Balami, Irefin, and

Naphtali, 2021), boundary adjustments, and border conflict resolution (Balami, 2015; Abass, 2018; Balami, Irefin, and (Tijani, 2013; Asiwaju and Barkindo, 2013). The impact of cross-border traders' operations, border markets dynamics and the government's unfavourable policy decisions on the provision of social services on residents of border communities have not received adequate attention. Scholars studying the Nigerian border appear to underestimate the dominating influence of trading activities, border market and particularly the health implications of these activities on border residents. To make up for this gap in research, this study mainly focused on border markets and traders' activities in the most popular border community in Nigeria, Seme. This is done by examining the dynamics of trading activities and their Health implications on residents in Nigeria and the Republic of Benin Boundary.

2 Theoretical Orientation

The socio-ecological theory is the theoretical foundation for this research and was developed by Urie Bronfenbrenner in the late 1970s. The socio-ecological model explains how people's behaviour is influenced by their physical and socio-cultural settings at various levels. These levels are revealed through the communication and synthesis of biological, behavioural, environmental, and social determinants, as well as the influence of organizations, significant others (such as family, friends, and peers), and public policies, which help individuals make healthy choices in their daily lives (Glanz and Rimmer, 2015). The Socio-ecological model emphasizes how changes and interactions among all environmental factors affect one's health and well-being throughout one's life or during the duration of the illness. Three aspects of the model are used to understand border markets. This model at individual level (as the ones who engage in trading operations), explain that their behaviour in the business process, and their physical surroundings (the convergence of traders in one place). Intrapersonal, interpersonal, organizational, community and policy analyses are all available for each dimension. The Socio-ecological model, according to Glanz and Rimmer (2015), presents a set of conceptual and methodological concepts for structuring comprehensive, community-based interpretations of human behaviour at all levels of their life, primarily drawn from systems theory. The ecological models related to the influence of the border environment in relation to trading activities. The theory explains how the structure and activities at the border encourage the development of market in a border like Seme. This has a multifaceted, focusing on environmental, behavioural, and social policy changes, allowing individuals to make decisions about whether to engage in business transacts in border communities.

3 Methodology

The study was conducted among residents of the Seme border community in Lagos, Nigeria, and was exploratory in nature. Seme is a community split into two (Nigeria and the Republic of Benin) by the colonial master's artificial boundary creation. On the seaside route between Lagos and Cotonou, it's a thirty-minute journey from Badagry. It is part of the Badagry-West Local Council Development Area in Lagos Nigeria, which is affected by the state's current political divide (LCDA).

This study employed a qualitative methodology to explore the context border market and traders in the Seme border community. Residents of both sides of the Seme border community provided information (Nigeria and Republic of Benin sides). Data was collected in the first quarter of the year 2021. Apart from the participant observation conducted by the researcher, 10 in-depth interviews and 10 Focus Group Discussions were conducted among border residents who were purposively sampled. This is due to the sensitivity of the location, being a border community. The IDIs include the following categories of people: 2 market leaders from both sides of the border, 4 traders were also strategically selected (2 from each side of the border), a community leader, and 3 border community residents. For the FGDs, discussants were strategically and purposively selected in the community to get detailed information about the border market and traders' activities in the Seme border. Generally, participants in the study were those who have been residents in the Seme border community for at least 5 years. This condition was given to get adequate data for the study. In the township, the research team crisscrossed to capture the general sociology of the community. The team consists of 4 research assistants and the lead researcher. Before the data collection exercise, the lead researcher trained the research trainees on how to conduct the interviews. We engaged the study themes in training. The research team leader discussed the themes with the research trainees for them to grasp a comprehensive understanding. While in Seme, the research trainees, under the leadership of the team lead, formed groups of twos in conducting the IDIs. In each group, a member (the facilitator) guided the discussion to ensure focus on the themes, while the other person did the recording and note-taking. Each research group obtained permission from study participants to record the interview.

The data generated through IDIs and FGDs were content analysed. First, each group transcribed the recorded interviews, and after comparing the transcription with notes taken during the interview, each team prepared a mini report on the data. The submitted interview data from each sub-team formed the basis of the analysis conducted. We went through the data to generate categories consistent with the study objectives, also noting memorable quotes used in demonstrating the findings, as evidence to support data discussion. In order not to violate the right of the discussants, the study sought verbal permission from each discussant before engaging them in the interview, and anonymity was crucial in the field investigation. At any point during the interview, each participant was given the opportunity and free will to end the discussion and withdraw their participation when necessary. Before the interview began, participants were advised on their right to privacy. Before recording the interview, express consent was also acquired. Furthermore, the participants' comfort was prioritized throughout.

4 Findings and Discussion

According to the socio-demographic characteristics of the discussants, both males and females participated in border market activities, men and women mix at border markets, just like they do in any other market. It is also unconcerned about religion. That is, religion is irrelevant, which is why both Muslims and Christians participated in border market activity. In Seme, a variety of people of various ages participate in the border market, with the bulk of them speaking *egun* language. This could be related to the location of the market in the Badagry local government region, where most of the population speaks *egun* language. Most people polled are illiterate, with little/no Western education.

4.1 *Patterns and Items of Trade in Seme Border Market*

The pattern of trade is determined mainly by the items of trade. What you are buying or selling would determine the modalities of the trading activities. In the view of one of the discussants, petrol, groceries, and textile materials were the most traded products. Jewellery, tyres/motor spare parts, reasonably old autos, plastics, and detergents were the next most popular items of trade in Seme border market. Electrical products and batteries were the least popular purchased. Consumer products such as rice, apples, tin tomatoes, and other

FIGURE 6.1 Border market in Seme border

consumable goods are stated to be widely available and inexpensive in the host country (Benin).

One of the informants has this to say:

> The two countries are neighbouring countries. Nigeria has onion, pepper, beans, etc., while Benin republic has rice, groundnut oil, palm oil, etc., the two countries both exchange their goods.
>
> Garri has become more expensive because of customs and immigration. Things bought in Benin come with a lot of bribes (bribery), and even products imported from Nigeria involve bribing companies and immigration agents. For instance, if you buy things for #10,000, you may have to pay up to $15,000 in a settlement. So, when we acquire from Benin and manage to get it into Nigeria's Seme market, we don't want to deal with the immigration hassles before selling elsewhere in Nigeria, so we sell at the Seme border market. When there is a shortage of tomatoes in Nigeria, they travel to Benin to purchase them and transport them to the Nigerian side of Seme, and vice versa. That is how the border market between neighbouring countries works.

The focus group discussion (FGD) revealed that cross-border business is multi-faceted since the majority of purchases are made outside of Nigeria. The primary goods smuggled out of Nigeria are gasoline, plastic, and wares.

The trading of gasoline was profitable and involved many retailers. The retailers provide gasoline on motorcycles rather than in large tankers. During the research, it was also discovered that petty trade was present in Seme border market. This was carried out by women traders who sell second-hand baby garments, groundnuts, and pepper regularly just inside the Seme border and across the border into the Republic of Benin.

One of the patterns in which cross-border trading occurs in Seme is that Seme youths aid smugglers in transporting their loads across the border by utilizing their "Lesz-passe" (passport) to deceive police into believing they are the owners of the items. It was discovered that security agents also assist smugglers by providing them with information on when it is safe to cross the border and when it is not.

It was also gathered during the interviews that:

> Smuggling at the Nigeria-Seme border was not just for non-disabled people; physically challenged people also participated in illegal businesses and traded near the border. The handicapped are said to cross the border in wheelchairs. They pretended to be begging for alms by covering their legs with wrapping under which they hid some things. One of our major sources (Mr Ajayi, the Oba's spokesman) claimed that Nigerian customs officers are aware of the tactics. They continue to overlook the crippled, enabling "kelebe" criminals to collect their own "dues" from the disabled smugglers.

Imported goods from Europe and the United States of America (USA) are not shipped directly to Nigeria. The items arrive at ports in neighbouring nations, such as Cotonun, in Republic of Benin, and Togo. When the goods arrive in the Republic of Benin, and for them to get to Nigeria, smugglers with the help of the corrupt customs officer do everything possible.

It was revealed during the focus group discussion (FGD) that.

> Smuggling products into the country is dangerous and difficult, but because of poverty, unemployment, and hunger, people are willing to journey kilometres through the wilderness carrying imported items throughout the day and largely at night.

Bullets were exchanged and lives were lost, according to a Nigeria Customs Service (NCS) spokesman, during one of their "cat-and-mouse" interactions between traffickers and border officials. He went on to explain that they engaged the smugglers last year and killed many of them. We (Customs officers)

FIGURE 6.2 Free movement of people and goods at Seme border post

have seized 384 bales of used apparel in the last four months. When someone loses millions of naira because their goods were confiscated, according to the NCS spokesman, they will not return to unlawful cross-border business. However, after these goods cross the border into Nigeria, most of the goods are sold in the Seme border market.

FIGURE 6.3 Free movement at a border post in Ilara border community in Nigeria

One of the border market traders stated that:

> People from Ibadan, Kano, Abia, and Enugu are among those who bring them in. Crossers are the ones who are familiar with the routes. The businessmen would pay them money and stay on the Nigerian side of Seme,

> where they will assist the crossers in purchasing Benin Republic items. The indigenous people are known as the crossers. The Hausas' base, for example, is G5; if you want to buy ten bags of rice, you will give them your money. They will cross the border on their "bike" to assist you in purchasing rice. G4 is also the Yoruba's foundation; if you need things like groundnut oil, turkey, rice, or other items, you can send them money and they would assist you in purchasing them. In addition, the Igbos live in Ogunba, while the Eguns are the indigenous population.
>
> Beninians are the ones that are assisting us to compensate customs officers. Customs officers will occasionally raid the market. Beninese people are assisting us in transporting them to Seme's border market.

Imported clothing marketplaces are in specific areas for rapid identification in the case of textile products. Bales of imported clothing are smuggled into the country overnight by bush paths and opened in Seme border market or carried straight to "katangwa" market in Abule-egba (Lagos) in the early mornings. According to one of the primary sources:

Traders congregate at the location to select the best pieces before they are taken by others.

> Merchants display the rumpled items on hangers and empty spaces in their stores, with customers coming in to buy them for personal use or resale. The border market sells used shirts, trousers, coats, jackets, boots, jeans, belts, socks, innerwear, nightwear, bedsheets, and other items for children and adults.

According to a discussant,

> Illegal products promote the border market, and they are carried into the country through a variety of methods. Transhipment is used by certain importers to get around quotas. By falsifying documentation or labels, they changed the country of origin of their goods. Some people employ an in-bond diversion strategy that involves putting bogus addresses on invoices. An importer might bring items into the country (Nigeria) and pretend that they will be shipped to another country. However, these commodities never leave the nation and end up in the Nigerian market.

The foregoing excerpt from FGD confirms that cross-border business in Seme follows various trends.

4.2 *Interpersonal Links and Cross-Border Trading in Seme Border Market*

The interpersonal and longtime socio-cultural affinity between the residents from both sides of the border to some extent, encourage trade link and this invariably encourage the existence of markets at the border. People from both sides of the border do not see themselves as belonging to different countries. This facilitates free movement of people and goods in most African borders, and this is mainly due to the artificiality of the creation of African boundaries.

The focus group discussions (FGD) conducted in Seme revealed that the interpersonal interactions between the traders and Seme border community residents facilitated illegal cross-border trading. The historical, cultural, and economic ties that linked the people on both sides of the border were examined in terms of the person or institution that facilitate and encourage the border market, their ethnicity and nationality and the form of assistance rendered by the community members. It was revealed that the family, social, and political ties between Nigeria and the Republic of Benin people facilitated cross border trading.

It was revealed during the focus group discussions (FGD) held in Seme that:

> Interactions between traders and members of the Seme community promoted illegal cross-border transactions, which in turn fueled the border market. One of the socio-cultural motivations for border trading is because of this. The historical, cultural, and economic ties that connected people on both sides of the border (people in Seme, Nigeria, and Seme, Republic of Benin) were investigated in terms of the person or institution that hosted the traders, their ethnicity and nationality, and the type of assistance provided by community members. It was discovered that these people's family, societal, and political ties aided the border market.

Apart from the above mentioned, the traders and the people who host them sometimes have the same nationality, which explains why their interpersonal interactions are so similar. Most of the hosts were Yoruba and Egun (from the Republic of Benin), with a handful from Togo, and Ghana. The traders were mostly offered economic and social aid. This included cash and gifts, as well as satisfactory negotiations and the provision of credit and currency exchange services. The next step is hospitality, with traders being offered lodging for a fee or for free.

> Seme's indigenous people have come to terms with their lot. Everything is dry in Seme; you can see immigration authorities monitoring people's

FIGURE 6.4 The researcher at Seme border post

movements if you stroll straight down to the bush where the indigenous people live. This makes unlawfully bringing in or taking out commodities more difficult for indigenous people. We have folks from Senegal, Mali, and even Niger in our market village. The indigenous people assist in the transport of products for foreigners. They have unrestricted access to the border, and they allow them to do so. The indigenes are those who purchase things from the Republic of Benin. On the other

> side, it's possible that the Benin people will bring the products in, and we'll pay them right away. So, those who bring it in from Benin already know what they're getting, and those who buy it already know what they're getting.

This study demonstrates that border trading is an integrative process that connects traders, border community residents, and neighbouring countries. The frequency and pattern of border commerce operations are consistent with what may be found in the most remote frontiers (Raji, 2022). Border trading, as far as the community members are concerned, takes place within their locality, which is an internal transaction rather than an international transaction, as evidenced by the business's high frequency and short duration.

4.3 *Unofficial Routes in Seme and Residents' Perceptions of Border Market*

Border traders used various unofficial routes. During one of the focus group discussions (FGDs), one of the discussants mentions "eti-koto" on the edge of the valley dividing the two countries (Nigeria and Republic of Benin), being the most popular. *G5, G4, the Bush route, Kumayon, Bebe, Sharp Corner,* and *Back of the Wire* are some of the other routes used by border traders. Unnecessary delays in customs checking were the main reasons mentioned for using the unofficial routes during the focus group discussion (FGD). The key reason for the high frequency of trading was proximity. Both Seme and Idiroko border settlements are immediately over the road from *Cotonou, Igolo,* and *Ifonyin.* They are 9 to 10 kilometres apart across the border, Porto Novo (43 kilometres) and Cotonou to Seme (less than 6 kilometres). However, the marketing appeal of Porto Novo and Cotonou invites more individuals to participate in border trading activities and the location of the border market in one way or another.

The study area is identified as a maximum borderland based on the available data and findings. Illegal cross-border trading was found to be widespread inside the research region, with little restraint, and was nearly accepted as a regular part of life by the people of Seme. The nature of border trading is complicated, as it is both internal and international. The location nearest to the border, in this case, Seme, has the highest volume of trading activity, as one might assume. The main port of call is Cotonou, a major commercial centre about a stone's throw from Seme, followed by Igolo, the nearest village to Idiroko on the way to Cotonou.

On the perception of the border residents, the residents of the Seme border community thinks that border trading is profitable. They do not see it as an illegal business, instead, they see it as a normal trading activity between two neighbouring communities. This is because the two communities were once one community where people move freely until colonization took place. Most individuals who took part in the focus group discussion (FGD) highlighted specific benefits. These include easy access to customers, low-cost items, and minimal hassle along the route; traders from the immediate area who were known to border officials found it easier to trade around the border than in other markets; the trade is profitable; cross-border interaction is simple, and the exchange rate is fair. During one of the focus groups, a participant said:

> There are issues with the way things are brought into this country. Because it is the indigenes and the people of the Benin republic who deal here in the market. Most of our ladies are married to Beninese men, and they are the ones that acquire Beninese items and sell them in Nigeria. Many officers will stop us and collect bribes at each checkpoint if we go to trade fare. Also, the money we used to pay the cops would have been more than the profit. And, because Benin is so close to us, bringing foods from there is preferred. People will also be selling things from Benin across the border.

Other focus group discussion (FGD) participants, on the other hand, had some criticisms. They claim that the presence of many immigration agents near the border, as well as their exploitative behaviour, forces most individuals to sell their wares on the outskirts. Another concern is that the checks are inconvenient, making legitimate cross-border trading difficult. The difficulty of getting travel documents, as well as the shifting exchange rate, have been noted as issues with border trading. Another point brought up was the linguistic barrier.

4.4 *Effects of Border Trading and Its Health Preference and Implication on the People of Seme*

Seme border community has often experienced inadequate healthcare services, insecurity, and illegal cross-border issues, simply because the border is porous, which produced severe economic, political and security challenges in the region. Armed groups, refugees, internally displaced individuals, and returning or deported migrants have all had a significant impact on border communities. An increase in crime, a high level of immorality, and so on are some of the consequences. The disparity between expanding demands and inadequate resources frequently leads to tensions and frustrations, which, if left uncontrolled, could lead to communal violence. Food, water, and medicine were in short supply; due to overcrowding, schools and health centres were congested, and basic sanitation facilities were missing. The issue of young unemployment was also prominent: rapid population growth mixed with a lack of infrastructure development has resulted in an ever-increasing number of unemployed youths, who supply fruitful services for the traders who reward the child with loot prizes.

Other challenges people faced in the Seme border community partly due to the market nature of the place include the proliferation of roadblocks (which hurts security and the movement of goods and people), widespread environmental degradation, social and moral exclusion, particularly for women, illegal exploitation of people, and the emergence of a culture of impunity concerning human rights violations due to the porosity, artificiality, and illicit activities taking place in the Seme community.

The flourish of border markets is mainly linked to the number of people tangled in the trade. One of the critical informants stated:

> Without an inventive community of traders participating in transnational business networks, border towns/communities can barely claim to be border markets; border towns/communities can hardly claim to be border markets. These entrepreneurs will strive to profit by connecting multiple nationally structured markets daily, using the various differentials that continue to characterize border regions.

The Republic of Benin operates an open border system where any goods could come into their country. Even when the Nigerian Government put some measures in place to restrict some of these goods from the Republic of Benin, the porosity and artificiality of the Seme border encouraged the illegal importation and access of most of the goods from the Republic of Benin into Nigeria. The first point of contact is the border community, where some traders sell off their goods right there.

Differences in countries policies and subsidy harmonization have also been linked to the growth of all sorts of business activities between Nigeria and the Republic of Benin.

According to one of the key informants:

> Informal traders on the Nigerian-Benin border are primarily motivated by variations in tax burdens and the resulting consumer sale price in a variety of items, beginning with petrol, second-hand clothing, and automobiles. The tariffs charged by Nigeria are greater than those charged by the Republic of Benin. This encourages traders to use the illicit method to sell their goods at the border market. The buyers' biggest issue is figuring out how the commodities would be used in Nigeria.

The structure of trade networks alters depending on whether trade takes place over the Nigeria-Republic of Benin border, which is an intriguing outcome of our study. Border trade is mostly facilitated by a linear chain of participants. Wholesalers in the Republic of Benin hire transporters to deliver items requested by their Nigerian counterparts to a store owner on Benin's side of the Seme border. The movement of imported products to another storage owner on the Nigerian side of Seme is subsequently facilitated by close family and cultural links between traders on both sides of the border. Imported items are then delivered to local wholesalers and this chain of the transaction will continue until they reach the final consumer on the Nigerian side of the Seme border market. This chain of business transactions is like what Howard (2020) posts about the pre-colonial Sierra Leone-Guinea commerce system, in which products were transported across vast distances and these transactions are done through private networks.

Almost all the key informants stated that their people have a high preference for traditional health care medicine. This is because while the border market encourages and experiences the huge influx of people from all over the world, western healthcare facilities are inadequately provided in most rural communities in Africa, particularly, border communities (Little, 2013; Raji, 2018). They explained the effectiveness of traditional medicine in the complete treatment/cure and prevention of illness. One of them captured the general view in this regard:

> Western healthcare is not sufficiently provided for us, and I cannot even use the available Western medicine; it will only provide a temporary solution to the health problem and after a while, the sickness will come back. Unlike when you use "*agbo*" (concoction from herbs), everything (the sickness) in your body will come out and you will be stronger than before.

> We were even told they (the white people) made their Western medicine from herbs. So, stop disturbing yourself and let us value and appreciate our own things.

The above response also supports the views of Ajala et al. (2019) that people in the rural area of Nigeria prefer the traditional medicine because of the availability and the efficacy of herbs in their environments. The inadequacy of the Western/government health care services in the border communities, despite the population due to the market around the border, redirects the health-seeking behaviouri of the people.

It was discovered that virtually all the informants argued that they would have preferred to use Western health care if they had a choice and that their utilization of the traditional medicine was partly since Western medicine was not available in their community. This is captured in the excerpt below:

> If there is a good government hospital in our community, I would prefer to use it than any other form of health care services. I am not saying that traditional medicine is not good in its own, but I prefer Western medicine because you know the dosage to be used and the expiring date will be written on it, but all these are difficult to know when it comes to the traditional medicine.

The above assertion revealed that the Seme border residents, to some extent, would have preferred Western health care, but the unavailability of such health care services made them to use traditional health care. It was also discovered that the people of Seme had high tendency of being influenced by their health care choices based on the everyday influx of people, both the traders and travelers, the social interactions, their educational level, and high level of socio-economic interactions taking place between them and other people all over the world might have been responsible for their high preference for Western health care. This was also why some of them cross the border to seek health care in Cotonou, Republic of Benin.

4.5 *Patterns/Networks of Cross-Border Trade within West Africa*

The pattern of trade networking is vital in the discussion of the border market. The network makes use of their cultural and linguistic affinities in ensuring that goods bypass all the border restrictions and barriers and are delivered to their destination accordingly. According to Raji (2021), the Nigeria Network, Subsidiary Network, and Coordinating Trade are the three key categories.

FIGURE 6.5 Ilara border post in Republic of Benin

– "For the Nigerian networks, the magnitude and volume of the Nigerian population and its diaspora in West Africa are their biggest assets. Nigerian networks are also divided into three categories. These include Nigeria, the Republic of Benin, Togo, and Ghana, as well as Cote d'Ivoire, where there are over 2,000,000 Nigerians, around 70% of whom are Yoruba who engages in micro-business such as retail trade, the Yoruba network is well developed even before the colonial era. They do deal in cosmetics and mostly high-end items like fabrics. This is one of the well-organized networks; networks of acquaintances from many locations coordinate and even regulate transactions. This structure is the foundation for the Cote d'Ivoire-Nigeria Chamber of Commerce, which is currently being established.

- The Hausa Kanuri group, which has a larger numerical presence, is mostly active in Nigeria, Niger, Chad, and North Cameroon. Their ties to other West African networks, particularly the Dioula networks, for livestock and cola trading, have grown significantly; they now have a global reach. For regional trade, they now use informal/illegal funding techniques. The Hausa constitute the backbone of the parallel forex market, which serves as both a means of coordination among all participants and a source of funding businesses for regional trade".
- -In the late 1960s, the Ibo network grew throughout the region. This network, which focuses mostly on international import-export, serves as a relay for the trading of used and counterfeit items, such as secondhand apparel, vehicles, tyres, and vehicle spare parts of all kinds.
- For the Subsidiary networks, it is networks that are separate from the main network. These are groups that operate as a connection between dist6ributors in other countries and the destination country.

Adedokun, Adepoju, and Ebigbola (2014) noted that trading at the border post frequently involves many local individuals individually moving little quantities—often merely as head loads or by bicycle rickshaw, dubbed bootleg smuggling or "*kelebe*" by the authors. At the other end of the spectrum, some trades entail unlawful tactics such as under-invoicing, misclassification, and bribery of customs and other agents, and are sometimes referred to as "technical smuggling."

Cross-border trade based on long-distance goods movements frequently entails a complex web of dealers, financiers, and shippers. Rather than simply market considerations like pricing and supply/demand, these circuits may be more essential in explaining the structure and flow of cross-border trade and border markets. While these networks help businesses succeed and border markets thrive, they can also be extremely exclusive, distorting supply and price circumstances (Peter, 2017). The complexity of these trade networks was described by Engola, and Harre, (2020):

> "Border marketing is far more sophisticated than the neoclassical concept of a producer selling to a customer at a negotiated market-clearing price, perhaps with the help of a wholesaler or retailer as market intermediaries," says the author. There are many market actors between

> primary producers and final consumers, partly because live animals are frequently included, partly because the trade is informal - even illegal - and crosses national borders, and partly because of the complex interrelationships between trade routes and clan territories. As a result, the marketing system is far from impersonal and anonymous. Instead, it's a web of personal and clean-based relationships, with each actor reliant on the others in ways that both safeguard and limit their options and chances
>
> Engola, and Harre, 2020:53)

These trade-based networks can connect many traders over long distances, making border markets and trading easier.

4.6 *Impact of Cross Border Trade/Market on Industrial and Agricultural Production in Africa*

One of the most divisive features of the border market and economic activity is this. Even though it is undeniable that in the border market transaction, both the traders and the customers profit handsomely and benefit from increased or maintained purchasing power, in this case, Nigeria as a country is always at the receiving and disadvantage. It is on record that government is most not gaining from the border market, and this is largely due to the artificiality and porosity of the African border. This situation might not be the same across countries, depending on the policy put in place by each country would determine what they gain or lose. For example, while the Republic of Benin might gain a lot due to the open-market policy strategies they operate, the Nigerian government continue to lose a huge amount, and this had led the Nigerian government to place a ban on the importation of many goods through their land borders. The Nigerian government might have discovered that the country is not gaining much from the ban and that is why the new government of President Tinunbu just open the importation of vehicles through the land border.

In Afolayan (2020)'s view, even when the overall contribution of border business transactions looks to be minimal to the Nigerian economy, the influence on industrial production in Nigeria has been significant. When one considers that petroleum exports account for more than 90% of Nigeria's foreign exchange revenues, the importance of cross-border trade flows in Nigeria's agricultural and manufactured products sectors becomes evident. Its neighbours are a little more difficult to deal with.

According to Raji, (2020), the effects of unlawful cross-border trading on Nigerian production have also been varied. He further argued that the inflows of European goods such as textiles, cigarettes, and worn clothing, as well as cheap Asian products like textiles, batteries, and electronics, have severely harmed local industries in Nigeria, particularly with the introduction of SAP. Simultaneously, increased demand for Nigerian goods in Franc Zone markets has helped several industries, including cement, textiles, cosmetics, and plastics.

4.7 *Government's Efforts in Reducing Cross-Border Trade in Nigeria*

Anti-economic and business games are played regularly throughout Nigeria's porous borders. Recently, Sally and Catherne, (2020), posited that the number of commodities being smuggled through the Nigerian borders was so huge that the Nigerian government had no choice but to contemplate establishing the Trans-border Trade Branch to combat the problem. To combat the intense high level of illegal cross-border trade which is encouraged by the border markets due to the porosity of the border, the Domestic Trade Department made the bold step in establishing trans-border marketplaces across the country, notably in areas where Nigeria shares borders with our neighbouring nations such as Niger, Benin, Cameroon, and Chad. *Seme, Pogi, Owode,* and *Idi-Iroko,* all in Lagos and Ogun States, Nigeria, were among the border towns chosen. The Domestic Trade Department conducted feasibility studies to determine the profitability and practicality of creating border markets in all these locations, according to the statement. "To achieve these goals, the Department and Ministry constructed the *Illela* border market in collaboration with the government of Sokoto State, and a similar market was established in *Jibiya i*n Katsina State, all in Nigeria. Nigeria and its neighbours have implemented an innovative marketing strategy to tackle informal and unrecorded border trade.

5 Conclusion

The study found that border markets and trading are quite common in Seme border community and are seen as a normal part of the community's way of life, because it is one of their key sources of income. They see it as an opportunity for individuals to work. Border commerce operations, on the other hand, have a variety of negative consequences of which include, high rate of morbidity due to fake drugs, increase insecurity, loss of traditional norms and values, high crime rate, and lack of social infrastructure. This is because the border market attracts individuals from both sides of the border, encouraging illegal activity in the border town. These deserve urgent government policy attention to eradicate these societal menaces.

References

Abass A.M. 2018. Socio-economic consequences of proximity to international boundaries: A case study of Ngala Local Government Area, Borno State, Nigeria. Unpublished M.Sc. dissertation, Department of Geography, University of Maiduguri.

Adedokun, A., Adepoju, A. and Ebigbola, J., 2014. "The Ife Labour Market: A Nigerian Case study". Population and Labour Policies Programme Working Paper No. 144.

Adekunle, Sule and Muturu, O. 2000. Socio-economic consequences of proximity to international boundaries: A case study of Ngala Local Government Area, Borno State, Nigeria. Unpublished M.Sc. dissertation, Department of Geography, University of Maiduguri.

Afolayan, A. 2020. Trans-Border Movement and Trading: A case study of a Borderland in Southwestern Nigeria. Oluben printers Ibadan pp. 33–89.

Asiwaju, A. I., and Adeniyi.1989. Borderland in Africa, University of Lagos Press, Nigeria.

Asiwaju, A.I. and Barkindo, B.M. 1993. *The Nigeria Niger trans-border co-operation.* Lagos: Malthouse Press.

Asiwaju A. 2004. Health-seeking behaviour and health service utilization in Pakistan: Challenging the policymakers.*Journal of Public Health,* 27(1): 49–54.

Balami D.H. 2015. Cross-border trade between Nigeria and her neighbours: A case study on Nigeria and its neighbours, A report submitted to the network on cross-border trade between Nigeria and her neighbours, Paris.

Dobler G. 2019. Oshikango: The dynamics of growth and regulation in a Namibian boom town. *Journal of Southern African Studies* 35(1): 115–131. DOI: 10.1080/03057070802685601.

Dobler G. 2014. Borderland actors: A typology and a conceptual framework. Paper presented at the *Association of Borderlands Studies (ABS) World Conference*, Joensuu, June 9.

Engola, W. and Harre, 2020. Illegal immigration: The Host-country problem in America. Economic Review 76(1), p. 567.

Tijani K. 2013. The Kanuri factor in Nigeria-Niger border relations. In Asiwaju, A.I. and Barkindo B.M. (eds.) The Nigeria – Niger trans-border co-operation. Lagos: Malthouse pp. 76–90.

Golub S. 2012. Government policies, smuggling, and the informal sector, in Benjamin N, Mbaye AA. (eds) *The Informal Sector in Francophone Africa. Firm Size, Productivity, and Institutions.* Washington, DC, The World Bank: 195–218.

Gregoire, A. and Labazee, F. 2014. Culture, Power, Place: Ethnography at the End of an Era. In Culture, Power, Place: Explorations in Critical Anthropology. Durham: Duke University Press.

Raji, S. O. 2018. Health Seeking Behaviour of Border Community Residents in Southwest Nigeria. Benin Journal of Social Sciences. Vol. 24, No, 1: 127–146.

Raji, S. O. 2019. Democratic governance and healthcare provosions in border communities of Southwest Nigeria. LASU *Journal of Social Sciences*. Vol. 13. 102–111.

Raji, S. O. 2020. Socio-economic Factors Influencing Healthcare Utilization among Border Residents in Southwest Nigeria. ABUAD *Journal of Social and Management Sciences*. Vol. 1, No., 1: 169–189.

Little, M. 2013. Cross-Border Livestock Trade and Food security in the Somalia and Northeastern Kenya Borderlands. Binghamton, NY: Institute for Development Anthropology.

Mahmane, F. 2013. The Establishment of the Nigerian/Benin Boundary, 1889–1989. *Geographical Journal* 157 (1) 62–70.

Mas, M. V. 2013. Vehicle Theft along the Texas-Mexico Border, (J.B.S), Vol. 11, No 2: 12–32.

Meagher, K. 2017. A Back Door to Globalization? Structural Adjustment, Globalization and Transborder Trade in West Africa. Review of African Political Economy 95:57–75.

Peter, D. 2017. Unofficial Cross-Border Trade in Eastern Africa. A paper presented at the PAD Workshop on "Staple Food Trade and Market Policy Options for Promoting Development in Eastern and Southern Africa", March 1–2, 2007, FAD Headquarters, Rome, Italy.

Ricca, N. 2019. International Migration in Africa (International Labour Organization, Geneva).

Sally, B. and Catherine, B. 2020. The impact of the second-land clothing trade on Developing counties pp. 4–19.

Walther O. 2012. Traders, agricultural entrepreneurs and the development of cross-border regions in West Africa. *Entrepreneurship and Regional Development* 24(3–4): 123–141. DOI: 10.1080/08985626.2012.670909.

World Bank. 2019. *World Development Report. Reshaping Economic Geography*. Washington, DC, The World Bank.

Zeller W. 2019. Danger and opportunity in Katima Mulilo: A Namibian border boomtown at transnational crossroads. *Journal of Southern African Studies* 35(1): 133–154. DOI: 10.1080/03057070802685619.

CHAPTER 7

Medicinal Herb Traders in Southwest Nigeria

Seun Mauton Ajoseh, S.O. Raji and I.O. Odejimi

1 Introduction

Medicinal herbs are plant parts used for prevention or curative purposes, especially in Africa. The word "*herb*" is derived from the Latin word "*herba*". They include plants consisting of fruit, stem, seed, flower, bark, stigma, root, and leaves. Aside from medicinal purposes, some of these herbs are also used as food flavours, perfume ingredients, and in spiritual activities that also have health implications and benefits (Shaheen et al., 2019). Ekor (2014) argued and estimated that over 80 percent of the world's population rely on herbal medicine for some aspect of their primary health care. An estimated 21,000 plant species are potential medicinal plants.

The use of herbal medicine has become a regular thing in the present day. Nigeria is said to possess rich resources that could be used in drug development, while some, such as ginger, garlic, turmeric, pepper, and green tea, among others, possess therapeutic values (Sofidiya, 2007). Plants and herbs have been used for medicinal purposes for centuries across the globe, long before the introduction of orthodox medicine, which is still made from plants but with more scientifically proven techniques and prescriptions. Indigenous cultures in places such as Rome, Africa, Egypt, Iran, China, India, and America used herbs in their healing rituals in the past, and some still combine various healing techniques in present times (Ahmad Khan & Ahmad, 2019). Most people who have taken herbal medicines prefer orthodox medicine to herbal medicine, even though most perceive herbal medication as safe and effective. As a result, most people purchase and use herbal medicine without professional consultation (Amorha et al., 2018).

Nigeria's health system has been plagued with challenges such as a high rate of maternal, child, and infant mortality, poor coverage of the National Health Insurance Scheme, inadequate health care quality, health inequality, little or no public funding, challenges of affordability, accessibility, and availability (Omoleke & Taleat, 2017), and recently the COVID-19 pandemic. Thus, the health care challenges along with the belief system favour traditional medicine,

 | DOI:10.1163/9789004692657_009

which makes a high proportion of the population use alternative medicine either alone or complementarily with orthodox medicine (Gyasi et al., 2016). Despite the contributions of traditional medicine to the health of citizens, some challenges have been identified in its administration, such as concerns about the quality, safety, and efficacy of herbal products, preservation, dosage, and measurement (Abdullahi, 2011). Amidst these areas of concern, traditional medicine has potential yet to be fully utilised due to ignorance and inadequate understanding of herbal medicine traders' operations and the informal economy of herbal medicine traders. Unorthodox medicine is an occupation, with the herb traders forming occupational groupings that expose only the insiders to the tricks and systems of the trade.

Adequate research attention has not been given to the medicinal herb traders and the tricks involved in the business; the study seeks to fill this knowledge gap. In Nigeria, traditional medicine is widely used; hence, medicinal herb trading is expanding and has received high patronage, especially in the southwestern part of the country. "Bode" Market is situated in the heart of Ibadan, located along Gate-*Molente* Road, precisely at "*Bode*", with thousands of stalls and shops. It is known as the Old Century International Herbal Market, which houses all kinds of herbs, roots, and branches that can cure different ailments. The *Bode* Market receives patronage across the states and neighbouring countries, including Togo, Ghana, Cameroon, Cote d'Ivoire, and some developing countries such as Brazil and London. There is a large inflow of people in and out of the market daily for other business purposes, but the buying and selling of herbs has a specific market day, usually every nine days (Waheed, 2018).

2 A Discourse on Trade in Herbs

Herbal Medicine is made from plant-derived materials that are proven to possess therapeutic or other human health benefits. They include processed ingredients from one or more plants, both in liquid and solid form. Herbal medicines have a long-standing history in Nigerian treatment of disease and illness. Although herbal medicine is perceived safe, it possesses some properties that could be potentially toxic, mutagenic, carcinogenic, or teratogenic. The safety of these herbs has become an essential concern for the health authorities. The policies and regulatory procedures of the herbal trade will determine the safety and quality of herbal medicines. Studies affirmed that a national policy on Traditional Medicine is in place in Nigeria, though in varying forms that need harmonisation (Awodele, Amagon, Wannang, and Aguiyi, 2014). In Nigeria, the National Agency for Food and

Drug Administration and Control (NAFDAC) currently only lists ethnomedicinal preparations on the market without issuing full registration status to most of these products. Herbal medicines in Nigeria have the exact same regulatory requirements for safety as conventional pharmaceuticals, which could hinder the proper administration of herbal medicine as the medicinal herb traders object to this policy and instead suggest that they should be treated differently (Awodele et al., 2014). The trade in Medicinal herbal products is unregulated.

In South Africa, people consult traditional healers as much as they consult medical practitioners. South Africa accounts for about 200,000 traditional healers that take care of over 27 million people (McFarlane, 2015). However, the herbal products must go through a complete drug evaluation with the Medicines Control Council (MCC) before they are marketed. There are no Specific regulations for the registration and control of new 'traditional' herbal medicines. Chukwuma et al., (2015) cited several leaves and their functions: Momordica charantia is used to take care of Ulcers, burns, skin infections, diabetes, convulsions, and pile; Momordica charantia cares for Ulcers, burns, skin infections, diabetes, convulsions, and pile; Baphia nitida Lodd takes care of Skin diseases, constipation, smallpox, and diabetes, among others.

In Nigeria, illnesses such as hypertension, dysentery, low sperm count, weak erection, coated tongue, pile, menstrual disorder, malaria, leucorrhoea, fevers, jaundice, guinea worm, venereal disease, Sores, skin infections, sore throat, ulcers, burns, skin infections, convulsions, cough, diabetes, night blindness, haemorrhoids, constipation, smallpox, diarrhoea, dysentery, epilepsy, goitre, gonorrhoea, and anaemia can be cured via the use of Medicinal herbs given by the practitioners (Olowokudejo, 2005). Medicinal herbs have made very significant contributions to the development of modern medicine; one of the many advantages of Medicinal herbs is that they play a synergistic role (Sofowora, Ogunbodede, and Onayade, 2013). While modern medicine focuses on one drug for one disease, traditional medicine has the capability of treating or preventing two or more diseases that may not be related, such as cardiovascular disease and diabetes, coupled with other therapeutic functions (Yuan et al., 2016).

A study conducted in the Limpopo, Kwa-Zulu Natal, and Northern Cape Provinces of South Africa found that most of the species of herbs being sold were those with multiple functions ranging from respiratory disorders, blood disorders, cardiovascular system disorders, cancer, diabetes, malaria, body cleaning, sexual health, fever, birth, magical uses, and dermatological problems (Rasethe et al., 2019). Although we have knowledged the effectiveness and challenges associated with the use of medicinal herbs in Nigeria, we still lack sufficient understanding of the trading procedures among herb traders.

3 Theoretical Orientation

The study adopted the social exchange theory developed by George Horman (1958). According to him, social exchange is the altercation of activities, tangible or intangible, rewarding, or costly, between at least two people. Exchange theory is based on the premise that human behaviour or social interaction is an exchange of activities, tangible and intangible (Homans, 1961), particularly rewards and costs. It treats the exchange of benefits, as the underlying basis of human behaviour (Homans, 1961),a phenomenon permeating all social life (Coleman, 1998; Zafirovski, 2005). Not only is the market permeated by exchange but also the non-economic realm—the social relations situated between extremes of intimacy, self-interest, or cost-benefit calculation and disinterested, expressive behaviour (Blau, 2017). Social exchange is composed of the actions of purposeful actors that presuppose the constellations of their interests and resources (Zafirovsky, 2005). Thus, trade in herbal medicine among traders, farmers, and customers is sustained via the principles of reciprocity, mutual respect, and cost-benefit analysis. It is purely economic, though there are traces of social relationships among them that exist in all traditional markets in Africa, such as celebrating with one another at social functions or buying the same outfit for a ceremony, among others.

4 Methodology

A qualitative methodology was adopted in this study. *The study purposefully selected the "Bode"* market in Ibadan, Southwestern Nigeria. "Bode" Market is situated in Ibadan, located along Gate-*Molente* Road, precisely at "Bode", with thousands of stalls and shops. Various kinds of herbs, roots, and stems are sold in the market. The Bode Market receives patronage across the states and neighbouring countries, including Togo, Ghana, Cameroon, Cote d'Ivoire, and some advanced countries such as Brazil and London. There is a large inflow of people in and out of the market daily for other business purposes, but the buying and selling of herbs has a specific market day, usually every nine days (Waheed, 2018). This "Bode" market was selected due to its popularity, centrality in Southwestern Nigeria, and the volume of medicinal herb traders therein. Forty-five (45) in-depth interviews were conducted among herb traders in the "*Bode*" Market. In addition, Key informant interviews (10) were also conducted among the stakeholders, such as the market leaders and buyers from outside Ibadan.

To factor in the ethical consideration, before starting the interviews, the study obtained verbal permission from each of the discussants, and confidentiality was critical in the field study. Each discussant was at liberty to stop the discussion and withdraw their participation at any stage of the interview. Participants were duly informed of this liberty before the commencement of the interview. Express permission was also obtained before recording the interview. In addition, the comfort of the participants was paramount throughout the discussion. Purposeful and convenient sampling techniques were used to select the study participants within the market. The data was collected, transcribed, and analysed via content analysis and ethnographic summaries.

5 Result/Findings

The qualitative data were analyzed thematically based on the study objectives.

5.1 *The Organisation of Trade in Herbs*

The organisation of trade in herbs involves the process of learning the trade, the requirements for joining the association, and the business transaction processes. This depends on the market and the association; there is no universal pattern of organisation. The association that determines the structure and modalities that the market will follow at every point in time.

The herb traders learned the trade through their familial relations, such as their mother-in-law, aunt, and mother. This suggests that the relationship will extend beyond the marketplace, strengthening the bond between them and wanting to understand the trade to receive approval from one's mother-in-law.

> I got to know about the herb trade from my mother-in-law, and I learned it from her. Initially, I sold clothes before I got married, but after marriage, my mother-in-law convinced my family to allow me to join her in the herb trade" (Female, 63 years, "Bode" Market).

Another Participant stated that she learned the trade from her aunt (her mother's younger sister) in the 1990s. During this period, when the trade was respected, relatives would be more inclined to give their children to people they trusted, family members. She has thus gotten autonomy from her aunt, and she is now doing fine in the business.

> I learned the trade from my aunt, who was like a mother, and the business was much more revered than it is now. I have gained my freedom from my aunt since the early '90s and am standing independently on my own" (Female, 55 years, "Bode" Market).

Another discussant stated that she is training her daughter, who caught interest in the business; hence, this could promote family business succession. Children are usually exposed to the trades of their parents during their formative years when they render help to the parents. During this time, the child took a special interest in the herb trade. More so, it is a thing of pride for parents when one of their children takes after them in their profession.

> I would love to have one of my children sell this product; it is a good thing. One of my twin children has caught an interest in this business; I am training her for the trade." (Female, 49 years, "Bode" Market).

Herb traders have their own association that helps promote their interests and protect the market, though it is not as decisive as it used to be or ought to be. Many of the traders complained that the specialty in the business is no longer protected, and this has the potential for developing quackery or shallow understanding among the traders. The requirement for joining the trade association is to get freedom after some years of apprenticeship and get a place to sell at the market.

> There are no special requirements to join the association, rather than, after apprenticeship, get a place to sell herbs, go to meetings, and do what the leadership requires of them, particularly registration and attendance. Every member is expected to play their roles and responsibilities to the association.

The association does not regulate the structure of the apprenticeship, like the entrance fees, autonomy fees, the kind of people to accept as apprentices, or the duration of the apprenticeship. All these decisions and many more are left to the individual trader's discretion.

> The trade has associations, but individual autonomy about what to sell, apprentices to take in, and the amount to collect has weakened the trade.
>
> Female, 53 years, "Bode" Market

There are different associations among the herb traders based on their specializations. The different groups are needed due to the peculiarities of their training and what they do. However, one can participate in many or all of these associations.

> There are different associations in the herb trade business, with their separate leaders, e.g., (dry animal parts) Olori-eku, (herbs) Alagbo, etc. They can only do what they are trained to do. Although you can do more than one just like me, I do all of them except for divination.
>
> Female, 59 years, "Bode" Market.

Moreover, to join the herb trade as an apprentice, one must pay money and give a few items to the master of the business, who will then expose one to the tricks of the trade. The entrance fee varies based on individual traders; the association does not regulate this.

> To learn the trade, an apprentice must pay a certain amount of money and bring items such as kola nuts and bitter kola, among others, for prayers, just as in the case of getting freedom from one's master.
>
> Female, 44 years, "Bode" Market.

The trade in herbs is part of the informal sector. Thus, there is no strict association's policy as to the necessary amount required for starting a business. The amount of money needed to start trading is dependent on the individual's ability. More finance give one leverage in trading with others.

> There is no specific amount to start the business, but "he who has money is he who has the business (olowo lo loowo).
>
> Female, 49 years, "Bode" Market

Another participant stated that to have stability and maximize profit in the business, one will need a minimum of #200,000 as startup capital. The different herbs, parts of animals, and other special items one will need vary, and to avoid travelling frequently for these items, one would need a sizeable amount of money.

> To start the business of selling herbs, one will need at least #200,000. However, including the sale of dry parts of animals will involve more than that.
>
> Female, 39 years, "Bode" Market

Moreover, a vivid understanding of business tricks and systems is critical for success in business, beyond the startup capital. There is an unwritten rule that does not favor apprentices changing masters among the herb traders in the "Bode" market.

> It is good that one learns and knows the trade very well before starting. More so, changing masters to learn as an apprentice is not so good because it will hinder the prosperity of the apprentice.
>
> Female, 49 years, "Bode" Market

Many of them find meaning and purpose in their trade since they perceive that it is their divine calling. Some of the traders have tried other things in which they failed, and they finally get back into the business as the only profession they can succeed in. The belief in trade as their calling gives them fulfilment and peace of mind, signifying the spiritual dimension of traders.

> This is the only work I am destined to do; I have done other work, but I did not prosper.
>
> Female, 60 years, "Bode" Market.

Several of the participants began the learning process when they were younger, learning from relatives, parents, in-laws, or family friends. When they gained independence from their master and subsequently joined the association for business protection, the learning process was successful. The association is criticized for not wielding enough power and control over individual traders.

5.1.1 Production and Procurement of Herbs, Roots, and Leaves

The herb traders do not have farms to cultivate herbs; instead, they approach different farm settlements to get supplies from them. Thus, the onslaught of the herdsmen on farm settlements around Oyo, Osun, and Ogun states brought scarcity to the market and price increases. The traders are not farmers; they do not cultivate the herbs themselves. They buy the herbs from farmers who cultivate them.

> I don't have a farm of my own where I cultivate herbs.
>
> Female, 52 years, "Bode" Market

The wholesale traders get animal parts from Northern Nigeria, where there is abundance and low demand, to get the goods at a cheaper rate. However, the roots and herbs are from farms in towns in southwest Nigeria.

> The roots, herbs, and other plants are gotten from the farm, e.g.,' Ijebu, Ife, while the animal parts are gotten from the Northern parts of Nigeria.
>
> Female, 43 years, "Bode" Market

The wholesale marketers go to other parts of Nigeria beyond the northern region if the herbs they are looking for are rare in the Southwest region. They travel to get them in other places. This suggests that a large sum of money is needed to travel to different places for herbs.

> However, some marketers go as far as Kano, Onitsha, and Benin to get herbs that are scarce in the western area of Nigeria. We could serve as both suppliers and buyers depending on the type that is available in a location.
>
> Female, 49 years, "Bode" Market

Channels of distribution exist among the traders; the large-scale wholesalers get the herbs from distant farms and distribute them among small-scale wholesalers or retailers, who then sell them to either final consumers or small-scale retailers—those who prepare concoctions with them. For a retail trader, they do not have to travel to the North or to distant farms; rather, they get the herbs from the wholesale traders in the "Bode" market.

> We buy herbs from within this "Bode" market through those who go to the farm directly, though we don't know the farm they get it from specifically, and those who go to Kano to get "Ori eku, dry rat head," birds, and other animal parts.
>
> Female, 52 years, "Bode" Market

Bode Market is a major distributor of herbs in the Southwest. Herb traders from different parts of the south-west region make transactions in this market. Thus, it is known for the volume of trade, centrality, and popularity of medicinal herb trades.

> "Bode" Market is the sole distributor of medicinal plants in the western region. However, it could serve the dual roles of suppliers and buyers.
>
> Female, 49 years, "Bode" Market

The herb traders do not have farms where they cultivate the herbs; rather, they get them from farmers nearby who do the cultivation, and the traders focus on the exchange of leaves, roots, and herbs. However, the animal parts are gotten from the city of Kano and other parts of the Northern part of Nigeria. There are various levels of traders, i.e., wholesalers and retailers. The retailers buy herbs from the wholesalers within the Bode market, while the wholesalers get theirs from distant farm settlements. The market serves as the mainstay of the buying and selling of herbs within the south-western region of the country.

5.1.2 Preservation of Herbs

Herbs, roots, leaves, and other medicinal plants need to be well dried to avoid attack by insects. It's difficult to predict how long the herbs will last before the traders spoil them. They shake these plants to measure their strength and rigidity. Due to the unpredictability of these herbs, traders are more likely to get dry plants because they are easy to preserve either in a basket, nylon, or any dry container, unlike wet herbs that are prone to insect attacks.

> When plants are well dried, they can be stored in a dry place in a basket or nylon, and nothing will happen to them. However, when they are still wet, they are open to several attacks by insects.
>
> Female, 43 years, "Bode" Market

Despite the sun drying method, there is the fear that some herbs can still spoil because the traders don't know the length of time post-harvest or where they have been stored in the past.

> There is no timeline as to when the herbs could get spoiled because we don't know how long they have spent in the bush and other places before they are sold to us.
>
> Female, 53 years, "Bode" Market

The fear of spoilage makes some of the traders buy a few herbal medicines and replace them when they are sold, especially among the retailers. However, wholesalers who buy large quantities are more likely to distribute them to their customers on time.

> We buy them little by little to avoid spoilage, and we sell those we can sell immediately and keep others for the next market pot.
>
> Female, 55 years, Bode market

Some of the traders detect roots that will not last by simply shaking them. Learning the skill of detecting good and bad roots is vital for the sustenance of the business and to minimize loss from spoilage.

> The roots that are still strong when shaken are good, but those that are shaky may not last long.
>
> Female, 42 years, Bode market

However, dry parts of the animal are preserved with kerosene and camphor. These could be dangerous to the health of the users, who may not wash the items thoroughly or dip them into cold liquid substances, i.e., alcohol, water, etc., for concoction.

> Kerosine is used to preserve dry parts of animals, and camphor (Kafura) is placed underneath the pot.
>
> Female, 51 years, Bode market

The chemical items are used to preserve the flesh used to prepare herbs, which can be harmful to health since some preparations of herbs are concoctions that do not include boiling. The durability of the herbs is quite unpredictable; hence, the traders put in some measures like sun drying, buying only dry herbs, buying a few items, distributing the items bought to customers on time, preserving them using kerosene and camphor, and developing the skills to detect bad roots by shaking them.

5.2 *Information about the Use of Herbs for the Cure and Prevention of Illness*

Several of the traders learned the trade from family and friends. They all contended that there are no discoveries in herbal medicine, but merely changes of names. Although they learn about treatment every day from interactions in the market and other parts of society, The loss of knowledge about herbs calls for concern when the young ones are not interested in learning about herbal medicine from the older ones, who are the custodians of wisdom.

> My mother-in-law taught me how to use herbs for different ailments, and there have been no discoveries. Rather, there are some roots, leaves, and herbs that we don't see again and whose information and knowledge have been lost due to the death of the person who has the information and knowledge and could not pass it on to their children.
>
> Female, 41 years, Bode market

A participant contended that there are no discoveries within the business; rather, what is experienced is just the change of names of the herbs, roots, and leaves among succeeding generations.

> There are no new herbs, leaves, or roots, but rather a change of names between different generations of pot.
>
> Female, 48 years, Bode market

Some of the herb traders have good knowledge of the uses of the herbs; hence, they prepare herbal drinks and concoctions for others and themselves. The concoctions they prepare are for more common illnesses among the populace, like malaria and pneumonia.

> I prepare herbs for myself when I am ill and prepare concoctions for others too, for instance, agbo-iba, an herbal medicine for malaria, and agbo Jedi, an herbal medicine for pile.
>
> Female, 39 years, Bode market

A participant indicated that some plants could work for many types of ailments as they were meant for multipurpose use within the household.

> There are some herbs that heal all kinds of ailments; they are called gbogbonise pot.
>
> Female, 43 years, Bode market

While some herbs may not cure all ailments, they can cure multiple ailments, such as mango roots. These kinds of herbs are popular among users because of their usage.

> There are some herbs that work for up to four types of ailments, such as 'egbooruwo', mango roots, and egboopoto (for sleeping and body increase pot).
>
> Female, 43 years, Bode market

However, not all herb traders know the uses of medicinal plants and dried animal parts. In such cases, they only sell it to the end-users who make use of these medicinal plants.

> I only know the names of the leaves, herbs, and roots you see here, but not what they used them for. The herbalist mainly knows the uses of pot.
>
> Female, 47 years, Bode market

There is no new discovery of herbs for treatment, though the traders learn new things from their peers. However, there is information that has been lost to antiquity due to the loss of interest of the younger ones and the demise of the custodian of the health information, which was not passed to the younger generation before death. Additionally, not all herb traders are aware of how to use medicinal plants for treatment, which is something that should only be known by end users.

5.3 *Marketing and Networking Style among Herb Traders' in "Bode" Market, Southwestern Nigeria*

The traders have a relationship with herbalists and other traditional healers that is based solely on economic reasons. The Yoruba traditional healers are diverse, including the herbalists (onisegun or adahunse), soothsayers (ala-sotele), traditional pharmacists (leku-leja), and many others. These traditional healing practitioners patronize the herb traders. The traders sell directly to the customers, sometimes through their children or by sending the items through motorcycle riders.

> We sell goods (Orieye, Ekete, orieku – animal parts) to herbalists, ada-hunse, onisegun, Islamic Clerics (alfa), and other customers who are involved in healing practices. Sometimes, we sell in bits and dozens through the customer's children or motorcycle riders, but in most cases directly to the customers themselves.
>
> Female, 39 years, Bode market

Sometimes, they sell directly to other places in bulk with the use of a vehicle, especially for the wholesalers who buy in bulk and distribute to other marketers in the southwest region.

> I supply herbal products to other places like Iseyin with the aid of a vehicle.
>
> Female, 47 years old, Bode market

A middle-aged woman believes that the relationship between the herb traders and the herbalists is economic. They buy and sell goods to them. She asserts that she could do other businesses, but she cannot leave the herb-selling trade.

> The relationship between herb traders, diviners, and herbalists is for economic reasons, i.e., buying and selling. I can do other kinds of business alongside herbs, but I can't leave herb selling.
>
> Female, 45 years, Bode market

The complementary businesses, such as pot selling and calabash, are supplied from elsewhere, and there are others who specialise in the sale of pots and other accessories attached to the herb trade.

> There are different pots, clay pots, and calabash supplied from Ilorin or Ibadan, while we buy from the wholesalers who specialise in any pot.
> Female, 51 years, Bode market

The specialisation is declining; while some encourage it, others frown at it as a weakness of the association. They believe that the association is not doing enough to protect the market.The association is weak, individuality is encouraged.

> The specialisations no longer exist; rather, people buy any item once they have money for it, which ought not to be so because they lack knowledge of it and could lead to quackery. If the association is strong enough, it should stop people from selling what they don't know about pot. Female, 43 years, Bode market

Another discussant who is favourably disposed to specialisations stated that there should be up to six specialisations among the herb traders:

> We ought to have up to six specialisations, such as Eleweomo (herbs and leaves trader); Olorieku (sellers of dry animal parts); Alape (traders in pots); Onileke (trader in herbs); Onisude (ide (snail shell), efun (Chalk), Osun, alum); and Olobi (sellers of Kolanut, bitter kola, etc.) pot.
> Female, 43 years, Bode market

A trader who supports it stated that it is based on the supply available and the money at hand that prompted the buying and selling of a particular product.

> I sell herbs and roots mainly, but when there is a supply for dry parts of animals, I purchase from them to pot.
> Female, 47 years, Bode market

The traders use daily or weekly contributions for the sustenance of their business. The thrift collection mechanism is vital to the growth of their business in terms of savings and getting the money for further capital to be invested in the business.

> I use thrift and assistance to sustain and rejuvenate the business pot.
> Female, 45 years, Bode market

The relationship the herb traders have with the herbalists and other healers they patronise is purely economic (an exchange of goods and services). They sell in bits to customers or through motorcycle riders to customers, and they sell in bulk with the use of the vehicle. Complementary goods such as pot and Calabash are supplied from villages elsewhere. However, the herb traders decry the decline of specialisation, which has encouraged impostors.

6 Discussion

The traders learn the trade from their family and friends, with little or nothing to pay for joining; this is because the family relationship is meaningful to them. A number of them perceive that trade is what they are divinely called to do in life. Awodele et al. (2014) opined that there are policies and regulatory policies and procedures for herbs in Nigeria, those policies are not implemented. Nigeria's health policies have not given herbal product full status or access to operate, just like in China, Ghana, and Korea, among others.

Most ofthe traders do not have a farm on their own; instead, they get medicinal plants from farms in Ife, Ijebu, and other southwestern areas of Nigeria; dried animal parts are gotten from the northern part of Nigeria. This supports the finding of Sofidiya et al. (2007), who argued that the herb traders are not the actual producers of the herbs, roots, leaves, and dried animal parts; instead, they have suppliers in other places. The sun-drying method is used for medicinal plants, and kerosene is used for preserving the dried animal parts; this contradicts the finding of Ozioma et al. (2019), who found out that the preservation methods among the herb traders include potash, extraction, boiling woody pieces, and filtration by the buyers. The findings support Sahar, Hala, and Elham's (2013) statement that sun drying and microwave drying processes are used in preservation. Still, it can lead to a reduction in the antioxidant properties of the herbs.

Studies show that traditional healthcare practitioners use different methods to diagnose diseases; these methods may include asking the patient about signs and symptoms, physical features, and pulse rate. Pulse rate was the most common method used to diagnose diseases. If the pulse rate is faster than usual, it is a sign of an acute infection. If the pulse rate is slow, it is a sign of heart disease, although it is impossible to detect the exact disease just by checking the pulse. Zahoor et al. (2021) Conventional medicine practitioners utilize herbs and roots, vegetables, medicine, charms or magic, healing tools, oracles or divination, sacrifice, drink-liquor or palm wine, and water, among others.

Many medicinal herbs are going extinct, and others are endangered due to infrastructural developments by individuals, organisations, and governments. They are no longer available, which may pose a danger to the citizens who depend on medicinal herbs. Policies on the conservation of herbs have not been efficiently implemented. More so, knowledge on the use of medicinal herbs for treatment is primarily held by the older generations, whose numbers are gradually decreasing (Chukwumna, Soladoye, and Feyisola, 2015).

Many herb traders can prepare concoctions and medicines for common ailments like malaria and piles. However, they only sell medicinal herbs to the end-users to do further processing on them; this contradicts the study of Chukwuma et al. (2015), where they assert that in Nigeria, medicinal herbs are used to treat different kinds of ailments such as diabetes, malaria, respiratory disorders, cardiovascular diseases, leucorrhoea and fevers, jaundice, guinea worm, venereal disease, sores, skin infections, sore throat, ulcers, burns, skin infections, convulsions, cough, diabetes, night blindness, haemorrhoids, constipation, smallpox, diarrhoea, dysentery, epilepsy, goitre, gonorrhoea, and anaemia, among others.

The medicinal herb traders collaborate with the herbalists, Islamic clerics, and Christian clergy, though it was reported that the relationship is purely on an economic basis. The finding corroborated the results of Alade and Ajibesin (2017) and Halder et al. (2021), where they assert that the market for herbal products is increasing in Nigeria with the collaboration of the two foreign religions, Christianity, and Islam, in the prevention and treatment of diseases (Alade & Ajibesin, 2017). More so, the internet and social media have increased the markets for traditional medicine products, though herb traders are yet to tap into this new resource (Mafimisebi, 2013). The medicinal herb traders have yet to tap into the full potential of social media in promoting their businesses.

The International Organisation of Herbs Trade Associations (2013), stated that to control and ensure the safety of herbs planted, harvested, and stored for commercial purposes, preservation means must be safe, free from bacteria, and do not cause harm to consumers. The processes include processing, sun drying, storage transportation, stuffing and shipping, pest monitoring, pesticides, processing aids, worker hygiene, field sanitation, and microbial contamination (Jayas, 2016).

A survey of anti-inflammatory plants carried out in an herb market in Lagos State, Nigeria, specifically in Mushin, Oyingbo, and Agege, reveals that medicinal herb traders, traditional healers, and patients seeking treatment meet at this market to perform various transactions. The market is known to have a designated market day where farmers bring fresh herbs from neighbouring towns and villages for the herb traders, who then resell them to their customers. The study also reveals that many of the herb traders are females who are also illiterate. The herbs being sold on the market perform numerous functions, but most are focused on curing inflammatory diseases. Most of the herbs being sold there are dried herbs, and, on a few occasions, when the customer requests a fresh herb, arrangements are made with the suppliers. The herb traders are of the opinion that their herb performs multiple healing functions and works effectively and faster when combined with other herbs (Sofidiya, 2007).

7 Conclusion

The medicinal herb traders have an association that helps to promote their welfare and wellbeing in the marketplace, though it is argued that the association is no longer as strong as it used to be. The association has failed to protectthe non-specialisations of herb traders. The informality of the business is shown by the fact that there is no regulation as to what to sell, and the number of specific amounts used to start and to gain autonomy is dependent on the individual master. The medicinal plants are gotten from the farmers; dried animal parts are from the north; and calabash and clay pots are brought from Ilorin and Ibadan. "Bode" market is the principal distributor of medicinal herb trade in western Nigeria; they can both serve as buyers and sellers simultaneously. The sun-drying method and kerosene are used to preserve medicinal plants and dry animal parts, respectively. Spiritual leaders such as diviners, herbalists, Islamic clerics, Christian clergy, and other end users patronise them consistently, while they are yet to utilise the potential of social media and the internet due to the low level of education of the traders. To fully maximize the potential of medicinal herbs in Nigeria, attention must be paid to the production, preservation, transportation of herbs, security of the farmers, and standardization of the training of the traders.

References

Abdullahi, A. (2011). Trends and Challenges of Traditional Medicine in Africa. *African Journal of Traditional, Complementary and Alternative Medicines*, *8*(5S). https://doi.org/10.4314/ajtcam.v8i5S.5.

Ahmad Khan, M. S., & Ahmad, I. (2019). Chapter 1 - Herbal Medicine: Current Trends and Future Prospects. In M. S. Ahmad Khan, I. Ahmad, & D. Chattopadhyay (Eds.),

New Look to Phytomedicine (pp. 3–13). Academic Press. https://doi.org/10.1016/B978-0-12-814619-4.00001-X.

Alade, G., & Ajibesin, K. (2017). Herbal medicine: Clerics' knowledge in a sub urban center in Niger delta, Nigeria - A pilot study. *Journal of Pharmacy and Pharmacognosy Research*, *5*, 200–216.

Amorha, K. C., Nwabunike, I. A., Okwumuo, B. M., Ayogu, E. E., Nduka, S. O., & Okonta, M. J. (2018). Use of herbal medicines in a Nigerian community and their reported adverse effects: A pilot study. *Tropical Journal of Pharmaceutical Research*, *17*(10), Article 10. https://doi.org/10.4314/tjpr.v17i10.

Awodele, O., Amagon, K. I., Wannang, N. N., & Aguiyi, J. C. (2014). Traditional medicine policy and regulation in Nigeria: An index of herbal medicine safety. *Current Drug Safety*, *9*(1), 16–22. https://doi.org/10.2174/1574886308666131126155434.

Chukwuma, E. C., Soladoye, M. O., & Feyisola, R. T. (n.d.). *Traditional medicine and the future of medicinal Plants in Nigeria.*

Coleman, J. (1998). *Foundations of Social Theory:* Belknap Press.

Ekor, M. (2014). The growing use of herbal medicines: Issues relating to adverse reactions and challenges in monitoring safety. *Frontiers in Pharmacology*, *4*, 177. https://doi.org/10.3389/fphar.2013.00177.

Gyasi, R. M., Asante, F., Abass, K., Yeboah, J. Y., Adu-Gyamfi, S., & Amoah, P. A. (2016). Do health beliefs explain traditional medical therapies utilisation? Evidence from Ghana. *Cogent Social Sciences*, *2*(1), 1209995. https://doi.org/10.1080/23311886.2016.1209995.

Halder, S., Anand, U., Nandy, S., Oleksak, P., Qusti, S., Alshammari, E. M., El-Saber Batiha, G., Koshy, E. P., & Dey, A. (2021). Herbal drugs and natural bioactive products as potential therapeutics: A review on pro-cognitives and brain boosters perspectives. *Saudi Pharmaceutical Journal : SPJ*, *29*(8), 879–907. https://doi.org/10.1016/j.jsps.2021.07.003.

Homans, G. C. (1961). *Social behavior: Its elementary forms* (p. 404). Harcourt, Brace.

Jayas, D. S. (2016). Food Dehydration. In *Reference Module in Food Science*. Elsevier. https://doi.org/10.1016/B978-0-08-100596-5.02913-9.

Kamel, S., Thabet, H. A., & Algadi, E. A. (2013). Influence of drying process on the functional properties of some plants. *Chemistry and Materials Research*, *3*, 1–8.

Mafimisebi, T. (2013). The Expanding Market for Herbal, Medicinal and Aromatic Plants In Nigeria and the International Scene. *Medicinal and Aromatic Plants*, 2. https://doi.org/10.4172/2167-0412.1000144.

McFarlane, C. (2015). South Africa: The Rise of Traditional Medicine. *Insight on Africa*, *7*(1), 60–70. https://doi.org/10.1177/0975087814554070.

Rasethe, M. T., Semenya, S. S., & Maroyi, A. (2019). Medicinal Plants Traded in Informal Herbal Medicine Markets of the Limpopo Province, South Africa. *Evidence-*

Based Complementary and Alternative Medicine: ECAM, 2019, 2609532. https://doi.org/10.1155/2019/2609532.

Olowokudejo, J., Kadiri, A., & Travih, V. (2008). An Ethnobotanical Survey of Herbal Markets and Medicinal Plants in Lagos State of Nigeria. *Ethnobotanical Leaflets, 2008*(1). https://opensiuc.lib.siu.edu/ebl/vol2008/iss1/116.

Omoleke, I. I., & Taleat, B. A. (2017). Contemporary issues and challenges of health sector in Nigeria. *Research Journal of Health Sciences, 5*(4), Article 4. https://doi.org/10.4314/rejhs.v5i4.5.

Ozioma, E.-O. J., NwamakaChinwe, O. A., Ozioma, E.-O. J., & NwamakaChinwe, O. A. (2019). Herbal Medicines in African Traditional Medicine. In *Herbal Medicine.* IntechOpen. https://doi.org/10.5772/intechopen.80348.

Shaheen, S., Ramzan, S., Khan, F., & Ahmad, M. (2019). Why Study Herbal Plants? In S. Shaheen, S. Ramzan, F. Khan, & M. Ahmad (Eds.), *Adulteration in Herbal Drugs: A Burning Issue* (pp. 17–33). Springer International Publishing. https://doi.org/10.1007/978-3-030-28034-5_3.

Sofidiya, M. O., Odukoya, O. A., Afolayan, A. J., & Familoni, O. B. (n.d.). Survey of Anti-Inflammatory Plants Sold on Herb Markets in Lagos Nigeria. *International Journal of Botany, 3*(3), 302–306. https://doi.org/10.3923/ijb.2007.302.306.

Sofowora, A., Ogunbodede, E., & Onayade, A. (2013). The role and place of medicinal plants in the strategies for disease prevention. *African Journal of Traditional, Complementary, and Alternative Medicines: AJTCAM, 10*(5), 210–229. https://doi.org/10.4314/ajtcam.v10i5.2.

World Health Organization (2019). World Health Organisation global report on traditional and complementary medicine 2019.ISBN 978–92-4–151543-6 © World Health Organization 2019, 3.0 IGO license (CC BY-NC-SA 3.0 IGO; *https://creativecommons.org/licenses/by-nc-sa/3.0/igo*).

Yuan, H., Ma, Q., Ye, L., & Piao, G. (2016). Traditional Medicine and Modern Medicine from Natural Products. *Molecules, 21*(5), 559. https://doi.org/10.3390/molecules21050559.

Zahoor, M., Yousaf, Z., Yasin, H., Shinwari, Z., Haroon, M., Saleh, N., Younas, A., Aftab, A., Shamsheer, B., Riaz, N., & Rashid, M. (2021). Ethnobotanicals and commercial trends of herbal markets in Punjab, Pakistan.*Journal of Herbal Medicine, 26*, 100425. https://doi.org/10.1016/j.hermed.2021.100425.

Zafirovski, M. (2005). The Influence of Sociology on Economics: Selected Themes and Instances from Classical Sociological Theory. *Journal of Classical Sociology, 5*(2), 123–156. *https://doi.org/10.1177/1468795X05053488.*

CHAPTER 8

Indigenous Usury Finance System and Informal Trader-Lendees in Ibadan Nigeria

Bernard Adeniyan and Ayokunle Olumuyiwa Omobowale

1 Introduction

Access to credit remains a major challenge to development in most developing countries of the world (Adebayo, 1992). This credit gap has been further exacerbated by the lending bias of formal financial institutions against the informal sector in most developing countries. Adams et al. (2003) noted that formal financial institutions have not been able to provide microcredit to most of the population, especially the poor who are largely described as informal and 'unbankable' (see also Mills, 2007). Banks and other modern financial institutions often argue that they incur substantial costs when providing credit to the poor and those in the informal sector of the economy. Such costs include loan processing, loan repayment, security monitoring, loan administration, and recovery of delinquent loans, among others. The poor who are at the receiving end of this credit vacuum usually fall back on other available alternatives. It is at this point that informal or traditional finance systems such as indigenous usury lenders become the beacon of hope for many individuals especially those in the low-income stratum of the society.

Indigenous usury credit also known among the Yoruba of southwest Nigeria as Owo ele has received relatively little attention as a system of informal credit and this is despite its popularity, especially among traders in the informal sector. Soyibo (1996; 1997) identified the indigenous usury system (also known as Moneylenders) as one of the six informal financial institutions found in urban Nigeria. Hitherto, the Owo ele system of finance has been studied by Adebayo (1992) and Falola (1993) but it must be noted that these scholarly works were archival as they investigated the system as practiced in the colonial Yoruba land. This is the central focus of this research work. This study focuses on the social interpretation of credit relations between contemporary usurers and their trader-clients, who exchange goods and services within the context traditional African marketplace.

At this point, the term 'usury' must be properly situated. Valeri (2011) identified two meanings of usury. The first refers to an exorbitant amount or rate

 | DOI:10.1163/9789004692657_010

of interest, especially more than the legally acceptable rate. In other words, it is the practice of lending at an exorbitant rate of interest. The second definition views usury as the act or practice of lending money at a particular interest rate. In other words, usury is interest paid on borrowed funds or money. According to Meeks (2011), usury involves an ever-changing array of exchange techniques which include taking any interest on a loan, making provisions for the payment of fees or late payment penalties, making commercial deals that, in effect, guarantee a profit to the lender and manipulating exchange rates for payment in foreign currency. In essence, usury can be described as a term used for financial transactions that involve the payment of interest, which was an unpopular practice, particularly in medieval Europe. This is understandable because the concept was condemned in Christian medieval Europe with a highly religious moral ethic that discouraged a high-interest rate (Mews and Abraham, 2006). The medieval description of usury lending based on the relatively expensive interest rate still constitutes a significant narrative of the system in contemporary informal microfinance. Jone (2008) however noted that moneylenders also finance routine health and social expenditures in a speedy and un-bureaucratic manner and with flexible repayment procedures.

The rest of this paper will proceed with a section on the informal sector and the traditional usury system. The next section deals with the research method and means of data interpretation while the paper proceeds with the analyses of findings and conclusions.

2 The Nigerian Informal Sector and Its Potentials for Development

Nigeria has the largest informal sector in Africa, and this can be attributed to her large population and decades of underdevelopment by agents of the state (Onyebueke and Geyer, 2011). Activities in the informal sector are generally described as unrecognized, unrecorded, unprotected, and unregulated by the government or its agencies (Onwe, 2013). According to Akintimehin et al, (2019), the Nigerian informal sector is defined in terms of employee size and ownership structure. Enterprises here are described as informal when they have less than ten (10) employees and are owned by an individual who enjoys the voluntary assistance of family members or occupational trainees popularly known as apprentices. Akintimehin et al further noted that the informal sector contributes 41.43% of Nigeria's GDP, and 57.9% to Nigeria's GNP at US$212.6 billion, and the sector is still growing in terms of national GNP up to this present moment. However, Atoloye (2007) warned about the need to put a figure on the size of the informal sector as it is still a growing phenomenon and several sectors have not been captured. Atoloye, however, noted that the sector is here to stay although it is largely unorganized, unregulated, and unregistered, falling outside of state regulations and control. However, it is important to note that there are non-state actors that have taken up the role of organising and regulating various sub-sectors within the informal sector of the economy. In 1972, The International Labour Organization further clarified the forms of enterprises that would be classified as informal to include those businesses that have easy entry and exit features; dependence on indigenous resources; family ownership enterprises; the small scale of operation; labour intensive and adopted technology; skills required outside the formal school system; unregulated and competitive market and lack of legal or government recognition (Adeyinka et al, 2006). Businesses that are captured within this context include small-scale retail and productive enterprises, artisans, retail–trading, hawkers, street traders, and food vending.

There are divergent views on how to situate the informal sector for the Nigerian economy vis-à-vis its potential for growth and development. Nwaka (2005) provided a clear analysis of these diverse perspectives on the informal sector of society. According to Nwaka, some see the sector as the major source of income for the poor, employment opportunities, the seedbed of local entrepreneurship, and a potent instrument in the campaign to combat poverty and social exclusion. On the other hand, some dismiss the sector as an anomaly, a source of disorder, and an obstacle to the development of a modern economy. They condemn the slums, health risks, insecurity, and exploitation associated with the sector, and hope that like other transitory phases during development, the informal sector will wither away with time and economic progress.

The fact however remains that the informal sector is where an overwhelming majority of the labour population earns their living, and this is true of most developing countries (Fapohunda, 2012). The growth of the informal sector has been attributed to the limited absorption capacity of the formal sector, economic hardship, poverty, unemployment, and underemployment, restriction of entry into the formal sector, demand for low-cost goods and services, have a broad spectrum of activities that fall outside the scope of the formal sector, among other (Sparks and Barnett, 2010; Onyebueke and Geyer, 2011; Nnabuife et al, 2020).

3 Indigenous Usury System as a Dimension of Informal Capital Formation

This section examines various studies that have identified the indigenous usury system as a dimension or aspect of informal lending. Most developing countries have a dual financial system comprising formal and informal financial institutions (Flora and Ray, 1997). The duality of sources of finance has long been a subject of scholarly discourse especially as it relates to credit in developing countries of the world (Boucher and Guirkinger, 2007). According to Shem and Atieno (2001), a formal finance system refers to the various forms of savings and credit flows that are recognised, controlled, and legally backed by the laws of a given country or region while savings and credit transactions that flow through unrecognised and uncontrolled systems without legal backing, are referred to the as informal financial system. However, Soyibo (1997) expanded the legality argument by stating that informal sources of finance such as moneylending or indigenous usury lenders are not illegal as there are laws in the state backing their existence and activities (see also Falola,1993; Eja and Bassey, 2001). The major concern is the inability of moneylenders to operate within the provisions of the laws regulating their activities. Soyibo (1996) thus described moneylending as a contract or agreement conducted between or among parties to any transaction where cash is exchanged in the present for the promise of another cash exchange in the future. In his study of the informal finance structure of Akwa, Ibe (1990) identified four major suppliers of funds for economic activities. These suppliers are individual moneylenders, village associations, unregistered cooperative societies, and traders' associations. The identified moneylenders were described as speculators who combined the business of moneylending with land and commodity trading. In an analysis of agricultural credits, Obeta (1992) also opined that the desire for credit before the advent of the formal credit system necessitated the evolution of informal credit systems in rural parts of Nigeria. These indigenous credit institutions include moneylenders, landlords, relatives, and friends, esusu, and age-grade associations. Obeta further stated that credits obtained from local money lenders were only second to loans obtained from friends and relatives. Adebayo (1992) noted that where the fund provided through Rotating Savings and Credit Associations (ROSCA) and credit from kins and friends were not sufficient, as was often the case, the African trader, craftsman, and farmer had to seek additional funds from the local moneylenders. The continuous existence of traditional moneylenders in post-colonial Yoruba society was due to the ability of the system to adjust to the new realities of the new world (Falola, 1993). The moneylending system is perhaps the only informal microfinance institution that does not focus its lending on distinct groups of clients (Nissanke, 2001).

In a study of informal credit in South Africa, James (2014) observed that the patronage of 'illegal' moneylenders was pervasive. Okurut and Bolthole (2009) also noted that the specific features of the moneylending system include the use of limited documentation during credit transactions, security based on trust, inter-personal knowledge of clients, and the fact that there is a high degree of secrecy surrounding their financial dealing. These features provide comfort and motivate the poor and traders to patronize their services. Chipeta and Mkandawire (1992) stated that finance for consumption and investment was carried out by several informal financiers such as moneylenders. The proximity to clients enables Moneylenders to rely on personal relationships, social sanctions, and collateral substitutes to overcome the problems of screening and enforcement (Jones, 2008). Buckley (1997) specifically noted that moneylenders tend to operate in highly localised markets, and they also have close interpersonal relationships with their debtors or clients. These two features consequently limit the number of loans that they are likely to extend at any time. This means that physical collateral is not of great importance in moneylending (Mohieldin and Wright, 2000).

Manig (1996) provided insights into why informal financial systems such as moneylenders have continued to enjoy patronage overtime. First, a credit relation in informal lending is just one component of a multi-stranded networking relation among people. Thus, credit relations between lenders and borrowers are embedded in the social, economic, and political relations of the people. Second, the embedding of credit relations in economic and social relations engenders trust between participants which also helps to enforce loan repayment. Third, there is the principle of reciprocity and the very often complementary character of informal credit which implies that, when credit is granted, the lender expects and receives something which is marked by the predominating relation. In the case of relations predominated by politics, the return service can consist of loyalty and support in political disputes. The possibility of further reciprocal exchange of value has continued to sustain the informal credit system (Olubiyo, 2009).

4 Dominant Views on Indigenous Usury as a Traditional System of Credit

There are two dominant schools of thought on the social relations of the indigenous usury system. The first perspective sees the system as exploitative and an obstacle to development while the other perspective views the system as a feature of most developing countries of the world, which addresses their peculiar financial challenges (Chavan, 2003). Reddy (2007) also categorized these perspectives as the positive and negative images of Moneylenders. The positive image sees the moneylender as a resilient entity that assists in the process of development. The negative image on the other hand sees the same moneylender as an exploiter who is responsible for rural distress and poverty (see also Schrader, 1992). According to Labet and Block (2012), the profession of usury lending has been a subject of conflict, morality, and religious scrutiny with claims at some point that the act should be penalised by a death sentence. The exploitative and bitter expression toward moneylending has often led to the establishment of laws that were meant to curtail the perceived exploitative tendencies of this form of lending (Falola, 1993; Schrader, 1994; Eja and Bassey, 2011; Saika, 2012).

Moneylenders have long been considered exploitative, monopolistic, and detrimental to socio-economic development (Sharma and Chamala, 1998). Gine (2011) also asserted that usury or money lending has traditionally been viewed as unfair by policymakers and development practitioners, who argue that lenders take advantage of their position to exploit poor borrowers. Gine, however, stated that several research works have shown that, despite the injection of formal credit, informal finance institutions such as indigenous usury is still patronised, and the interest rates charged by usurers have not been affected by the increased presence of formal credit and related institutions.

Shah et al (2007) noted that moneylenders in pre-colonial and colonial India for instance engaged various mechanisms that ensured the continued exploitation of the hapless peasants who through repeated borrowings were trapped in perpetual debt relations. Eboh et al (1991) observed that one major problem facing those who borrow from moneylenders is the high rates of interest relative to institutional or formal interest rates. Falola (1993) described moneylending in colonial Yoruba society as the most detested of all sources of credit. The various features of exploitation according to Falola included high-interest rates, forcible collections of debts were notorious, and the use of various ways to cheat the borrower. Interest rates charged by private money lenders have variously been described as "usurious". The most common reasons for the negative perception of moneylenders have to do with the high-interest rate that the lenders charged and the behaviour of the lender during the period of default (Buckley, 1997).

The exploitative image of moneylenders is being questioned because traditional moneylenders are more effective than formal banking institutions, particularly in reaching out to the poor (Sharma and Chamala, 1998). While the banks have not been successful in displacing the moneylenders in rural areas, they have also failed in convincing villagers about their sympathetic disposition regarding the credit problems and needs of the rural people. Sharma and Chamala (2003) noted that there is a rising positive image paradigm of moneylenders in contemporary times. This perspective has provided the most forceful challenge to the negative image paradigm. This paradigm strongly advocates the involvement of moneylenders in the development process. Rahman (1992) noted that informal finance systems such as moneylending are not necessarily as exploitative as they are usually depicted in development literature. For Rahman, the weight of the evidence rather supports the argument that they play a positive role in the process of development, which could be enhanced by a more positive approach towards this sector. Fernando (1988) also asserted that the hypothesis that informal finance sources are highly exploitative cannot be supported by the evidence available in a place like Sri Lanka. According to Patole and Ruthven (2001), far from being exploited, the borrower is said to be aware of the price of patronising usurers, especially considering the unbeatable convenience and short turn-around time that the moneylender offers in finance service delivery.

Schrader (1994) introduced the modernisation perspective to the discourse by stating that the notion that informal finance such as moneylenders are obstacles to development reflects the white and black dichotomy of modernisation theorists regarding developing countries. This negative perspective of moneylending reflects the modernisation perspective that anything that is not Western is bad and detrimental to development (Sarker, 2006). Modernisation and consequent development of the formal economy notwithstanding, the informal financial markets have remained relevant and constituted part and parcel of the domestic economic framework of many African countries (Oladeji and Ogunrinola, 2001).

The positive paradigm of moneylending is predicated on the fact that it provides credit alternatives to the other formal means of securing credit which is relatively inaccessible to the low class and the vulnerable in the society. Informal financial institutions are known to serve both economic and social goals by helping to redistribute income among community members and provide a form of social security by meeting their fluctuating liquidity needs (Soyibo, 1997). Another fact is that they can be accessed at a time, be it at night or during the day (Schrader, 1994). In addition, small loan amounts or capital can be obtained from usury lenders and repayment can be adapted to the peculiarities of the borrowers especially the poor and women, who depend on the usury lenders as their source of finance (Swaminathan, 1991; Siyongwana, 2004). Bastelaer (2000) also observed that moneylenders, who were typically landowners or traders, were often the only source of credit available to the poor in most developing countries, especially in rural areas. The moneylenders' loans are extended quickly and for short periods. Okurut and Botlhole (2009) noted that some key features of the informal credit market include accessibility, simple procedures and the flexibility of credit, and its adaptability to many purposes. Women are sometimes subjected to socioeconomic deprivations, but the highlighted features of informal credit make credit accessible to these women. The study also noted that moneylenders in Botswana target mainly clients from the medium income to low-income category thereby suggesting that most of their clients belong to the economically active categories of the population of the study. The patronage of usury lenders is however not limited to the poor as their clientele cut across the low to middle and even the high-status borrowers (Sharma and Chalama, 1998). These features of indigenous usury or moneylenders tend to affect the perspective of their clients, especially in a positive way and this may explain the trend toward the positivity perspective of usury lending.

5 Method

5.1 *The Study Area*

Given the peculiarities of indigenous usury lending as an underground system of microfinance, this study adopted the qualitative research method. The study population is the indigenous usury lenders and clients who are traders in traditional markets located within the city of Ibadan. Qualitative data were collected for this study, using an In-depth Interview (IDI). The urban markets that were purposively selected were Bodija market, Bola Ige International market (New Gbagi market), and Agbeni market. The actual interviewees were selected using the snowballing sampling method. It is important to note that the rationale for the use of traditional African markets is because these selected markets had huge trading populations, relatively large capital base required by traders, the dominance of traders who are likely to access funds from informal microfinance sources such as indigenous usurers and the presence of lendees in the market. Usury lenders were also selected, using the snowball method. Snowballing was used because usury lenders do not have conspicuous locations such as offices or shops. This can be attributed to the fact that their operations are illegal because they prefer to operate outside the prescription of the laws covering their activities. Usury lenders cannot be easily recognised except when identified by their previous or present clients. Further, usury lenders prefer not to advertise their activities because of the fear of an armed robbery attack. The lenders have the assumption that people generally have the perception that they are always with cash either at hand or at home.

6 Data Collection and Analysis

In-depth interviews were conducted with lendees and lenders in the three selected major markets within the Ibadan metropolis. In each of the three markets, 10 trader-lendees were interviewed, making a total of 30 trader-lendees across the 3 selected markets. Likewise, a total of 10 lenders were also interviewed. Data were collected using a specially designed IDI guide. Also, the study made use of a voice recorder for ease of data collection and transcription. Data from the field were subjected to content and interpretive analysis. The analyses took the form of data codification, chronicles, repeated reviews, and verbatim transcriptions. The presentation of findings was done by using words in summary forms. This involved the use of keywords, phrases, and sentences that explained the interviewees' dispositions and actions within the context of the indigenous usury system.

7 Findings

7.1 *The Social Relations of the Indigenous Usury System*

From the Weberian perspective, Mucha (2003) noted that social relations take place when the social actions of several people are oriented toward each other in such a way that there is a chance that the social action of one actor will be met by the reaction of the other. Mucha further stated that the content of social relations is therefore guided by the mutuality of consent on values, norms, cultural or traditional prescriptions, associational or communal affiliations, length of interaction, economic exchange, and the repetitive nature of such relations. The actions of rational participants are thus dependent on the subjective content of social relations. The relationship of rational actors within the context of the indigenous usury system is based on individual self-interest objectives, which can be achieved either by cooperation or conflict.

The most popular description of social relations between usury lenders and their clients has been based on the notion that such relation is skewed in favour of the moneylenders who detects the terms and conditions of lending (Sarap, 1990). This subsequently feeds into the narrative that the lenders often exploit the perceived or real desperation of the borrowers by charging them extremely high-interest rates when compared with those charged by formal financial institutions (Shah et al, 2007). According to Falola (1993), the notion of exploitation is usually based included the high-interest rates charged by the lenders, the means of cheating the borrowers, and the methods of collecting debts from defaulting clients. However, the notion that social relations can also be positive in the sense that it is seen as mutually beneficial to the lending actors is prominent in this study. Commenting on the mutuality of benefits in indigenous usury system, one of the lenders interviewed stated:

> It is easy to access indigenous usury credit if the lender and the borrower see each other as partners in progress. With this sense of partnership, both parties would overtime establish a good relationship that is based on trust and mutual benefits.
>
> IDI/Lender/2nd February 2015

The mutuality of benefits relies on the fact that the borrower has rationally weighed all options and has calculated the benefits that approaching or taking the loan will bring to them. The popular view among the clients of the lenders is that an agreement is reached on the terms and conditions before the loans can be accessed. However, the accessibility and quick turnaround time make the moneylenders, an attractive form of lending for most borrowers. One of the moneylenders interviewed in this study confirmed the quick turn-around-time for accessing credit from as stated by this lender:

> It is easy to access loan from us if the collateral is satisfactory because this would assure us that the money will be repaid. In contemporary times, there is nothing secretive about our business. Once we have provided loan to someone, it will spread to others. So, the customers that we have helped before or our friends who know what we do will introduce us to them.
>
> IDI/ Lender/4th May 2015

The data above is an indication that quick access to credit is predicated on existing information or informal relations between the lenders and their borrowers or the source of referral. The purpose of the loan, terms of repayment, and collateral arrangement are issues that can be easily addressed and concluded between the lender and related parties or actors within a very short period. The quick process points to the wealth of information of the lenders have on their clients which enables them to ascertain the creditworthiness of clients.

The credit relationship persists because both lenders and lendees have something to gain from their interaction. The benefits can be social or economic in nature. Evidence of the mutuality of benefits can also be found in the ability of traders to use the funds for their businesses and thus, able to stock their shop. One of the traders interviewed stated that:

> The borrower would agree on the percentage of interest that will be paid to the lender and signs the dotted lines after which the lender will give the client the money. It affords the lendee the opportunity to meet most pressing needs at that time.
>
> IDI/Formal-Worker-Lendee/24th November 2014

This purposive use of the loan even at the shortest notice was further explained by this trader who stated that:

> The Moneylenders are very important because it helps my business. For instance, when there is an urgent need to stock my shop, and this purchase is unexpected, I quickly run to these lenders, and because they know that I have been faithful in the past by making repayment as and when due, they will lend me the money again.
>
> IDI/Trader-Lendee/3rd June 2015

Thus, in these transactional and sometimes, enduring social relations, the borrower counts the benefits from the standpoint of quick access and ability to use the fund to achieve the unstated goals which may sometimes be different from the stated objectives. This is because this study also found evidence that loans are diverted for other social but equally important uses. One of the lendees attested to the prevalence of this practice by stating thus:

> We have situations where lendees will get these loans from their lenders and divert them to activities such as burial or other social events. This can make it difficult for the lendees to repay the loan when it is due. So, the usury lender will always advise and warn the lendees to keep to their existing businesses and use the loan strictly for their present line of business.
>
> IDI/Trader-Lendee/21st February 2015

One of the Moneylenders in this study recounted his experience on the diversion of business-oriented-loans into non-business needs in the statement below:

> I recently had a case where a woman collected a loan from me for business purposes, but she eventually used the loan for her parent's burial

> with the hope that the people she would invite will give her money as a 'gift' during the burial ceremony. But the people she invited did not give her the money as expected because their shops had been destroyed by the government a few days before the burial. Now, she is having a problem repaying the loan because she has not used the money for the real purpose of the loan.
>
> IDI/Lender/5th January 2015

The traders argue that there are other competing social needs for which they may not have the financial capacity at the material time and knowing that Moneylenders mostly do not fund some of these social needs, they use their business to get the money and then use it for other purposes.

From the perspective of the Moneylender, they are in the business to make money and grow their sources of income. Scholars have noted that the traditional usurer does not collect the deposit and often depends on the profit from the lending businesses, other related businesses, and personal savings as sources of capital formation (Toby, 1991; Falola, 1993; Soyibo, 1997; Nissanke, 2001). Thus, loans must be given and repaid based on agreed terms including the interest element of the transaction. In alluding to the importance of profit, the lenders also added the notion that their financial services are a form of help. One lender opined that:

> I lend money to people for various purposes but most especially for trading or business purposes. My calculation is that by using the loan for their businesses, they would make profit and so, I also deserve to get a share of the profit.
>
> IDI/Lender/24th January 2015

The consensus among the lenders is that they are expected to make profit from lending because the traders who patronize them also use their money to make a profit. This explanation sounds rational considering the economic gains that guide transactions. However, a high-interest rate by lenders may also serve as a backup in case the loan can never be fully recovered. In other words, in charging high interest, the lender had implicitly made provision for loan losses as well as the inherent operational risk of the business. One lender stated that:

> Another major challenge of this our profession is the risk involved in the business. While I would give loan to people before noon, when some of them want to return the money, they would bring the money to my house at night. And if I do not collect the repayment, the person may not repay

> the loan again. And when I collect the money, I stand the risk of robbers attacking me because information may spread that I have money or cash in the house.
>
> IDI/Lender/8th April 2015

One of the usury lenders reaffirm this position of risk and repayment probabilities when he stated that:

> If a lendee collects a loan of ₦20,000.00, the repayment at the end of the month would be ₦25,000.00 and if the loan is ₦50,000.00, the lendee would have to repay ₦60,000.00 at the end of the month. But based on my evaluation, if I think that the business is very profitable, I will give a higher interest such that even if the person eventually defaults on the principal, I would have collected enough money to cover my principal in the first place.
>
> IDI/Lender/5th June 2015

This justification for high rate of interest reconfirms the position that high risk evaluation and profitability orientation drive indigenous usury system and this is still the case in contemporary usury credit (Adebayo, 1992; Fernando, 1998). The lendee knows that a reliable credit history will propel the lender to engage in repetitive and incremental lending (Nadan, 2005). A cooperative and mutually beneficial relation ensures repetitive access to credit such that future loans can also be obtained. The mutually beneficial relationship of this system does not preclude elements of exploitation which may persist even in contemporary times. This is reflected in the rate of interest and the mode of loan recovery. Concerning the high rate of interest which usury lendees must pay on their loans, one of our interviewees stated that:

> The challenge that I see in money lending is in the high interest that we must pay on loans collected from moneylenders. For instance, if I borrow ₦100,000 from the local moneylender, I will have to pay back ₦150,000 in three months. I would have to sell a lot of goods to cover the interest rate of this loan, but we have to repay the loan once we have taken it.
>
> IDI/Trader-Lendee/10th April 2015

The high cost of borrowing from the usury lender was also echoed by this worker in the organised formal sector who added that:

> If you borrow from the local moneylenders, they will not want you to pay back the principal. So, most times you end up paying just the interest

> element every month such that you may end up paying an interest amount that is far more than the principal sum itself.
>
> IDI/Trader-Lendee/1st February 2015

Social relations of usury lending have two forms. The first is based on reputational trust which creates a mutually beneficial credit relationship. The second form shows that a mutually beneficial relationship can also turn into a conflicted relationship and can therefore be viewed as exploitative depending on the contextual realities of the lendees. The lender in such conflict relation uses coercive methods to intimidate and eventually make repayment possible. However, what this study discovered is that the actors within the system would always want to maintain a conflict-free relationship. For lendees, this ensures relatively quick, easy, and future access to credit. For the lenders, it secures the patronage of existing and new credit relationships and for the alternative collateral, it strengthens the de-collateralization process and increases reputational trust and the referral system.

7.2 *The Contextual Interpretation of Usury System in Contemporary Informal Credit*

The mutual benefit perspective relies on an underlining idea that indigenous usury credit is a form of financial assistance during financial uncertainties and limited access to credible sources of credit. In other words, while it may be true that the parties in usury credit have some form of benefits no matter the disproportionality, such benefits find their sustenance in the idea that the system is a means of providing financial 'help'. There is a prevailing interpretation of indigenous usury lending as a form of merciful-help or benevolent-assistance (known in Yoruba as *aanu*) among lendees who patronise the system. This has been crucial to the existence of the system in contemporary Yoruba society.

Usury lenders also deliberately promote this concept of *aanu* in their communication with actors within the system. The concept of *aanu* within the context of the indigenous usury system explains the crucial role the system plays in providing financial help to lendees, who may have been deprived of credit by other sources of lending, most especially the formal financial institutions. The interpretation of usury lenders as benevolent helpers provided the basis for patronage as clients tend to rationalise indigenous usury lenders as benevolent creditors. This interpretation of usury lenders as merciful helper was echoed by one of the interviewees who stated that:

> The fact is that the bulk of the money that people use to trade in our society today is from moneylenders. Moneylenders will remain relevant

> because it is a form of help and that is why the rate of borrowing from moneylenders has continued to be on the increase in our contemporary society. We cannot run away from the fact that indigenous usury lenders have been very helpful to us, no matter what anybody wants to say.
>
> IDI/Trader-Lendee/14th April 2015

Another interviewee also reiterated the help perspective by stating thus:

> … indigenous usury system is a form of help that enables the trader to have advantage in terms of getting access to loan to buy goods, trade with it and make profit. We see the moneylenders as our source of mercy (*alaanu wa ni won*), hence we must keep to our terms of agreement by repaying the loan as and when due while the moneylender will always provide the fund whenever we need it.
>
> IDI/Trader-Lendee/17th October 2014

Reiterating this notion of help, another trader stated emphatically that:

> Indigenous usury lending remains very important because we see it as a form of help. When you need money in our present society, please tell me who will borrow you money. Even your family members will present their problems when you approach them for financial assistance. So, it is very difficult to get money anywhere, not even from the government. So it is on this basis that local money lenders are good sources of loans for our businesses, and they have been very helpful to us.
>
> IDI/Trader-Lendee/15th September 2015

Apart from the traders, the moneylenders at every opportunity often make it a duty to reaffirm that they are in the business primarily to help others who are in financial problems. The statement below points to this claim as one of the lenders interviewed noted that:

> People that we help would usually call on us to help other people too. When there is a problem that requires financial help, people that we have helped in similar situations will now tell those in such problems: why go to the bank when they know that they cannot solve your problem. They know that the moneylenders can quickly solve their financial problems.
>
> IDI/Lender/ October 4th, 2014

Another lender also alluded to the idea of 'help' when he stated that:

> Once we have provided a loan to someone, it will spread to others. So, the customers that we have helped before or our friends who know what we do will introduce us to them. How quickly you get the money will depend on how much you want to borrow, the collateral arrangement, the purpose of the loan, and your guarantor.
>
> IDI/ Lender/4th May 2015

Some lenders and clients alike even justify the idea that the system is a form of help that had been divinely instituted. The following comment from one of the lenders, who is also a usury lender, typified the existence of this belief that usury lenders are forms of 'help' sent by God:

> The Indigenous usury system is a form of lending money to people who need money urgently for business purposes. It is a system where some of us who God has blessed with certain savings try to help people who need to raise money for their businesses and other needs. We make sure that we use the money that God has given us to help others so that these lendees would use the loan to run their businesses and pay back the principal and interest as they get the money and as agreed.
>
> IDI/Lender/December 12th, 2014

Another trader reechoed the divine mandate to lend, and she noted that:

> Moneylenders are very important because they are God-sent such that when you have a problem, they would help you out by providing money so that you can solve your problems. The reason I believe they would continue to exist is because the system has been a form of help for a long time and that is why they still exist to date.
>
> IDI/Trader-Lendee/14th May 2015

The historical conditions that facilitated the existence of the indigenous usury system are still present in contemporary times. These conditions include the demand of the family, pressure to fulfill social obligations, and economic activities that require financing among others (Falola, 1993). The difficulties in accessing formal credit also created for the informal credit structure market to fill the vacuum created by the modern financial system inadequacies.

The lendees invariable see the informal lenders as valuable parts, which consequently create opportunities for exploitation as well as building on the notion of financial intervention in distress, also known as help. This is possible because the lender can ascertain the creditworthiness of their clients much quicker than formal financial institutions (Mohieldin and Wright, 2000). Thus, the success of the lendee's business is attributed to the financial intervention of informal lenders like the Moneylenders.

The success of the business that is attributed to the funds obtained from usury lenders creates social prestige, particularly among borrowers or clients. Clients are thus able to relate with their peers and family members based on being economically engaged, and respected. This restoration and affirmation of social prestige can also be tied to the prevention of social shame which some of the interviewees have alluded to as the covert benefit of patronising indigenous usury lenders. The following statement from a lender supports this position:

> Now there was a woman who happens to be the last born of her mother and the mother died. She needed to do the burial of this her late mother before the end of the month and she approached us for assistance. The problem was that the date of the burial was within the month, and she will only collect her salary by the end of the month. So, we assisted her by giving her a loan so that she could perform the burial rites of her late mother and we collected our money plus interest when her salary was paid at the end of the month.
>
> IDI/Lender/January 19th, 2015

A usury lendee also affirmed this position thus:

> … the system allows those with limited cash to have access to fund so that their businesses and lives can improve such that they would be accepted among their peers in the community (*la ti ba egbe pe*). So, I see usury lending basically as form of help from people who really love and care for us.
>
> IDI/Trader-Lendee/10th March 2014

This study confirms the position of Guerin (2014), that debt from moneylenders can among other things prevent social shame. In other words, social acceptability is derived either from the lendee's ability to meet socially expected expenses or the success of businesses financed with loans from moneylenders. The expression that usury lenders 'love and care' for their clients by providing funds that assist these clients' businesses to grow or prevent them from dying has implications for the future action or perception towards this institution.

8 Conclusion

Access to credit especially in developing countries poses a serious challenge to the developmental drive of this class of countries. For traditional or informal sources of credit, the evidence has shown that their resilience is based on the concrete process of financial problem-solving. This study shows that traditional usury lenders and their clients engage in a continuum of social relations of mutual benefits with tendencies for exploitation, depending on the situation and interpretation. A more significant part of this study is the interpretative understanding that has sustained this form of lending, which has been popularly vilified as extremely exploitative and brutal. Clients and lenders alike share the common understanding that at some point, the existence of this system of lending can be credited to its interpretation as a form of financial help rather than exploitation.

References

Adams, J., Brunner, H., and Raymond, F. (2003). Interactions of informal and formal agents in South Asian rural credit markets. *Review of Development Economics* 7(3), 431–444.

Adebayo, A. (1992). Pre-colonial institutional frameworks for moneylending and loan repayment among the Yoruba. *Paideume Bd 38, 163–176.*

Adebayo, A. (1994). Money, credit and banking in pre-colonial Africa: The Yoruba experience. *Anthropos 89, 379–400.*

Adeyinka, A., Omisore, O., Olawuni, O. and Abegunde, A. (2006). An evaluation of informal sector activities and urban land use management in south western Nigeria. In *Shaping the Change XXIII FIG Congress Munich, Germany, Oct*: 8–13.

Akintimehin, O., Eniola, A., Alabi, J., Eluyela, F., Okere, W. and Ozordi, E. (2019). Social capital and its effect on business performance in the Nigeria informal sector. *Heliyon*, 5(7), 1–13.

Atieno, R. (2001). Formal and informal institutions' lending policies and access to credit by small–scale enterprises In Kenya: An Empirical Assessment. *AERC Research Paper 111, African Economic Research Consortium, Nairobi.*

Atoloye, A. S. (2007). The informal sector and employment generation in Nigeria. *CBN Economic and Financial Review*, 45(2), 1–43.

Bastelaer, T. (2000). Does social capital facilitate the poor's access to credit? a review of the microeconomic literature. *The World Bank Social Development Family Environmentally and Socially Sustainable Development Network* 1–36.

Boucher S. and Guikinger, C. (2007). Risk rationing and wealth effects in credit markets: theory and implications for agricultural development. *American Journal of Agricultural Economics* 90(2), 409–423.

Chavan, P. (2003) Moneylender's positive image: regression in development thought and policy. *Economic and Political Weekly* 38(50), 5301–5304.

Chipeta, C. and Mkandawire, M. (1992). The informal financial sector in Malawi. *African Review of Money Finance and Banking* 2, 121–157.

Eboh, E; Ugama, O and Okereke, O (1991). Nigeria village money lenders and their usurious interest rate: an analysis of intervening factors. *Savings and Development* 15(4), 361–372.

Eja, E and Bassey, E. (2011). Moneylending law and regulation of consumer credit In Nigeria. *Journal of International Law and Jurisprudence* 2(1), 196–211.

Falola, T. (1993). ''My friend the shylock'': money-lenders and their clients in southwestern Nigeria. *The Journal of African History* 34(3), 403–423.

Found, M. (2012) Women and the informal sector in Nigeria: Implications for development. *British Journal of Arts and Social Sciences*, 4(1):35–45.

Fernando N. (1988). The interest rate structure and factors affecting interest rate determination in the informal rural credit market in Sri Lanka. *Savings and Development* 13(3), 249–269.

Floro, M. and Ray, D. (1997). Vertical links between formal and informal financial institutions. *Review of Development Economics*, 1(1), 34–56.

Giné, X. (2011). Access to capital in rural Thailand: an estimated model of formal vs. informal Credit. *Journal of Development Economics* 96, 16–29.

Guerin, I. (2014). Juggling with debt, social ties, and values: the everyday use of microcredit in rural South India. *Current Anthropology* 55(S9), S40-S50.

Ibe, A. (1990). The structure of the informal credit market in Nigeria: lessons from Awka town of Anambra State. *African Review of Money Finance and Banking* 1, 5–14.

James, D. (2014). "Deeper into a hole?" borrowing and lending in South Africa. *Current Anthropology* 55(S9), S17–S29.

Jones, H. (2008). Informal finance and rural finance policy in India: historical and contemporary perspectives. *Contemporary South Asia* 16(3), 269–285.

Labat, A and Block, W. (2012). Money does not grow on trees: an argument for usury. *Journal of Business Ethics* 106(3), 383–387.

Manig, W. (1996). The importance of the informal financial market for rural development financing in developing countries: The Example of Pakistan. *The Pakistan Development Review* 35(3), 229–239.

Meeks, M. (2011). The peril of usury in the christian tradition. *Interpretation 65*(2), 128–140.

Mews, C. and Abraham, I. (2006). Usury and just compensation: religious and financial ethics in historical perspective. *Journal of Business Ethics, 72*(1), 1–15.

Mills, S. (2007). The Kuyasa fund: housing microcredit in South Africa. *Environment and Urbanization* 19, 457–469.

Mohieldin, M. And Wright, P. (2000). Formal and informal credit market in Egypt. *Economic Development and Cultural Change, 48*(3), 657–670.

Mucha, J (2003). The concept of social relations in classic analytical interpretative Sociology: Weber and Znaniecki. Paper Presented at the 6th ESA Conference, Murcia 2003.

Nadan, A. (2005). The competitive advantage of moneylenders over banks in rural Palestine. *Journal of the Economic and Social History of the Orient, 48*(1), 1–39.

Nissanke, M. (2001). Financing enterprise development in Sub-saharan Africa. *Cambridge Journal of Economics. Special Issue on African Economic Development In A Comparative Perspective.* 25(3), 343–367.

Nnabuife, K., Okoli, N., and Anugwu, C. (2020). Informal sector and Nigerian economic prospects: The Covid–19 experience. *European Journal of Business and Management Research*, 5(4), 1–5.

Nwaka, I. (2005). The urban informal sector in Nigeria: towards economic development, environmental health, and social harmony. *Global Urban Development Magazine*, 1(1), 1–11.

Obeta, M. (1992). Agricultural credit in Nigeria: performance at farm level. *African Review of Money Finance and Banking* 2, 173–184.

Okurut, N. and Botlhole, A (2009). Informal financial market in Botswana: a case study of Gaborone city. *Development Southern African* 26(2), 255–270.

Oladeji, S and Ogunrinola, I. (2001). Determinants of informal savings in south-western Nigeria. *Savings and Development* 25(2), 225–251.

Olubiyo, S. (2009). The changing phase of farm credit delivery in Nigeria: a review of nature, characteristics and accessibility. *Savings and Development* 33(2), 133–151.

Omobowale, A. (2011). Social capital and ajo system among working class traders in Ibadan Nigeria. *The Journal of Labour and Society,* 14, 333–346.

Onwe, J. (2013). Role of the informal sector in development of the Nigerian economy: Output and employment approach. *Journal of Economics and Development studies,* 1(1), 60–74.

Onyebueke, V. and Geyer, M. (2011). The informal sector in urban Nigeria: Reflections from almost four decades of research. *Town and Regional Planning*, 59, 65–76.

Patole, M. and Ruthven, O. (2001). Metro moneylender: microcredit providers for Delhi's poor. *An Output of a project funded by Finance and Development Research*

Programme funded by DFID and directed by institute of Development Policy and Management (IDPM).

Rahman, A. (1992). The informal financial sector in Bangladesh: an appraisal of its role in development. *Development and Change 23, 147–168.*

Reddy, S. (2007). Diary of a moneylender. *Economic and Political Weekly 42(29), 3037–3043.*

Saikia, A. (2012) The moneylenders and indebtedness: understanding the peasant economy of colonial Assam, 1900–1950. *Indian Historical Review 37(1), 63–88.*

Sarap, K. (1990). Interest rates in backward agriculture: the role of economic and extra-economic control. *Cambridge Journal of Economics 14(1), 93–108.*

Sarker, D. (2006). Development theory and gendered approach to development: a review in the third world perspective. *Sociological Bulletin 55(1), 45–66.*

Schrader, H. (1992). The socioeconomic function of moneylenders in expanding economies: the case of the Chettiars. *Savings and Development 16 (1), 69–82.*

Shah, M., Rao, R and Vijay-Shankar, P. (2007). Rural credit in 20th century India: overview of history and perspectives. *Economic and Political Weekly 42(15), 1351–1364.*

Sharma, S and Chamala, S. (1998). Moneylender and banker in rural India - the images from below. *Savings and Development 22(1), 107–130.*

Sharma, S and Chamala, S. (2003). Moneylender's positive image: paradigms and rural development. *Economic and Political Weekly 38(17), 1713–1720.*

Siyongwana, P. (2004). Informal moneylenders in the Limpopo, Gauteng and Eastern Cape provinces of South Africa. *Development Southern African 21(5), 581–866.*

Soyibo, A. (1996). Financial linkage and development in Sub-Saharan Africa: the informal financial sector in Nigeria. *Working Paper 90, Overseas Development Institute, Regent's College.*

Soyibo, A. (1997). The informal financial sector in Nigeria: characteristics and relationship with the formal sector. *Development Policy Review 15, 5–22.*

Sparks, L. and Barnett, T. (2010). The informal sector in Sub-Saharan Africa: out of the shadows to foster sustainable employment and equity? *International Business & Economics Research Journal (IBER)*, 9(5):1–12.

Swaminathan, M. (1991). Segmentation, collateral undervaluation, and the rate of interest in agrarian credit markets: some evidence from two villages in south India. *Cambridge Journal of Economics 15(2), 161–178.*

Toby, R. (1991). Both a borrower and a lender be. from village moneylender to rural banker in the tempo era. *Monumenta Nipponica, 46(4), 483–512.*

Valeri, M. (2011). The Christianisation of usury in early modern Europe. *Interpretation 65(2), 142–152.*

CHAPTER 9

Graduates in the Informal Sector of Southwestern Nigeria

Adepeju Olubukola Odunlami, Ephraim Ifediri Nwokporo and Olayinka Akanle

1 Introduction

Unemployment has remained a significant problem in Nigeria. Over the years, it has spurred many innovative and creative coping mechanisms and survival strategies among the many unemployed graduates. Against this background, this chapter contributes to knowledge on the interfaces of graduate unemployment in the informal economy/sector. This is to enable a better and more sustainable understanding of resilience and formidability of the informal sector not only in Nigeria and Africa but globally. This chapter contributes to knowledge on the global problem of youth unemployment through the empirical case study of Nigeria. The incidence of youth unemployment in the 21st century is gradually becoming ubiquitous irrespective of levels of socioeconomic development and advancement in technology. About 60 million young people worldwide are looking for a job but are still looking for one (International Labour Organisation, 2019). Young people are three times more likely to be unemployed than adults. Around 226 million young people between the ages of 15 and 24 make up 19 per cent of the estimated youth population in Africa. This number is expected to increase by 42 per cent by 2030 (United Nations, 2018).

However, unemployment across Africa is a profound problem. Labour poverty, including under-employment or low-wage employment, is equally profound, and young people are often exposed to unemployment, under-employment, or low-wage employment. The rate of under-employment or low-wage employment among youth in sub-Saharan Africa is almost 70% (International Labour Organisation 2020), inferring that youth suffer from unemployment, underpayment, and poor quality of work (International Labour Organisation, 2019). Relatively high youth unemployment in Africa directly impacts poverty among the youth population that needs to work to sustain a living and may, in some cases, need to support others. The teeming young Nigerian population strongly desires to be educated to high levels. They

 | DOI:10.1163/9789004692657_011

are attending tertiary institutions, consisting of Universities, Mono-technics, Polytechnics, and Colleges of Education, and deservedly, expecting to occupy high occupational and professional job positions upon graduation only to find themselves in the scourge of unemployment and under-employment.

In Nigeria, unemployment has been a problematic issue for many years. Youth and graduate unemployment are particularly endemic. According to data from the Nigerian Bureau of Statistics (NBS), the age group with the most significant rate of unemployment is the youth (15–34 years), with the second quarter unemployment data of 2020 indicating an unemployment rate of 34.9%, an increase from 29.7% from the previous survey. Hence, about 2.9 million of Nigeria's unemployed hold graduate and postgraduate degrees from tertiary institutions (National Bureau of Statistics, 2021). The current unemployment rates generally, and among the youth and graduates, are identical to the (graduate) unemployment situations of the mid-1980s during the Structural Adjustment Programme (SAP) era when there was an embargo on employment and the collapse of industries. Even though there is no official embargo on employment currently in Nigeria, counterproductive policies and misrule in the country have resulted in massive unemployment, particularly among the youth.

Unfortunately, regardless of such unemployment and underemployment levels confronting graduates of tertiary institutions, these numerous institutions continue to admit and produce thousands of well-educated and supposedly deserving youths annually who have continued to cramp the labour market (Educational and Employability Survey Report, 2014). As a result, the pace of growing unemployed graduates in the country has increased steadily. It has, over time, become a common phenomenon that graduates seek alternatives to structured jobs and recondition themselves to create businesses, learn a new skill, or enter professional business practices that allow them to thrive and survive in society. Graduates train in new ventures, introduce and evaluate new businesses by incorporating knowledge from functional and external experiences in terms of their expanded worldview from the structured formal education they have gotten before and launch out to create options for their employment. Such a venture could be unusually uncertain and ambiguous.

This is a reality of new business ventures. By and large, some of these young graduates get involved in a broad range of self-employed activities in areas such as parts manufacturing, textiles, and services companies, as well as in masonry, shoe production, and machine tool production and the likes, requiring different levels of preparation in skills development. Gruber-Muecke and Hofer (2015) opined that these moves enable graduates to set up various artisanal businesses and create employment opportunities. Accordingly, becoming artisans and independent workers are wellsprings of new openings and monetary dynamism for graduates and can improve youth occupations and financial autonomy. As such, to run a personal business effectively and contribute to the growth of society, graduate artisans work for themselves. They are responsible for generating their profits, providing their workplace and all their facilities, materials, and equipment, subcontracting, and having to use, primarily, skills that may have been hurriedly acquired outside of what was in their undergraduate school curricula. In the process, they must also become contractors and developers, attending to every required infrastructure or service when starting a business or creating a product or service (Nwosu & Ojo, 2015).

The antecedents of unemployment and under-employment have created a void among Nigerian graduates. Most of them have been filled with their involvement in artisanal works, which in some cases are unrelated to their courses of study in tertiary institutions. To ensure that the young generation is not lost to these societal challenges but can learn, improve, and practice skills, maintain their engagement (commercially) and make a decent living, society needs to take a particular interest in this growing phenomenon of graduate artisanship that is fast becoming a viable escape route from unemployment, underemployment, and poverty. Also, societal severe interest is required to ensure the proper guidance and support to the younger generation as they make such choices. In this light, this study investigated the forms of artisanal enterprise that tertiary institution graduates are involved in, explored the push, and pull factors for their involvement in artisanal work, and unveiled the lived experiences of graduate artisans in their artisanal and entrepreneurial ventures.

2 Literature Review

The dearth of available white-collar jobs in Nigeria has given rise to 95% of college graduates being unemployed within 12 to 24 months of graduation (Odunlami & Akanle, 2021; Oladokun & Ayodele, 2015). This has resulted in many national, social, and economic challenges, including but not limited to the increased rate of criminal activities, drug trafficking and abuse, and worse of all, suicide (Akhuemonkhan et al., 2014). Ineffective economic policies, corruption, policy inconsistencies, and low human capital development in Nigeria have kept the economy in unstable conditions, with unemployment rising every quarter while under-employment abounds due to continued inflation. The Nigeria Bureau of Statistics (2021) puts the unemployment rate at 23.1% and under-employment rate at 16.6%.

Entrepreneurship and involvement in artisanal works have become the golden path guiding and stemming the tide in the right direction to self-employment and possible wealth creation. Studies show that Nigeria has a young, vibrant population and a competitive, innovative, and result-oriented private sector. Critical situations, such as economic and political power-sharing, legal systems, history, party prestige, colonial legacy, and unique institutional context, all affect business development in Nigeria (Adegbite et al., 2007; Mambulu, 2002; Oyelaran-Oyeyinka, 2002). According to Ray (2007), inept and bureaucratic institutions stifle entrepreneurship in Africa, and Nigeria continues to score poorly on the ease of doing business owing to weak infrastructures, such as electricity, and transportation, a challenging business climate, and limited access to capital (Schoof, 2006).

Understanding why Nigerian youths are starting artisanal careers, trading, or developing their entrepreneurial skills is crucial. However, there is a lack of empirical and systemic literature that provides this knowledge (Chigunta, 2002; Green & Amat, 2012). Understanding the 'why' will lead to creative ways to promote creativity among young people. Chigunta (2002) found that the degree of youth entrepreneurship and self-employment in sub-Saharan Africa is higher than in other developing countries but lower in adults. According to the Africa Commission (2009), men are more likely than women to participate in entrepreneurial activities. However, the NBS/SMEDAN (2010) report found that more Nigerian women work in the informal and micro industries than men. The Africa Commission (2009) also furthered that older youth handle more business endeavours than younger ones. While these studies need further research to determine their applicability to Nigeria, the NBS/SMEDAN (2010) Nigerian survey shows that youths dominate the small business market. However, we must remember that Nigerian youth, like most African categorisations, are those aged 15 to 35.

According to Chigunta (2002), 92.3% of youth enterprises started to solve socio-economic challenges. Other reasons young people venture into entrepreneurship include unemployment, a desire to supplement household income, hunger, and the desire to make wealth. In Malawi, young entrepreneurs cite insecurity and poverty as reasons for starting a company (Chigunta, 2002). According to Gallup, most Nigerian youth would want to start their own business. (Beeka, 2015). As a result, Chigunta argues that while it is tempting to ignore African entrepreneurs, entrepreneurship ambitions result from a lack of alternatives. The truth is that many factors play a role, including shifts in the political, economic, and social climate and lower wages in the traditional economy.

3 Theoretical Framework

This study has the theory of planned behaviour, entrepreneurial event theory, and the push/pull dichotomy as theoretical leaning. The Theory of Planned Behaviour (TPB) is based on Ajzen and Fishbein's theory of Reasoned Action, published in 1980 (Ajzen, 2012). It is widely accepted as the most prominent and common method for human behaviour prediction. According to the TPB, attitudes toward behaviour, subjective norms, and presumed behavioural discipline influence entrepreneurial intentions (Ajzen, 2005; Ajzen & Cote, 2008). An individual's decision to start a company is based on a positive or negative assessment of doing so, perceived personal capacity, and perceived social pressure to conduct or not perform the behaviour. However, the relative value of these antecedents of entrepreneurial purpose varies depending on the intention under investigation, as well as from individual to person and community to population (Ajzen, 2005).

The Entrepreneurial Event Model (EEM) is concerned with the decision to undertake entrepreneurial action, which necessitates a pre-existing mindset that regards the activity as attractive and practicable and the willingness to act on an incentive (Shapero & Sokol, 1982). The degree to which people believe they can successfully launch a company is described as perceived viability. It alludes to the allure of ideas when starting a company (Shapero & Sokol, 1982). According to Krueger (1993), perceived viability is the most significant predictor of an entrepreneurial purpose. Perceived viability and entrepreneurial motive have a meaningful and constructive relationship (Fitzsimmons & Douglas, 2005). Similarly, Segal, Borgia, and Schoenfeld (2002) found a strong correlation between perceived viability and entrepreneurial ambitions among business students. In various ways, literature revealed that perceived viability is positively and substantially linked to entrepreneurial purpose.

The Push-Pull model has been used in the study of entrepreneurship. The Push-Pull Entrepreneurship hypothesis resembles the Push-Pull Mooring Paradigm of Human Migration in several ways. According to Giacomin, Janssen, Pruett, Shinnar, Llopis, and Toney (2007), the formation of new companies corresponds to the movement of people from salaried jobs or unemployment to self-employment. As a result, entrepreneurship can be described as a person's desire to switch from unemployment or salaried jobs to self-employment. According to the migration perspective of push-pull, negative factors such as discontent with one's existing employment, life, or status, inability to find work, harsh economic situations, social recognition, or an inflexible work schedule influence one's desire to pursue an entrepreneurial career path, leading to self-employment (Segal et al., 2005). These critical causes are thought to be the driving forces behind an individual's present state, like his or her origin.

The push effect happens if there are contradictions between an individual's current situation and their aspiration, causing them to become self-employed (Uhlaner & Thurik, 2007). Push effects have been linked to certain levels of discontent with one's current life status and have been shown to inspire entrepreneurship (Giacomin et al., 2011). Any constructs of the push factors from migration literature have methodological parallels with push theory. On the other hand, the 'Pull' principle applies to attractions at the destination that entice people to pursue self-employment or entrepreneurship. This could be the search for freedom of time, innovation, riches, and fulfilment. Pull factors draw people mainly because they want to start a company (Ritsilä & Tervo, 2002). The pull factors are described in migration literature as attractions at the destination that draw migrants (Moon, 1995). Entrepreneurship is the 'destination.' The entrepreneurial drive is influenced by pull factors (Giacomin et al., 2011). Independence, profit search, and market opportunity are examples of pull variables in the entrepreneurship literature. Regardless of the forces that drive or charm people into entrepreneurship, those factors make it attractive (e.g., cultural and social norms) and practical (e.g., skill availability) (Hisrich et al., 2005).

4 Methodology

The study that informed this article adopted the cross-sectional and analytical survey research design while combining quantitative and qualitative data collection methods. Data for the study was derived from questionnaires and in-depth interviews. The research was conducted in four selected South-Western states of Nigeria. They included Lagos, Ogun, Oyo, and Ondo. The choice of South-West Nigeria for this study was based on the nature of the zone in terms of overall economic, educational, financial, and trade advancement. The study population comprised university and polytechnic graduate artisans in the selected states. While universities award degrees, polytechnics award Ordinary National Diplomas and Higher National Diplomas (OND/HND). HND is equivalent to the second year of a bachelor's degree internationally. HND can also be seen as equivalent to a foundation degree. OND is lower than HND, and it is usually equivalent to A-Levels. A multi-stage sampling technique was utilised in this study. In the first stage, four states within Southwestern Nigeria were selected by balloting. A purposive selection of the capitals of each chosen state followed this. Nonetheless, the study did not discriminate against any craft or business or on the line of gender, as long as a subject fit into the inclusion sampling criteria of this study.

Respondents in this study were also stratified based on the type of tertiary institution they attended. This was to ensure a representative of graduates across all tertiary institutions. Finally, snowball sampling was used to select artisans who had graduated from tertiary institutions. The questionnaire was administered to four hundred and fifty (450) respondents, distributed thus: 150 in Lagos State, 100 in Ogun State, 100 in Ondo State, and 100 in Oyo State. Two (2) in-depth interviews were held in each state, making up eight (8). A pilot study was carried out in Ibadan, Oyo State, to check for the reliability of the research instruments. This formed the basis for improvements in the instruments. Three field experts in the areas of entrepreneurship and artisanry also assisted with a review of research instruments. Their comments further guided the final revision of the instruments. The researchers employed trained research assistants and divided them into groups of 3 comprising 1 Supervisor and 2 Research Assistants for each of the selected states. The collected quantitative data were analysed using the Statistical Package for Social Sciences (SPSS), while content analysis was used to analyse the qualitative data. Global best practices in research ethics were carefully implemented at every stage of this research.

5 Findings and Results

Administered questionnaires for this study received an 89% response rate representing 400 well-filled questionnaires by the respondents. The socio-demographic characteristics of the respondents show that generally, the proportion of respondents in each age group increase as age increases, peaking at 35.8% (28–32 age group) in Lagos, 38.6% (23–27 age group) in Osun, 44.9% (23–27 age group) in Oyo, and 41.2% (23–27 age group) in Ogun, and declining thereafter. This reflects the comparatively young age structure of the population. More than half of the respondents were males in Lagos (57.5%), Osun (62%), and Oyo (50.6%), while females were the majority population in Ogun (53.8%). Most of the respondents in Lagos (47.8%), Osun (51.2%), Oyo (70.6%), and Ogun (56.7%) were single, while most of the rest in Lagos (38.1%), Osun (26.2%), Oyo (23.5%) and Ogun (40.2%) were married. Consequently, more than half of the respondents in Osun (52.4%), Oyo (77.4%) and Ogun (67%) have no children, while 47.8% in Lagos also had no children; one out of three respondents in Lagos (34.3%) and Osun (32.1%) had 1–2 children.

There was diversity in terms of the academic qualifications of respondents across the states. About half of the respondents in Lagos (44%) and Ogun (42.3%) had attained their Bachelor of Arts or Bachelor of Science degrees, with 1 out of 3 respondents in Osun (34.5%) and Oyo (35.8%) attaining the same degree. Most of the respondents in Lagos (53%), Osun (57.1%), Oyo (71.6%), and Ogun (66%) graduated from a tertiary institution 1–5 years ago, while about one-third of the respondents in Lagos (29.5%) Osun (31%), Oyo (19.8%) and Ogun (28.7%) had graduated 6–10 years ago. Most of the respondents in Lagos (73.3%), Osun (76.2%), Oyo (76.2%) and Ogun (58.8%) practice Christianity, 22.1% (Lagos), 15.5% (Osun), 23.8% (Oyo) and 38.1% (Ogun) practise Islam. Many of the respondents in Oyo (70.7%) and Ogun (57.7%) were from the South-Western zone of Nigeria, while 36.9% in Osun were from the South-East zone and 32.1% in Lagos were from the South-West zone of Nigeria.

The qualitative data was derived from interviewing eight graduate artisans across the selected Oyo, Ogun, Ondo, and Lagos states. The average age of respondents was 28 years, with the youngest being a 23-year-old Fashion Designer. Only one of the respondents was married and one practised the Islamic religion, while the others were single and practised Christianity.

5.1 *Forms of Artisanal Work That Graduates Are Involved In*

Table 9.1 presents the forms of artisanal work that graduate artisans are involved in. It is structured based on gender and state. It reveals that graduate artisans are involved in a variety of artisanal work. One out of five (20%) females in Osun are hairdressers. One out of 3 (31%) females in Oyo and 21.2% of the females in Ogun are tailors/fashion designers. One out of five (20.9%) males in Oyo are photographers/videographers.

In the period when the graduate artisans started learning their artisanal skills, results show that 3 out of 4 (77.4%) respondents in Osun started learning during their tertiary education, 42.2% in Oyo started learning before their tertiary education, 37.5% in Ogun started learning after their tertiary education, and 37.4% started learning during the period of their tertiary education. The respondents' opinion on graduate artisanship reveals that almost all the respondents in Lagos (88.7%), Osun (92.9%), Oyo (94%), and Ogun (91.8%) agree that graduate artisans are becoming a more frequent phenomenon. Also, most of the respondents in Lagos (71.6%), Osun (88.1%), Oyo (84.1%), and Ogun (58.8%) agree that graduates take up these artisans' careers as full time than as supplementary careers. Four out of five interviewees in Ogun (75%) agree that there are more male artisans than female artisans, 38.1% in Lagos and 42.1% in Ogun also agree, 31.8% in Oyo and 33% in Ogun disagree, while about one-third-of the respondents in Lagos (35.8%) and Oyo (38.8%) are

TABLE 9.1 Forms of artisanal work by gender and state

Variable	Lagos		Osun		Oyo		Ogun		Total	
	Female N (57)	Male N (77)	Female N (30)	Male N (49)	Female N (42)	Male N (43)	Female N (52)	Male N (45)	Female N (181)	Male N (214)
Aluminum Fabrication	–	–	–	–	-	–	–	2.2%	–	0.5%
Appliances Repairer	–	1.3%	–	2%	–	–	–	2.2%	–	1.4%
Art & Signs	1.8%	–	–	–	2.4%	2.3%	–	–	1.1%	0.5%
Auto-mechanic	–	1.3%	–	–	2.4%	–	–	2.2%	0.6%	0.9%
Baker	–	1.3%	6.7%	2	7.1%	2.3%	11.5%	4.4%	6.1%	2.3%
Barber	–	7.8%	–	6.1%	–	11.6%	–	4.4%	–	7.5%
Basket Weaver	1.8%	–	–	–	–	–	–	–	0.6%	–
Bead/Bag Maker	7%	1.3%	–	–	2.4%	11.6%	5.7%	–	4.5%	–
Block Maker	–	3.9%	–	–	–	–	–	–	–	0.5%
Bricklayer	–	–	–	2%	–	–	–	–	–	0.5%
Carpentry	–	3.9%	3.3%	10.2%	–	11.6%	–	2.2%	0.6%	6.5%
Catering & Confectioneries	7%	9.1%	13.3%	6.1%	11.9%	–	5.8%	–	8.8%	4.7%
Chef	3.5%	–	–	–	–	2.3%	–	–	1.1%	0.5%
Cloth Weaver	–	–	–	–	–	–	1.9%	–	0.6%	–

(*Continued*)

TABLE 9.1 Forms of artisanal work by gender and state (*cont.*)

Variable	Lagos		Osun		Oyo		Ogun		Total	
	Female N (57)	Male N (77)	Female N (30)	Male N (49)	Female N (42)	Male N (43)	Female N (52)	Male N (45)	Female N (181)	Male N (214)
Computer/Phone Repair	–	1.3%	–	–	–	–	–	–	–	0.5%
Decorator	1.8%	1.3%	6.7%	–	–	–	7.7%	–	3.9%	0.5%
Electrician	1.8%	5.2%	3.3%	2%	2.4%	4.7%	–	4.4%	1.7%	4.2%
Event Planner	8.8%	2.6%	–	2%	–	7%	3.8%	–	3.9%	1.4%
Fine Artist	1.8%	–	–	2%	–	–	–	2.2%	–	0.9%
Florist	–	–	–	–	–	–	–	2.2%	–	0.5%
Goldsmith/Jewellery	–	–	3.3%	–	–	–	–	–	0.6%	–
Graphic Designer	1.8%	–	3.3%	–	–	7%	1.9%	–	1.7%	1.4%
Hairdresser	12.3%	5.2%	20%	2%	14.3%	–	7.7%	2.2%	12.7%	2.8%
Hairdresser & Wig Maker	1.8%	–	–	–	–	–	1.9%	–	1.1%	–
ICT Appliances Installer/ Repairer	–	2.6%	–	–	–	4.7%	–	–	–	1.9%
Interior Designer	1.8%	2.6%	–	2%	–	–	–	2.2%	0.6%	2.3%
Jewellery Maker	–	–	–	–	–	–	1.9%	–	0.6%	–

Makeup Artist	10.5%	2.6%	10%	2%	7.1%	2.3%	15.4%	4.4%	0.6%	–
Manicurist/Pedicurist	5.3%	–	–	–	–	–	3.8%	2.2%	2.8%	0.5%
Metal Works	–	–	–	4.1%	–	–	–	–	–	0.9%
Milliner	–	–	–	–	2.4%	–	–	–	0.6%	–
Painter	3.5%	2.6%	–	8.2%	–	9.3%	–	15.6%	1.1%	7.9%
Phone Repairer	–	2.6%	–	–	–	2.3%	–	–	–	1.4%
Photographer/ Videographer	3.5%	13%	3.3%	12.2%	2.4%	20.9%	1.9%	8.9%	2.8%	13.6%
Plumber	–	1.3%	3.3%	10.2%	–	2.3%	–	8.9%	0.6%	5.1%
PoP Maker	–	1.3%	–	–	–	–	–	–	–	0.5%
Potter	–	1.3%	–	–	–	–	3.8%	–	1.1%	0.5%
Printer	–	2.6%	–	2%	–	–	–	2.2%	–	1.9%
Rewire	1.8%	–	–	–	–	–	–	–	0.6%	–
Sculptor	1.8%	–	–	–	–	–	–	–	0.6%	–
Shoemaker	–	2.6%	–	2%	4.8%	2.3%	–	6.7%	1.1%	3.3%
Soap/Cream/Cosmetic Maker	5.3%	1.3%	–	–	2.4%	–	3.8%	–	3.3%	0.5%
Tailor/Fashion Designer	14%	13%	10%	6.1%	31%	9.3%	21.2%	8.9%	19.3%	9.8%
Textile Designer	1.8%	1.3%	–	–	–	–	–	–	0.6%	0.5%
Tie & Dye Maker	1.8%	3.9%	–	–	–	–	–	4.4%	0.6%	2.3%
Tiler	–	–	–	–	–	4.7%	–	2.2%	–	1.4%

(*Continued*)

TABLE 9.1 Forms of artisanal work by gender and state (*cont.*)

Variable	Lagos		Osun		Oyo		Ogun		Total	
	Female N (57)	Male N (77)	Female N (30)	Male N (49)	Female N (42)	Male N (43)	Female N (52)	Male N (45)	Female N (181)	Male N (214)
Vulcanizer	–	1.3%	–	–	–	–	–	–	–	0.5%
Watchmaker	–	–	–	2%	–	–	–	–	–	0.5%
Welder	–	1.3%	3.3%	4.1%	–	–	–	2.2%	0.6%	1.9%
Wig Maker	–	1.3%	10%	4.1%	4.8%	–	–	–	2.8%	1.4%
Woodwork	–	–	–	–	–	–	–	2.2%	–	0.5%

SOURCE: DATA GATHERED FROM FIELDWORK BY THE AUTHORS IN 2021

undecided. About half of the respondents in Lagos (52.2%) and Osun (50%) agree that university graduates are more involved in artisan careers than polytechnic graduates, 36.6% in Oyo and 51.5% in Ogun disagree, while 38.1% in Osun and 35.3% in Oyo are undecided.

About 44.5% of the respondents in Ogun and 37% in Oyo were found to become artisans to create a successful company (and not necessarily becoming a big public company). One out of three (31.8%) in Lagos is an artisan and shares the dream of building giant companies like Microsoft, Apple, or Google, and 27.7% in Ogun became artisans to operate business predominately by innovation and focused on using their company to improve the society.

5.2 *Push and Pull Factors Explaining the Involvement of Graduates in Artisanal Work*

Table 9.2 presents the push factors influencing involvement in artisanal work by graduate artisans. It shows that 83.3% of the respondents in Ondo and 48.5% in Ogun became artisans because they were unable to find paid white-collar jobs, while about half of the respondents in Lagos (51.5%) and Oyo (47.6%) did not become artisans because they were unable to find paid white-collar job. While 47% of the respondents in Ondo and 41% in Oyo became artisans because the salary, they got from their previous employment was not enough to sustain their family. Also, more than half of the respondents in Lagos (65.4%) and Ogun (62.9%) did not become graduate artisans because the salary in their previous employment was not enough to sustain their families.

Most of the respondents in Ondo (73.8%), Ogun (50.5%), Lagos (49.3%), and Oyo (48.2%) became artisans because it was the only way they could make a living, while 41.8% in Lagos, 45.9% in Oyo and 44.3% in Ogun did not become artisans because it was the only way they could make a living. Two-thirds of the respondents in Lagos (71.4%), Oyo (63.5%), and Ogun (71.6%) did not become artisans to continue a family tradition, while 53.6% of the respondents in Ondo became artisans to continue a family tradition. Most of the respondents in Ondo (84.3%), Oyo (80.7%), Ogun (72.7%), and half (50%) in Lagos became artisans to have something of their own as they could not rely on their spouse's income.

Table 9.3 presents findings on pull factors influencing involvement in artisanal work by graduate artisans. It reveals that most of the respondents in Lagos (60.4%), Ondo (90.5%), Oyo (73.8%), and Ogun (53.6%) became artisans because they can do the kind of work they want to do. Similarly, most of the respondents in Lagos (65.7%), Ondo (89.3%), Oyo (77.6%), and Ogun (58.8%) became artisans because they can be their own bosses and avoid having to work for others. Also, most of the respondents in Lagos (72.7%), Ondo (89.3%),

TABLE 9.2 Push factors influencing involvement in artisanal work by graduate artisans

Variables	Lagos			Ondo			Oyo			Ogun			Total		
	A	UD	D	A	UD	D	A	UD	D	A	UD	D	A	UD	D
	(%)	(%)	(%)	(%)	(%)	(%)	(%)	(%)	(%)	(%)	(%)	(%)	(%)	(%)	(%)
I became an Artisan:															
Because I was unable to find paid white-collar job	44.0%	4.5%	51.5%	83.3%	3.6%	13.1%	44.0%	8.3%	47.6%	48.5%	7.2%	44.3%	53.4%	5.8%	40.9%
Because my salary in my previous employment was not enough to sustain my family	28.6%	6.0%	65.4%	47.0%	7.2%	45.8%	41.0%	15.7%	43.4%	32.0%	5.2%	62.9%	35.9%	8.1%	56.1%

Because it was the only way I could make a living	49.3%	9.0%	41.8%	73.8%	10.7%	15.5%	48.2%	5.9%	45.9%	50.5%	5.2%	44.3%	54.5%	7.8%	37.8%
To continue a family tradition	20.3%	8.3%	71.4%	53.6%	28.6%	17.9%	24.7%	11.8%	63.5%	20.0%	8.4%	71.6%	28.2%	13.4%	58.4%
To have something of my own, I could not rely on my spouse's income	50.0%	7.8%	42.2%	84.3%	8.4%	7.2%	80.7%	10.8%	8.4%	72.7%	5.7%	21.6%	69.4%	8.1%	22.5%

SOURCE: DATA GATHERED FROM FIELDWORK BY THE AUTHORS IN 2021

TABLE 9.3 Pull factors influencing involvement in artisanal work by graduate artisans

Variables	Lagos			Ondo			Oyo			Ogun			Total		
	A (%)	UD (%)	D (%)	A (%)	UD (%)	D (%)	A (%)	UD (%)	D (%)	A (%)	UD (%)	D (%)	A (%)	UD (%)	D (%)
I became an Artisan:															
To be able to do the kind of work I really want to do	60.4%	9.7%	29.9%	90.5%	6.0%	3.6%	73.8%	9.5%	16.7%	53.6%	8.2%	38.1%	67.9%	8.5%	23.6%
To be able to be my own boss and avoid having to work for others	65.7%	9.7%	24.6%	89.3%	6.0%	4.8%	77.6%	10.6%	11.8%	58.8%	9.3%	32.0%	71.5%	9.0%	19.5%
To make more money than I would otherwise make as a formal sector employee	72.7%	13.6%	13.6%	89.3%	7.1%	3.6%	89.3%	4.8%	6.0%	97.9%	1.0%	1.0%	85.9%	7.3%	6.8%

To build a successful business enterprise	78.9%	7.5%	13.5%	96.4%	1.2%	2.4%	96.5%	1.2%	2.4%	91.8%	4.1%	4.1%	89.5%	4.0%	6.5%
To achieve a higher position for myself in society	64.9%	18.7%	16.4%	92.9%	2.4%	4.8%	85.7%	4.8%	9.5%	93.8%	2.1%	4.1%	82.2%	8.3%	9.5%
To follow the example of a person I admire	31.3%	9.0%	59.7%	61.9%	23.8%	14.3%	56.5%	18.8%	24.7%	32.3%	7.3%	60.4%	43.4%	13.8%	42.9%
In order to have more control of my time	62.7%	16.4%	20.9%	79.8%	9.5%	10.7%	79.8%	4.8%	15.5%	76.3%	4.1%	19.6%	73.2%	9.5%	17.3%
In order to be innovative	78.9%	6.8%	14.3%	83.3%	6.0%	10.7%	79.8%	9.5%	10.7%	90.6%	1.0%	8.3%	82.9%	5.8%	11.3%
So that I can use my special talents effectively	68.4%	21.8%	9.8%	92.9%	4.8%	2.4%	85.9%	7.1%	7.1%	87.6%	8.2%	4.1%	82.0%	11.8%	6.3%

(*Continued*)

TABLE 9.3 Pull factors influencing involvement in artisanal work by graduate artisans (*cont.*)

Variables	Lagos			Ondo			Oyo			Ogun			Total		
	A	UD	D	A	UD	D	A	UD	D	A	UD	D	A	UD	D
	(%)	(%)	(%)	(%)	(%)	(%)	(%)	(%)	(%)	(%)	(%)	(%)	(%)	(%)	(%)
Because I saw an opportunity/incentive that I could benefit from	83.6%	6.7%	9.7%	83.3%	3.6%	13.1%	83.5%	8.2%	8.2%	66.0%	3.1%	30.9%	79.3%	5.5%	15.3%

SOURCE: DATA GATHERED FROM FIELDWORK BY THE AUTHORS IN 2021

Oyo (89.3%), and Ogun (97.9%) became artisans because they make more money than they would otherwise make as formal sector employees. Consequently, 78.9% of the respondents in Lagos, 96.4% in Ondo, 96.5% in Oyo, and 91.8% in Ogun became artisans to build a successful business enterprise. More than two-thirds of the respondents in Lagos (64.9%), Ondo (92.9%), Oyo (85.7%), and Ogun (93.8%) became artisans to achieve a higher position for themselves in society. More than half of the respondents in Lagos (59.7%) and Ogun (60.4%) did not become artisans to follow the example of a role model, while 61.9% in Ondo and 56.5% in Oyo became artisans to follow the example of a person they admire.

Furthermore, most of the respondents in Lagos (62.7%), Ondo (79.8%), Oyo (79.8%), and Ogun (76.3%) became artisans to have more control of their time. Similarly, most of the respondents in Lagos (78.9%), Ondo (83.3%), Oyo (79.8%), and Ogun (90.6%) became artisans to be innovative. A vast majority of the respondents in Lagos (68.4%), Ondo (92.9%), Oyo (85.9%), and Ogun (87.6%) became artisans so that they could use their unique talents effectively. Finally, more than two-thirds of the respondents in Lagos (83.6%), Ondo (83.3%), Oyo (83.5%), and Ogun (66%) became artisans because they saw an opportunity/incentive that they could benefit from.

5.3 *The Experiences of Graduate Artisans in Their Artisanal Journey*

This study revealed that 63% of the respondents in Oyo, 55.7% in Ogun, 45.9% in Lagos, and 43.9% in Ondo trained for 1–2 years in their line of artisanship. About 1 out of 3 respondents in Oyo trained for 3–4 years, while 34.6% of the respondents in Lagos trained for less than a year. The study also revealed that about half of the respondents in Oyo (50.6%), Ondo (50%), and Ogun (49.5%) had their artisanal training funded by a family member, while 52.2% of the respondents in Lagos, 46.4% in Ondo and 43.3% of the artisans in Ogun funded their artisanal training themselves. Upon completion of training, 46.4% of the respondents in Ogun and 40.5% in Ondo had their artisanal business funded by a family member, while 40.3% of the respondents in Lagos, half (51.2%) in Ondo, 34.1% in Oyo, and 37.1% in Ogun funded their artisanal business themselves. Furthermore, this study shows that about half of the respondents in Ondo (52.7%) and Oyo (46.6%) have been earning with their artisanal skill for 1–2 years, while 35.1% in Ondo, 31.5% in Ogun, and 28% in Lagos have been earning with their artisanal skill for 3–4 years.

Most of the respondents in Lagos (59%), Ondo (87.5%), Oyo (66.3%), and Ogun (70.2%) found it easy to learn the artisanal skill they chose. The bulk of the respondents in Ondo (95.2%) and Ogun (72.9%), and slightly more than half in Lagos (56.4%) and Oyo (59.5%) were prepared by their tertiary education for the realities of artisanal work. Most of the respondents in Lagos (68.7%), Ondo (91.7%), Oyo (82.1%), and almost all (99%) in Ogun have experienced growth in their artisanal enterprise since they started. Nonetheless, most of the respondents in Lagos (55.2%), Ondo (86.6%), Oyo (67.5%), and Ogun (26.8%) experienced discouraging issues with their artisanal enterprise. More than half of the respondents in Lagos (53.7%), Ondo (67.5%), and Oyo (51.3%) face the same challenges in their business as their non-graduate counterparts, while 36.5% in Ogun do not face the same challenges. Most of the respondents in Lagos (73.7%), Ondo (96.4%), Oyo (74.1%), and Ogun (92.7%) opine that being educated make their artisanal work easier for them to do. Finally, most of the respondents in Osun (81.9%) and Ogun (67%) agree that their non-graduate counterparts see them as a threat to their business, while 34.8% in Lagos disagree.

5.3.1 Working Schedule Experiences of Respondents

From the qualitative data (in-depth interviews), the study found that graduate artisans have different work schedules. However, one major thing common to all is the flexibility of their work schedules and business structure. Compared to white-collar jobs that require a specific resumption and closing time, mostly between 8:00 am and 5–6 pm daily, enforced by the organisation, entrepreneurs determine their own time and when it is convenient for them to work. Some have a time frame within which they work daily, leaving room for flexibility. In other cases, entrepreneurs also experience having to work overtime, depending on the nature of the work. For example, an entrepreneur who makes aluminium products explains that depending on the work, they might work longer or shorter hours and sometimes shift location to building sites where they will install the aluminium products.

> Ah, in this our work, there are no special days for work. Let us say we work from Mondays to Saturdays between the hours of 8 am to 6 pm. Sometimes, we work more than that; sometimes, we go to the site; sometimes, we work at the shop where we fabricate our works and then move them to the site. Yes, it is how work comes, and it depends on what we have at hand
>
> IDI/Ogun/ 38 years/Aluminium products

This fashion designer also stated that sometimes not every day is a workday, especially when business is slow, and there is no demand for her services.

> I do not have specific working days; my working days are always depending on the demand of customers ..."
>
> IDI/Ondo/ 23 years/Fashion Design

For the photographer, workdays also mean and include working all around the week, including weekends; on some weeks, there is more job to be done during the weekends than on weekdays.

> Well, I work round the week. In most cases, I work during the weekdays and times during the weekends, but the specific time of my work cannot be stated ...
>
> IDI/Oyo/27 years/Photography

5.4 *Respondents' Positive and Negative Experiences in Artisanship*

Interviewees also expressed the advantages and disadvantages of working as entrepreneurs. Although they had earlier stated that they were motivated for the job and preferred to be self-employed, they also reported facing some challenges that disadvantage businesses. This disadvantage for most of them is the country's economy which slows down the patronage of their respective businesses. An entrepreneur believed risk is a disadvantage in every business, but for those who are self-employed, it is higher because they bear the risk alone.

> The disadvantage I will say is that there is no business without risk; when you are self-employed, you bear the risk alone.
>
> IDI/Oyo/24 years/Milliner/Import and Export

For the photographer, while he knows he is good at his work' in some ways, he is limited because of the lack of necessary equipment to scale up the business. In a way, there is also a higher demand, thus necessitating him to think outside the box and surmount these limitations to get ahead in the business.

> Yeah, there are challenges. People demand more from you. I covered a football match of recent; two prominent football clubs in Ibadan. After finishing the work, the management appreciated it; they loved it not until a new development came, and they needed to state something the work needed to carry, which required advanced technology to execute. So that is one of the challenges we face as media practitioners because

> innovations keep creeping in every now and then, and it demands you to think outside of the box. You know, being proactive, being smart and being futuristic in your way of reasoning.
>
> IDI/Oyo/27 years/ Photography

Being good at one's craft is necessary for those who must make ends meet through their skill, as it would help them gain more clientele through recommendations. However, while the economy is a disadvantage, this interviewee believes that the flexibility of earning and the steady stream of income within the month is an advantage compared to waiting till the end of the month to receive a salary.

> Yes. Sorry, you see this handiwork we are doing; once you are perfect, no one is 100% perfect, but once you know what you are doing, it is what you did that person would see, and self-recommendation is not the best, it is other people that will recommend you. So, if you do yama-yama, you will see yama-yama. That is the way I see this thing. But the economy is the major and only disadvantage, and the reason why I am saying the advantages are many is that see, you cannot compare me to a salary earner who will have to wait till the month's end.
>
> IDI/Ogun/ 38 years/Aluminum products

This interviewee also talked about the opportunities for more exposure and how things are done elsewhere as an advantage of being self-employed.

> The advantage of being self-employed is that it opens your eyes to many things, it open's your eyes to many businesses and opens you more to the world.
>
> IDI/Oyo/24 years/Milliner-Import and Export

5.5 *Willingness to Go Back to Paid Employment*

The responses about the disadvantages of entrepreneurship also created the need to investigate the willingness of the interviewees to go back to working under an employer. The responses ranged from a vehement no to those who were yet considering it and others who thought it was a good option.

> No. I am not even considering it.
>
> IDI/Ogun/ 38 years/Aluminum products

For this interviewee, instead of returning to working for someone, he would instead focus on expanding the current business to earn more.

> No ... what I just consider is for a way to build the business at hand. The plan I have for this business is for me to see it grow. The plan is for me to see me having different branches all over the states. No, I do not. Like I said earlier, what I am into now, I prefer to build it by using my knowledge and not to work for another person.
>
> IDI/Oyo/24 years/Import and Export

Some showed uncertainty and reported that if there is a better offer, she could consider putting the business on hold for a while and go into paid employment to gather some funds, which can then be used to fund the business.

> I am not sure for now
>
> IDI/Ogun/ 27 years/Caterer

> The country is not encouraging for job employment and to be non-idle, if I get a better offer, I could stop for a while to gather some funds for the business.
>
> IDI/Ondo/ 23 years/Fashion Design 1

In the same light, another respondent stated that the current work can be used as a "side hustle" as the current economy does not allow for only one income stream.

> The situation of the economy as of now is not encouraging for job opportunities and also looking at the aspect of side hustle even if eventually there is a white-collar job
>
> IDI/Ondo/ 23 years/Fashion Design 2

Sometimes, young people who are entrepreneurs consider paid employment, especially when they see and know people around who are doing well for themselves financially and who work with a well-paying company or institution. However, the reluctance to go into paid employment could be a matter of pride where one as an employer does not want to work under someone else. Money is, however, a significant factor that could tilt the decision.

> I have never, but sometimes, I would want to be sincere when I see friends working in a high echelon of entities; sometimes, I will want to envy them. When you see your friends earning six digits as salary, you want to think of quitting, but the drive has kept me on. Well, as you know, I think I have been paying salaries to people for a while now and having to collect

> salary is not something I pray for. Moreover, even if I am going to collect salary, I should collect it in big scale in huge nine digits, not even six digits. So, the point is we all pray for progress, not regression, so the point is having to be paid as an employer is not the best; you pay your employees.
>
> IDI/Oyo/27 years/Photography

6 Discussion of Findings

The findings of this study, supported by the theories of Planned Behaviour (TPB), Entrepreneurial Event Model (EEM), and the Push-Pull Model (PPM), espoused the understanding of 'why graduate artisanship is a major and growing phenomenon. In the demographic data obtained from the fieldwork, an interesting angle as to the sex dichotomy of the respondents seem to corroborate the report from the African Commission (2009:24) that men are more likely than women to participate in entrepreneurial activities. Though entrepreneurship is the bigger umbrella term under which artisanship is subsumed, the research result produced a 54.2% male respondents' rate compared to the female respondents at 45.8%. Only in Ogun state were female respondents marginally more than male respondents at 53.8%.

For graduate artisan's favoured professions, more graduates are involved in Tailoring/Fashion design, which carries a total of 29.1%, more than a quarter of the entire respondents of the study. Next to tailoring are Photographers at 16.2%, while Hairdressers came next to it at 15.5%. Caterers/Confectioners and Painters are at 13.5% and 9%, respectively, with these two professions having more male than female respondents. Overall, the profession of choice seems to be Tailoring, with female respondents doubling their male counterparts, in this profession, under this study. Most respondents are approximately 40% of university graduates with B. A, B. Tech, and B.Sc. degrees. 28.8% of the graduate artisans are graduates with Higher Diplomas (HND), 20.7% have Ordinary Diplomas (OND), and 10.6% have post-graduate degrees. If the polytechnic graduate's sub-population is summed, it amounts to 49.5% of the respondents. This can be an area necessitating further studies.

The study that informed this chapter showed that 33% of the respondents are motivated by economic survival and the quest to stay afloat in business. For this category of artisans, becoming artisans was mainly born through the non-availability of jobs related to their graduate disciplines or lack of financial and emotional satisfaction in their previous white-collar jobs. Their typology in artisanship is 'Lifestyle' focused. Though they desire growth in their respective businesses, becoming a large public company or conglomerate does not seem important to this category's respondents. Their motivation is to be employed, make a profit, and control their time and business enterprise. This category of artisans corroborates the Entrepreneurial Event theory's salient factors that require the artisanal enterprise to be attractive and practicable, in addition to the willingness to act on an incentive" (Shapera & Sokol, 1982).

Closely following the 'Lifestyle' artisans is the 'Innovator' category of artisans who believe they have ideas that can transform their career spaces and give room for innovative creativity and distinguish them from their colleagues in their industry. They are 31.4% of the respondents. The typology of artisans with the least of respondents is the 'Serial' artisans. This category of artisans seems to tilt to the areas of business where the money is at the time. Many in this category mix their artisanship with another trending, money-making activity of the season. Those within this category are 13% of the respondents. It is observed that at specific periods of their business life, the main artisan business takes a backseat to a momentary money-making venture, which is often trading. 21% of the respondents fall within the 'Empire builders' typology. Respondents that fall within this category from the study seem to have mentors within their chosen artisan career field. Their business plan is grander, with aspirations geared towards building big conglomerates.

An individual's decision to start a business is based on an expectation that the intention with which the individual established the business will be met. The relationship between the theory of Planned Behaviour (TPB) and the Entrepreneurial Event Model (EEM) has well explained the motivating factor why graduates instead go into skilled artisanship than go for white-collar jobs. From the study, the motivation factor was majorly the country's economic situation which reduced employment opportunities for the teeming number of tertiary institution graduates. There is already established personal capacity that has been honed through the experiences garnered from school and skills training, and there is established social pressure for the need to earn an income and contribute meaningfully to themselves, their families, and their respective communities.

Therefore, to survive, graduates have instead gone for training in any artisanal skill of choice to provide employment for themselves. Other factors that pushed graduates into artisanship are insufficient remuneration that they received when they worked at structured white-collar companies, tight work schedules, high-stress levels, and the inability to have sufficient time for themselves or any other activities of their interest. It is influenced by assumptions about the expectations of significant others, the desire to meet those expectations, and the availability of stimuli that could help or hinder the behaviour's success. According to Ajzen and Cote (2008), when real influence is elevated, the impact of intention on behaviour is heavy.

Of the total number of respondents, 84% can be said to find satisfaction in their artisanal careers because they submitted that it has been easier and better for them to achieve their goals. 73.2% of respondents in both Oyo and Ondo states are not worried about the financial risks that artisans and entrepreneurs face, while a marginal 54.6% of respondents from Lagos and Ogun states expressed their worry about the financial risks of being an artisan. Be that as it may, most of the respondents (80.4%) in all the states stated that they would encourage their relatives and friends instead to become artisans than take up a white-collar job.

7 Conclusion

The theoretical framework for understanding the graduate artisanship phenomenon can be best summed up by the AOI (Ability, Opportunity, and Intent) Model. The motivating factors for any educated young person to choose artisanship over white-collar jobs are the 'Ability' to make that choice, the 'Opportunity' to follow through with the choice, and the 'Intent' to make what he/she chooses from the business. These seem in agreement with the perspective of the Theory of Planned Behaviour (TPB)'s 'presumed behavioural discipline' and 'attitudes towards behaviour'. Simply put, perceived personal capacity and Entrepreneurship Event Model (EEM). 'Perceived social pressure' is the ability of a person to quickly grasp a new skill without being frustrated; and, the ability to raise the financing of the Artisanal startup. 'Opportunity' is the summation of EEM's factors, such as perceiving an opportunity to enter entrepreneurship. This is the ability to deduce the attractiveness of artisanship and understand its practicability in solving the individual's economic desires. 'Pull' factors are summarily explained by Opportunity. The intent could be to build a business empire, effect a particular change by solving issues, and or make a profit. The elements that comprise the EEM or TBP and PPModel are all subsumed within the AOI Model. Intent' envelopes EEM's factor of the willingness of a graduate to act on an incentive and Perceived Viability of the artisanal business enterprise.

References

Adegbite, S.A., llon, M.o., Irefin, IA., Abereiji, I. o And Aderemi, H. o. (2007) Evaluation of the impact of entrepreneurial characteristics on the performance of small scale manufacturing industries in Nigeria. Journal of Asia Entrepreneurship and Sustainability, 3 (1), 90–109.

Ajzen, I. & Cote, N.G. (2008).'Attitudes and the prediction of behaviour', In Crano, W.D. &Pnislin, R. (Eds), Attitudes and Attitude Change. New York: Psychology Press.

Ajzen, I. (2005). Attitudes, Personality, and Behaviour (2nd edition). Berkshire, England: Open University Press.

Odunlami, P. and Olayinka Akanle, (2021). *The Youth Unemployment Quagmire of Africa: Graduates in Artisanal Sector of Southwestern Nigeria.* Paper Presented at the 2nd ARUA centre of excellence for unemployment and skills development international conference, Cape Town, South Africa. Theme: The drive for innovative solutions to youth unemployment in Africa: Policy and practice imperatives. Cape Town, South Africa. 24th–26th August 2021.

Akhuemonkhan, I., Raimi, L., Patel, A. M., &Fadipe, A. O. (2014). Harnessing the potentials of technology incubation centres (TICs) as tools for fast-tracking entrepreneurship development and actualisation of the vision 20:2020 in Nigeria, Humanomics, 30, 349–372.

Beeka, B. H. (2015). Entrepreneurship as a viable career choice for Nigerian youth. Doctoral, Sheffield Hallam University (United Kingdom). Retrieved on March 5th 2021, from http://shura.shu.ac.uk/19336/1/10694217.pdf.

Chigunta, F. (2002). The Socio-economic Situation of Youth in Africa: Problems, Prospects and Options. Retrieved on March 5th 2021, http://www.yesweb.org/gkr/res /bg.africa.reg.doc.

Educational and Employability Survey Report. 2014. "Report of National Needs Assessment Surveys. Labour Market Expectation of Nigeria Graduates." Retrieved (Retrieved from National Unit .com on 4/4/201 9.).

Giacomin, O, Janssen, F, Pruett, M, Shinnar, R., Llopis, F, Toney, B. (2010). Entrepreneurial intentions, motivations, and barriers: Differences among American, Asian and European Students. *International Entrepreneurship Management Journal,* 7, *pp.* 219–238. https://doi.org/10.1007/s11365-010-0155-y.

Gilad, B, & Levine, P. (1986). A behavioural model of entrepreneurial supply. Journal of Small Business Management, 24(4), 45–51.

Green, W. S & Amat, S. W. (2012). Entrepreneurship as a career. *Innovations,* 7 (2), 63–66.

Hisrich, RD, Peters, MP, Shepherd, D (2005). *Entrepreneurship* 6th ed. New Delhi: Tata McGraw-Hill Publishing Company Limited.

International Labor Organisation. 2019. "World Employment Social Outlook: Youth. Trends for Youth 2019. Geneva: ILO," Retrieved from http: //www. ilo.org/wcmsp5 /groups/public/---dgreports/---dcomm/---publ/ documentsfpublication/wcms5l 3741.pdf.

International Labour Organisation. 2020. *"Global Employment Trends for Youth 2020: Youth exclusion from jobs and training on the rise, International Labour Office.* Geneva, Switzerland. "Retrieved from hftp://www. ilo.org/wcmsp5/groups/public /-- -dgreports/---dcomm/documents/publication/ wcms2 12423. pdf.

Krueger, NJ, &Carsrud, A. (1993). Entrepreneurial intentions: applying the theory of planned behaviour. Entrepreneurship and Regional Development 5, 315–330.

Mambulu, C. (2002). Perceptions of SME Growth Constraints in Nigeria. *Journal of Small Business Management*, 40 (1), 58–65.

National Bureau of Statistics (NBS). 2020. *Nigerian graduates and employment.*Retrieved from https://www.nigerianstat.gov.ng/pdfuploads/ANNUAL%20ABSTRACT%20STATISTICS%20VOLUME-1.pdf.

National Bureau of Statistics NBS. 2020. *Total Population of Unemployed Youth in Nigeria.* Retrieved from hftps://nigerianstat.gov.ng/elibrary.

Nwosu, B. O. & Ojo, K. E. (2015). "Improving Self-Employment Awareness and Opportunities through the Business Education Programme in Nigeria." *International Journal of Education and Evaluation* 1(8).

Oladokun, T. T., & Ayodele, T. O. (2015). Students' perception of the relevance of work experience scheme to real estate education in Nigeria. Property Management, 33, 4–18.

Oyelaran-Oyeyinka, B. (2002). Manufacturing Response in a National System of Innovation: Evidence from the Brewing Firms in Nigeria. Discussion Paper Series of The United Nations University, Institute of New Technologies (INTECH), pp. 1–57. Retrieved on March 5th 2021, from http://www.intech.unu.edu.

Ray, D. (2007). Development Economics. Retrieved on March 5th 2021, from http://www.econ.nyu.edu/user/debraj/Papers/RayPalgrave.pdf.

Ritsilä, J, &Tervo, H. (2002). Effects of unemployment on new firm formation: Micro-level panel data evidence from Finland. Small Business Economics, 19(1), 31–40.

Gruber-Muecke, T., and Hofer, K. M. 2015. "Market Orientation Entrepreneurial Orientation and Performance in Emerging Markets," *International Journal of Emerging Markets.* Doi 10, 560–570. doi: 10.11 08/IJOEM-05–201 3–0076.

Salami, C. G. E. (2011). Entrepreneurship and youth unemployment in Nigeria: The missing link. Global Journal of Management and Business Research, 11 (5), 21–26.

Schoof, U. (2006). Stimulating Youth Entrepreneurship: Barriers and Incentives to enterprise start-ups by young people. Series on Youth and Entrepreneurship. International Labour Organisation, (76), pp. 1–12.

Segal, G, Borgia, D, Schoenfeld, J. (2005). The motivation to become an entrepreneur. International Journal of Entrepreneurial Behaviour & Research, 11(1), 42–57. Retrieved on March 5th 2021, https://doi.org/10.1108/13552550510580834.

Shapero, A (1982). Social dimensions of entrepreneurship.In C Kent, D Sexton, K Vesper (Eds.), *The Encyclopaedia of Entrepreneurship*, (pp. 72–90). Englewood Cliffs: Prentice Hall.

SMEDAN (2011). Our Functions. Retrieved on March 5th 2021, http://www.smedan.gov.ng/.

Uhlaner, L, & Thurik, R. (2007).Post-materialism influencing total entrepreneurial activity across nations. Journal of Evolutionary Economics, 17(2), 161–185.

United Nations. (2018). "Population Facts: Youth Population Trends and Sustainable Development. United Nations Department of Economic and Social Affairs. Population Division." *UN Publications.*

CHAPTER 10

Gender, Education and Informal Employment in Togo

Dossè Mawussi Djahini-Afawoubo

1 Introduction

The informal sector is the main source of employment in Togo. Informal employment accounts for 87.9% of employment in the non-agricultural sectors in Togo, with a disparity between women (95.6%) and men (78.3%). For all informal jobs, more than two-thirds of the workforce (69.7%) is made up of women. Only 30.9% of informal sector workers have an employment contract, which is a sign of the precariousness of these jobs. This precariousness is even more pronounced in rural areas, with only 29.3% of workers having a contract, compared with 32.3% in urban areas. The average hourly wage rate is estimated at only 235 CFA francs, or about US $0.42. The minimum monthly wage is estimated at 1,640, or nearly half the minimum wage in the formal sector (INSEED 2019).

The informal economy is a major concern for developing countries as it hinders the mobilization of tax revenues, which poses problems for the financing of public goods and social protection (Fortin, Marceau, and Savard 1997; Leal Ordóñez 2014)we study the effects of taxation and wage controls in a developing economy with an informal sector. For that purpose, we build a model with firm heterogeneity, in which a formal and an informal sector endogenously emerge in some productive branches of the economy. Based on the assumption that the marginal cost of tax and regulation evasion increases with the size of the firm, our model offers an explanation for the observed discontinuity in the distribution of firms size (the `missing middle' and therefore for the provision of basic social services needed to effectively combat poverty in all its forms as recommended by the SDGs. The informal economy can also serve as a haven for criminal activities, fostering illicit financial flows that have damaging effects on African economies. It is therefore important to identify the main determinants of informal employment in order to propose appropriate reforms to reduce the size of the informal economy. Despite the fact that informal employment represents an important part of the Togolese

 | DOI:10.1163/9789004692657_012

economy, there is surprisingly little research on its determinants in Togo. This study aims at filling this gap.

The main objective of the study is to analyse the determinants of informal employment in Togo. Specifically, the study seeks to answer two questions. Firstly, does education enable one to escape informal employment in Togo? Secondly, are women more likely to participate in informal employment than men? To address these questions, this paper applied a logit model to analyse data collected in 2015 from households in Togo by the Community Based Monitoring System (CBMS) research program implemented by the Partnership for Economic Policy (PEP).

Aside from this introduction, this article is structured in four sections. The second section presents a related review of the literature on informal employment. The third section presents the empirical strategy and data source. The fourth section presents and discusses the results. Finally, the fifth section concludes.

2 A Related Literature Review on Informal Employment

There are two conflicting views in the literature on why individuals work in the informal sector. On the one hand, informal employment is the result of competitive market forces. Informal employment is seen as a voluntary choice by workers based on income or utility maximization. On the other hand, informal employment is more the result of labour market segmentation. It is a last-resort strategy to escape involuntary unemployment.

The competitive model considers that individuals are employed in the informal sector because they lack the characteristics that generate high returns in the formal sector. In this view, wage differences between the formal and informal sectors do not imply that the labour market is segmented since individuals can freely move between these two sectors (Dickens and Lang 1985). It is therefore assumed that individuals voluntarily choose to work in the informal sector (Maloney 2004; Rosenzweig 1988), given, for example, the desirable non-wage characteristics of the informal sector. Thus, individuals maximize their utility rather than their earnings (Maloney 2004). In addition, workers may have an individual comparative advantage in the informal sector (Gindling 1991; Maloney 2004). For example, women may choose to work in the informal sector if the formal jobs available do not offer them the flexibility to combine them with family responsibilities.

Several empirical works have demonstrated a competitive labour market in developing countries (Gindling 1991; Pratap and Quintin 2006). Using an integrated microeconomic model derived from a labour supply model in a four-sector labour market with explicit demand constraints, (Magnac 1991)"plainCitation":"(Magnac 1991 demonstrates the presence of comparative advantages for individuals across economic sectors. An application of the model to data on women's participation in the labour market in the main cities of Colombia in 1980 using multivariate techniques confirms the hypothesis of a competitive labour market. Addressing the same issue, (Pratap and Quintin 2006), using semi-parametric methods, show, using data from a developing country such as Argentina, that estimates of the premium for working in the formal sector are either small and insignificant or negative. Similarly, they do not find significant differences in measures of job satisfaction between the formal and informal sectors. Based on these results, they question the assumption that labour markets are segmented along formal and informal lines in developing countries.

However, the competitive model and its extensions failed to explain the persistence of inequalities between groups and between individual intra-group wages despite economic growth and improved initial training. This has contributed to the emergence of the segmentation theory of the labour market. The traditional dualism theory of the labour market (Doeringer and Piore 1971), developed in the United States, holds that jobs are divided into two groups: those with low wages, poor working conditions, unstable employment, and few opportunities for advancement (secondary jobs), and those with relatively high wages, good working conditions, and opportunities for advancement into higher-paying jobs (primary jobs). Advocates of this view have argued that primary jobs are rationed and that, in particular, women, blacks, and other minorities have difficulty obtaining primary employment. Based on the dualism theory of the labour market, the informal sector is the disadvantaged sector that workers enter to escape unemployment once they are rationed out of the formal sector, where wages are set above equilibrium market prices (Harris and Todaro 1970; Stiglitz 1976). Thus, in contrast to competitive labour market theory, dualism theory posits that individuals are pushed into informal employment because of barriers to entry into the formal sector.

There are several empirical studies that have highlighted the segmentation of the labour market. For example, (Gindling 1991), using Chow tests, shows that there is no single wage structure that explains wage determination in the formal and informal sectors in San Jose, Costa Rica. His results are therefore consistent with the hypothesis of labour market segmentation between the public and private formal sectors and the hypothesis of labour market segmentation between the private formal and informal sectors in San Jose. (Günther and Launov 2012) found a heterogeneous informal sector. Using an econometric labour market model that accounts for unobserved heterogeneity in earnings and sample selection caused by the self-selection of individuals in the labour market, they show that the informal sector is composed of two segments with a distinct wage equation in each segment. Using data for Côte d'Ivoire, they reject the hypothesis of unrestricted sectoral mobility of workers, detecting a considerable number of informal workers who would be better off in another segment of the labour market. However, they also find that a larger share of informal employees appears to have a comparative advantage in the informal sector. Therefore, they conclude that the informal sector includes both individuals for whom informality is a last-resort strategy to escape unemployment and individuals who have a comparative advantage in the informal sector.

3 Empirical Strategy for Analyzing the Effect of Education on Informal Work and Data Source

3.1 *Empirical Strategy*

The general model is as follows:

$$Y_i = \alpha_0 + \alpha_1 E_i + \alpha_2 B_i + \varepsilon_i \qquad (1)$$

where Y is a dichotomous variable indicating whether or not an individual is informally employed. E is the level of education attained by individual i and B is the set of other explanatory variables in the model; the α are the parameters to be estimated; ε is a random error term. Given the dichotomous nature of the dependent variable, a logit model is used. Previous studies have also used the binary model (logit or probit) to analyse the determinants of informal employment in Africa (Adair and Bellache 2012; Başbay, Elgin, and Torul 2018; Kouadio and Gakpa 2020) Elgin, and Torul 2018; Kouadio and Gakpa 2020. The estimated model is therefore as follows:

$$Prob(Y = 1|X) = \alpha_0 + \alpha_1 E_i + \alpha_2 B_i + \varepsilon_i \qquad (2)$$

The parameters of equation (2) are estimated using the maximum likelihood technique. It is of interest to know whether the effect of the level of education attained by the individual on his or her chances of having an informal job differs according to gender or place of residence. To test this hypothesis, we include in the model not only the main effect of the level of education attained, but also its interaction with each of these factors. The model is then written as follows:

$$Prob(informal = 1|x) = \alpha_0 + \alpha_1 E_i + \alpha_2\, group_i + \alpha_3\, (E_i \times group_i) + \gamma B_i + \varepsilon_i \tag{3}$$

where *E* denotes the individual's level of education; group, the socio-demographic group (such as gender and place of residence); *B* denotes all other explanatory variables in the model. The total effect of education is obtained by deriving equation (3) as follows:

$$\frac{\partial Prob(informal = 1|x)}{\partial E_i} = \alpha_1 + \alpha_3 group_i \tag{4}$$

3.2 *Description of the Main Variables of the Model*

Dependent variable. The dependent variable in this study is informal work. Informality can include a wide range of situations, such as the non-declaration of the firm's activities or its employees, non-compliance with the labour code, or the non-payment of taxes or social contributions (Albertini et al., 2020). It is also possible for a firm to have a formal existence but hire workers informally. Similarly, most of a firm's activity may be carried out within the legal framework, while a minor part escapes regulation. For the purposes of this study, an individual is considered to be working in the informal sector when that individual is working in an enterprise that is not registered with the business formality center or when the individual does not benefit from at least one service offered by the National Social Security Fund (CNSS).

Independent variables. The selection of independent variables was made with reference to the literature presented above. The independent variable of interest is education. To measure education, the following questions were used: "Has the individual ever attended school in his or her life?" and "What is the highest grade completed?". From these questions, we constructed a polytomous variable that takes the values 0 when the individual has never attended school, 1 when the individual has reached primary school, 2 when the individual has reached secondary school, and 3 when the individual has reached university level. It is expected that poorly educated individuals are more likely to work in the informal sector either because they lack characteristics that generate high returns in the formal sector or because they are pushed into informal employment because of barriers to entry in the formal sector.

Besides educational attainment, we control for the effects of the usual variables such as age, gender, residential background, social capital, marital status, and job satisfaction. These variables are widely retained in the empirical literature on the determinants of informal employment (Adair and Bellache 2012; Aikaeli and Mkenda 2014; Başbay et al. 2018; Kouadio and Gakpa 2020)"plainCitation":"(Adair and Bellache 2012; Aikaeli and Mkenda 2014; Başbay et al. 2018; Kouadio and Gakpa 2020. Age is an indicator of seniority. As a result, the older one gets, the more experience one gains, which strengthens one's human capital. As a result, one should be less likely to work in the informal sector. Gender is a dichotomous variable that takes the value 1 when the individual is male and 0 if he is female. It is expected that women will be more likely to work in the informal sector than men, either because women find it easier to work in the informal sector than in the formal sector due to the fact that available formal jobs do not offer the flexibility for women to combine them with family responsibilities or because women are pushed into informal employment due to barriers to entry into the formal sector. Social capital is a part of an individual's human capital. We therefore expect its coefficient to have a negative sign. It is a binary variable, taking the value 1 when the individual participates in meetings of syndicates, NGOs, or associations and 0 otherwise. We consider that individuals who are satisfied with their job are not looking for an additional job. We therefore measure satisfaction using a binary variable that takes the value 1 when the individual is not looking for an additional job and 0 otherwise. Table 10.1 presents the matrix of simple correlations between the main explanatory variables in the model. Overall, the correlations between the main explanatory variables are low.

3.3 *Data Source*

The data used in this study were collected in 2015 from households in Togo by CBMS research program. CBMS is part of the PEP network. This data collection was funded by the UK Department for International Development (DFID) and the International Development Research Centre (IDRC) of Canada. In total, data were collected from 7,436 households, including 4,296 informal sector workers (2,374 in urban areas and 1,922 in rural areas). Three questionnaires were submitted to the respondents: the household questionnaire, the annex questionnaire, and the community questionnaire. The household questionnaire covered information on household members such as population, education, multidimensional characteristics of poverty, access to basic services, etc. The annex questionnaire collected additional information on social protection. Finally, the community questionnaire was completed by district and zonal leaders, representatives, and resource persons in the health, education, and other sectors. Table 10.2 presents the descriptive statistics for the main variables.

TABLE 10.1 Correlation matrix of main explanatory variables

Variables	(1)	(2)	(3)	(4)	(5)	(6)	(7)	(8)	(9)	(10)
Education (1)	1.0000									
Gender (2)	0.2919	1.0000								
Age (3)	-0.3423	-0.0060	1.0000							
Place of residence (4)	0.3484	-0.0966	-0.1731	1.0000						
Household size (5)	-0.1077	-0.0384	0.0173	-0.1895	1.0000					
Number of elderlies (6)	-0.1661	-0.0420	0.4259	-0.1559	0.0408	1.0000				
Number of children under 5 (7)	0.0174	-0.0483	-0.1962	-0.0842	0.5422	-0.0721	1.0000			
Marital status (8)	-0.3424	-0.2257	0.4489	-0.1559	0.0640	0.1589	0.0082	1.0000		
Job satisfaction (9)	-0.0741	-0.0497	0.1566	-0.0185	0.0069	0.1146	-0.0246	0.0519	1.0000	
Social capital (10)	0.0366	0.0547	0.0382	-0.0731	0.0512	0.0013	0.0070	0.0007	-0.0845	1.0000

TABLE 10.2 Descriptive statistics of main variables

Variables	N	Mean	Std. errs.	Min	Max
Age	4,736	38.56	12.59	15	92
Number of children under 5	4,736	0.338	0.595	0	4
Number of elderlies	4,736	0.0665	0.262	0	3
Informal employment	4,736	0.904	0.295	0	1
Education	4,736	1.117	0.929	0	3
Marital status	4,736	2.053	0.730	1	4
Household size	4,736	2.473	1.481	1	10
Social capital	4,736	0.132	0.338	0	1
Job satisfaction	4,736	0.344	0.475	0	1
Gender	4,736	0.431	0.495	0	1
Place of residence	4,736	0.568	0.495	0	1

4 Results and Discussion

4.1 *Descriptive Statistics*

Table 10.3 presents some employment statistics by level of education, gender, and place of residence. The results show that, overall, the informal sector accounts for more than 90% of employment. Disparities are highlighted according to the level of education attained. Individuals with no formal education represent the largest proportion of informal jobs (35.9%). Conversely, individuals with university education represent only 3.15% of informal jobs. On the other hand, they account for 15.37% of formal jobs, although they represent only 4.33% of the total sample considered. Similarly, individuals with secondary education account for 36.7% of the sample but represent 57.5% of formal jobs. It would seem, therefore, that education increases the chances of working in the formal sector and that informal jobs are reserved in greater proportion for workers with little or no education. This suggests that individuals with low levels of education are pushed into informal employment because of barriers to entry into the formal sector according to labour market segmentation theory (Doeringer and Piore 1971) or that they are employed in the informal sector because they lack characteristics that generate high returns in the formal sector according to competitive labour market theory (Maloney 2004; Rosenzweig 1988). Regardless of the explanation, these results seem to reveal the important role that education might play in determining the sector (formal or informal) in which an individual is employed.

TABLE 10.3 Type of employment by level of education, gender, and place of residence

Sociodemographic characteristics	Formal	Informal
Education		
No formal education	12.50	35.93
Primary	14.69	26.45
Secondary	57.46	34.46
University	15.35	3.154
Gender		
Men	61.84	41.12
Women	38.16	58.88
Place of residence		
Urban	66.89	55.75
Rural	33.11	44.25
Total	9.63	90.37

The results also seem to suggest that women are more likely to work in the informal sector (58.9%) than men (41.1%). This seems to confirm the hypothesis that informal employment offers comparatively more opportunities to women than to men (Priest 1993), which could be explained by the fact that women find it easier to work in the informal sector than in the formal sector. It may be that the formal jobs available do not offer women the flexibility to combine them with family responsibilities. This situation may also reflect labour market segmentation, in which women are pushed into informal employment because of barriers to entry into the formal sector. These barriers may lie in the unequal distribution of educational opportunities between men and women and between rural and urban residents. As noted above, the illiteracy rate is twice as high among women (56.2% of women versus 28.8% of men) and in rural areas (56.6% in rural areas versus 26.6% in urban areas).

4.2 *Determinants of Informal Employment*

Table 10.4 presents the results of the estimates based on equations (2) and (3) using the logit model (coefficients, marginal effects, and odds ratios are reported). Two specifications were made. In the first one, interaction effects between education and gender and between education and place of residence are not taken into account. In the second one, we include not only the main effect of education but also its interaction with gender and place of residence to test whether or not the effect of education on informal employment differs for each of these factors. Before interpreting the results, it is worth saying a few words about the quality of the estimation. For all models, the Wald test shows that the null hypothesis (that all regression coefficients are jointly zero) is rejected at the 1 percent significance level. This implies that the variables included in the regression create a statistically significant improvement in model fit. For both specifications, the predictions are correct in more than 90% of the cases, which is a sign of a good fit.

The results of the first specification show that the chances of having an informal job decrease as the level of education increases. Indeed, all other things being equal, the probability of having an informal job decreases by 1.7 percentage points (statistically significant at the 5% level) when the individual has attained a primary education level compared to individuals with no formal education. When the individual has attained a secondary education, his or her chances of working in the informal sector decrease by 11 percentage points (significant at the 1% level), while they decrease by 30 percentage points (significant at the 1% level) when he or she has attained a university education compared to individuals with no formal education. This result is consistent with our expectations and is consistent with the literature (Başbay et al. 2018; Kouadio and Gakpa 2020; McCaig and Pavcnik 2015; Williams, Shahid, and Martínez 2016) we empirically investigate the relationship between informal sector employment and micro-level socio-demographic characteristics, political acts and attitudes, and individual norms. Using self-reported individual micro-level data from the World Values Survey for seven developing countries (China, Ecuador, Egypt, Mexico, Peru, South Africa and Yemen. This result that individuals with low levels of education are more likely to work in the informal sector could be explained by the existence of barriers to entry in the formal sector (labour market segmentation theory) or by the fact that individuals with low levels of education lack characteristics that generate high returns in the formal sector (competitive labour market theory). In any case, this result reveals the importance of education in the search for formal employment. This suggests that special emphasis should be placed on equity in people's access to education so that everyone has an equal opportunity to access formal employment.

The results show with statistical significance at the 1% level that as age increases, the probability of working in the informal sector decreases, all else being equal. This result is consistent with our expectations because age is an indicator of seniority. Thus, the older one gets, the more experience one acquires, which strengthens one's human capital, and thus the less likely one is to work in the informal sector. The positive sign of age squared is also consistent with our expectations and suggests a U-shaped relationship between informal

TABLE 10.4 Main determinants of informal employment in Togo

Variables	Specification 1			Specification 2		
	Coefficient	Odds ratio	Marginal effect	Coefficient	Odds ratio	Marginal effect
Dependent variable=informal employment						
Primary education	-0.396**	0.673**	-0.0172**	-0.659***	0.517***	-0.0235***
	(0.193)	(0.130)	(0.00837)	(0.211)	(0.109)	(0.00739)
Secondary education	-1.491***	0.225***	-0.109***	-2.219***	0.109***	-0.166***
	(0.175)	(0.0393)	(0.0114)	(0.269)	(0.0293)	(0.0214)
University	-2.611***	0.0735***	-0.302***	-4.070***	0.0171***	-0.549***
	(0.240)	(0.0176)	(0.0381)	(0.469)	(0.00800)	(0.0741)
Gender = male	-0.425***	0.654***	-0.0342***	-1.100***	0.333***	-0.0902***
	(0.118)	(0.0773)	(0.00958)	(0.237)	(0.0789)	(0.0202)
Gender x education				0.419***	1.521***	0.0337***
				(0.127)	(0.193)	(0.0103)
Age	-0.0959***	0.909***	-0.00773***	-0.102***	0.903***	-0.00819***
	(0.0345)	(0.0313)	(0.00276)	(0.0347)	(0.0313)	(0.00278)
Age squared	0.00112***	1.001***	9.05e-05***	0.00120***	1.001***	9.62e-05***
	(0.000429)	(0.000429)	(3.44e-05)	(0.000431)	(0.000432)	(3.46e-05)
Place of residence = urban	0.0154	1.016	0.00124	-0.537**	0.584**	-0.0415**
	(0.125)	(0.127)	(0.0101)	(0.245)	(0.143)	(0.0182)
Education x place of residence				0.369***	1.446***	0.0297***
				(0.143)	(0.206)	(0.0115)

Household size	-0.00248	0.998	-0.000200	-0.000958	0.999	-7.70e-05
	(0.0450)	(0.0448)	(0.00362)	(0.0450)	(0.0449)	(0.00362)
Number of elderlies	0.0164	1.017	0.00132	-0.0193	0.981	-0.00155
	(0.272)	(0.276)	(0.0219)	(0.277)	(0.272)	(0.0223)
Number of children under 5	0.0759	1.079	0.00611	0.0859	1.090	0.00691
	(0.111)	(0.120)	(0.00895)	(0.111)	(0.121)	(0.00896)
Marital status = married	-0.378**	0.685**	-0.0280**	-0.350**	0.705**	-0.0259**
	(0.162)	(0.111)	(0.0110)	(0.160)	(0.113)	(0.0110)
Statut matrimonial = divorced	-0.672***	0.511***	-0.0553**	-0.660***	0.517***	-0.0547**
	(0.249)	(0.127)	(0.0226)	(0.249)	(0.129)	(0.0227)
Marital status = widowed	-0.134	0.874	-0.00906	-0.184	0.832	-0.0128
	(0.342)	(0.299)	(0.0237)	(0.343)	(0.285)	(0.0249)
Job satisfaction = yes	0.0124	1.013	0.001000	0.0235	1.024	0.00188
	(0.111)	(0.112)	(0.00889)	(0.111)	(0.113)	(0.00886)
Social capital	0.0399	1.041	0.00318	0.0412	1.042	0.00328
	(0.153)	(0.159)	(0.0120)	(0.153)	(0.159)	(0.0120)
Constant	5.611***	273.3***		6.185***	485.4***	
	(0.653)	(178.5)		(0.675)	(327.6)	
Prob > chi2	0.00			0.00		
Pseudo R^2	0.10			0.11		
Correctly predicted	90.42%			90.44%		
Observations	4,738	4,738	4,738	4,738	4,738	4,738

ROBUST STANDARD ERRORS IN PARENTHESIS
*** P<0.01, ** P<0.05, * P<0.1

employment and age. This result could be explained by the fact that retirees are mainly employed in undeclared jobs in order to receive a full pension from the government and that young workers may need to spend some time in the labour market before they are able to get a formal job. This U-shaped relationship between age and informal employment is also consistent with the existing literature (Başbay et al. 2018; Williams and Martinez 2014)we empirically investigate the relationship between informal sector employment and micro-level socio-demographic characteristics, political acts and attitudes, and individual norms. Using self-reported individual micro-level data from the World Values Survey for seven developing countries (China, Ecuador, Egypt, Mexico, Peru, South Africa and Yemen.

The results also show that, other things being equal, men are less likely to work in the informal sector than women. All else equal, the likelihood of working in the informal sector decreases by 3.4 percentage points when the individual is male compared to female. The gender effect thus has the expected sign and is consistent with previous work showing that women and less educated workers are more frequently employed in the informal sector in developing countries (Başbay et al. 2018; Kouadio and Gakpa 2020; McCaig and Pavcnik 2015; Williams et al. 2016)we empirically investigate the relationship between informal sector employment and micro-level socio-demographic characteristics, political acts and attitudes, and individual norms. Using self-reported individual micro-level data from the World Values Survey for seven developing countries (China, Ecuador, Egypt, Mexico, Peru, South Africa and Yemen. This result may be explained either by women choosing to work in the informal sector because it offers more ease in combining employment with their family responsibilities or by women being pushed into informal employment because of barriers to entry into the formal sector. This could reflect inequalities in access to education between men and women. These results remain robust when we control for interaction effects between education and gender and between education and residence (specification 2). The fact that the coefficients of the interactions are statistically significant at the 1% level suggests that the effect of education on informal employment differs by gender and residence.

An interesting question is what effect each level of education has on informal employment. To answer this question, we created binary variables for each level of education (primary, secondary, and tertiary) and entered them separately into the equations, resulting in specifications (1) through (3) in Table 10.5. For specification (4), we consider an individual to be educated if he or she has a level of education above the primary level. Otherwise, he is considered uneducated. Only marginal effects are reported in Table 10.5. The results show that

TABLE 10.5 Effect of different education levels on informal employment (marginal effects are reported)

	(1)	(2)	(3)	(4)
Variables	**Primary**	**Secondary**	**University**	**At least secondary**
Dependent variable=informal employment				
Primary	0.0366*			
	(0.0209)			
Gender = male	-0.0700***	-0.110***	-0.0688***	-0.0826***
	(0.0102)	(0.0147)	(0.00971)	(0.0165)
Primary x gender	-0.00739			
	(0.0254)			
Age	-0.00784***	-0.00879***	-0.00725***	-0.00853***
	(0.00281)	(0.00283)	(0.00276)	(0.00280)
Age squared	0.000104***	0.000109***	9.49e-05***	0.000102***
	(3.49e-05)	(3.54e-05)	(3.41e-05)	(3.50e-05)
Place of residence = urban	-0.0453***	-0.0617***	-0.0344***	-0.0258*
	(0.00985)	(0.0121)	(0.00899)	(0.0150)
Primary x place of residence	0.0438*			
	(0.0251)			
Household size	0.000855	0.000408	0.00120	-0.000510
	(0.00367)	(0.00369)	(0.00359)	(0.00369)

TABLE 10.5 Effect of different education levels on informal employment (marginal effects are reported) (*cont.*)

	(1)	(2)	(3)	(4)
Variables	**Primary**	**Secondary**	**University**	**At least secondary**
Number of elderlies	0.000629	-0.000530	-0.000768	-0.000749
	(0.0223)	(0.0226)	(0.0218)	(0.0226)
Number of children under 5	0.00102	0.00545	0.00197	0.00699
	(0.00924)	(0.00930)	(0.00914)	(0.00917)
Marital status= married	-0.0128	-0.00914	-0.0238**	-0.0160
	(0.0121)	(0.0118)	(0.0118)	(0.0113)
Marital status = divorced	-0.0307	-0.0323	-0.0457**	-0.0411*
	(0.0224)	(0.0227)	(0.0227)	(0.0226)
Marital status = widowed	0.0214	0.0100	0.00912	-0.00277
	(0.0210)	(0.0234)	(0.0212)	(0.0246)
Job satisfaction = yes	0.000616	0.000253	0.00273	-0.000139
	(0.00919)	(0.00918)	(0.00896)	(0.00912)
Social capital = yes	-0.00724	-0.00332	-0.00304	-7.02e-05
	(0.0129)	(0.0125)	(0.0128)	(0.0122)
Secondary education		-0.193***		
		(0.0284)		
Secondary education x gender		0.0879***		
		(0.0180)		

Secondary education x place of residence		0.0784***		
		(0.0186)		
University			-0.633***	
			(0.117)	
			(0.0303)	
University x place of residence			0.127**	
			(0.0499)	
Educated (at least secondary level)				-0.166***
				(0.0250)
Educated x gender				0.0555***
				(0.0191)
Educated x place of residence				0.0282
				(0.0199)
Prob > chi2	0.000	0.000	0.000	0.000
Pseudo R^2	0.055	0.039	0.067	0.087
Percentage correctly predicted	90.38%	90.38%	90.44%	90.38%
Observations	4,738	4,738	4,738	4,738

ROBUST STANDARD ERRORS IN PARENTHESIS
*** $P<0.01$, ** $P<0.05$, * $P<0.1$

primary education has a positive effect on informal work, while secondary and university education have negative effects. All else being equal, primary education increases the odds of informal employment by 3.6 percentage points. The effect of primary education does not differ by gender or by place of residence, as the coefficients of the interactions are not statistically significant at the 5 percent level. All else being equal, the probability of having an informal job decreases by 2.67 (−0.267= −0.193 + 0.0879 + 0.0784) percentage points when the individual has a secondary education. The effect of secondary education differs by gender and place of residence, as the coefficients of the interaction effects with gender and residence are statistically significant at the 1% level. University education reduces the probability of being informally employed by 43 (−0.4276 = −0.633 + 0.0784 + 0.127) percentage points, ceteris paribus. The effect of university education also differs by gender and residence.

5 Concluding Remarks

The informal sector accounts for a large proportion of employment in developing countries in general and in Togo in particular. However, there is very little empirical evidence on the main factors driving the expansion of informal employment in Togo. This study aims to fill this gap. Previous studies have analysed the effect of individuals' socio-demographic characteristics on their chances of being employed in the informal sector without highlighting the effect of education. The purpose of this paper was to highlight the effect of different levels of education on informal employment. To achieve this goal, survey data from the Community Based Monitoring System (CBMS) implemented in Togo in 2015 by the Partnership for Economic Policy (PEP) are used. Using a logit model, the results showed that the level of primary education increases the odds of being employed in the informal sector, while secondary and university levels reduce the odds of being employed in the informal sector. The effect of university education is larger than that of secondary education. Women are more likely to work in the informal sector than men. The same is true for rural residents.

In light of these results, inequalities in access to all levels of education should be reduced to give everyone an equal opportunity to escape informal employment. Indeed, inequalities in access to education can have lifelong effects on individuals and are likely to perpetuate and exacerbate inequalities between different population groups. Inequalities in access to and retention in school today between girls and boys, between rural and urban residents, or, in short, between different socio-demographic groups, translate later into inequalities in access to formal employment. This situation perpetuates poverty and inequality between these different groups. Economic policy should therefore target disadvantaged groups such as girls, the poorest populations, and rural residents not only for universal primary education but also for other levels of education, since the benefits of education in terms of access to formal employment are higher for higher levels of education. The policy of universal primary education is certainly useful since it is primary education that provides access to higher levels of education. However, it is important that the education system give students from disadvantaged backgrounds equal opportunities to remain in the system until they reach university level.

References

Adair, Philippe, and Youghourta Bellache. 2012. "Emploi et secteur informels en algérie: déterminants, segmentation et mobilité de la main-d'œuvre." *Region et Developpement* 35:121–49.

Aikaeli, J., and B. K. Mkenda. 2014. "Determinants of Informal Employment: A Case of Tanzania's Construction Industry." *Botswana Journal of Economics* 12(2):51–73. doi: 10.4314/boje.v12i2.

Başbay, Mustafa Metin, Ceyhun Elgin, and Orhan Torul. 2018. "Socio-Demographics, Political Attitudes and Informal Sector Employment: A Cross-Country Analysis." *Economic Systems* 42(4):556–68. doi: 10.1016/j.ecosys.2018.03.003.

Dickens, William T., and Kevin Lang. 1985. "Testing Dual Labor Market Theory: A Reconsideration of the Evidence."

Doeringer, Peter B., and Michael J. Piore. 1971. *Internal Labor Markets and Manpower Analysis*. Lexington MA: Heath.

Fortin, Bernard, Nicolas Marceau, and Luc Savard. 1997. "Taxation, Wage Controls and the Informal Sector." *Journal of Public Economics* 66(2):293–312. doi: 10.1016/S0047-2727(97)00013-3.

Gindling, T. H. 1991. "Labor Market Segmentation and the Determination of Wages in the Public, Private-Formal, and Informal Sectors in San José, Costa Rica." *Economic Development and Cultural Change* 39(3):585–605. doi: 10.1086/451892.

Günther, Isabel, and Andrey Launov. 2012. "Informal Employment in Developing Countries: Opportunity or Last Resort?" *Journal of Development Economics* 97(1):88–98. doi: 10.1016/j.jdeveco.2011.01.001.

Harris, John R., and Michael P. Todaro. 1970. "Migration, Unemployment and Development: A Two-Sector Analysis." *The American Economic Review* 60(1):126–42.

INSEED. 2019. "Enquête Régionale Intégrée sur l'Emploi et le Secteur Informel, 2017, Togo." Retrieved July 25, 2023 (https://inseed.tg/download-page/).

Kouadio, Hugues, and Lewis Landry Gakpa. 2020. "Micro-Determinants of Informal Employment in Cte DIvoire: The Role of Socio-Demographic Factors." *Journal of Economics and International Finance* 12(3):95–104. doi: 10.5897/JEIF2020.1060.

Leal Ordóñez, Julio César. 2014. "Tax Collection, the Informal Sector, and Productivity." *Review of Economic Dynamics* 17(2):262–86. doi: 10.1016/j.red.2013.07.004.

Magnac, Th. 1991. "Segmented or Competitive Labor Markets." *Econometrica* 59(1):165–87. doi: 10.2307/2938245.

Maloney, William F. 2004. "Informality Revisited." *World Development* 32(7):1159–78. doi: 10.1016/j.worlddev.2004.01.008.

McCaig, Brian, and Nina Pavcnik. 2015. "Informal Employment in a Growing and Globalizing Low-Income Country." *American Economic Review* 105(5):545–50. doi: 10.1257/aer.p20151051.

Pratap, Sangeeta, and Erwan Quintin. 2006. "Are Labor Markets Segmented in Developing Countries? A Semiparametric Approach." *European Economic Review* 50(7):1817–41. doi: 10.1016/j.euroecorev.2005.06.004.

Priest, George L. 1993. "The Ambiguous Moral Foundations of the Underground Economy." *Yale Law Journal* 103:2259.

Rosenzweig, Mark R. 1988. "Chapter 15 Labor Markets in Low-Income Countries." Pp. 713–62 in *Handbook of Development Economics*. Vol. 1. Elsevier.

Stiglitz, Joseph E. 1976. "The efficiency wage hypothesis, surplus labour, and the distribution of income in L.D.C.s." *Oxford Economic Papers* 28(2):185–207. doi: 10.1093/oxfordjournals.oep.a041340.

Williams, Colin C., Muhammad S. Shahid, and Alvaro Martínez. 2016. "Determinants of the Level of Informality of Informal Micro-Enterprises: Some Evidence from the City of Lahore, Pakistan." *World Development* 84:312–25. doi: 10.1016/j.worlddev.2015.09.003.

Williams, Colin, and Alvaro Martinez. 2014. "Is the Informal Economy an Incubator for New Enterprise Creation? A Gender Perspective." *International Journal of Entrepreneurial Behavior & Research* 20(1):4–19. doi: 10.1108/IJEBR-05-2013-0075.

CHAPTER 11

Gig Economy: the Experience of Nigerian Digital Freelancers

Adeola O. Opesade

1 Introduction

Advancements and pervasiveness of the information and communication technologies have greatly impacted on people's ways and states of living (Nath, 2017). The spread of the Internet to over five billion people worldwide (Internet World Stats, 2021) has among many other things given rise to a range of outsourcing practices. One of such practices is the adoption of digital platforms that connect millions of people across the globe, in order to exchange money for labour in the form of digital gigs (Wood, Graham, Lehdonvirta, & Hjorth, 2019b; Bukht & Heeks, 2018). Digital gigs are a host of contingent, independent contracting, freelancing or temporary works that happen through, via, and on digital platforms (Woodcock & Graham, 2020). They are a new form of informal economy characterised by the delivery of economic activities that have market value through digital platforms, whereas workers are not formally registered with the government (International Monetary Fund, 2021). Similar to the traditional informal sector workers, there are no legal protections for digital gig workers; there is no minimum wage, and no requirements around working hours, safety, benefits, or registration for government programs like health insurance or pensions (Ng'weno & Porteous, 2018).

The involvement of digital platforms in the organisation of work and financial transactions is a significant and common element of this new economy (Duggan, Sherman, Carbery, McDonne, 2020; Barratt, Goods, & Veen, 2020). Rapid adoption of these platforms for various services has led to the emergence of the new gig economy and the dominance of some of its new economic processes, systems and sectors, such as Uber (world's largest taxi company), Facebook (world's most popular media company), Alibaba (world's biggest and most valuable retailer) and Airbnb (world's largest hotelier) (Bukht & Heeks, 2018). The 'gig' in the term 'gig economy' has its origin in the short-term arrangements that are characteristic of a musical event where an ambitious musician might celebrate getting a gig or tell a friend that they have got a gig in the back room of a pub or other venue. Such that their performance in the

 | DOI:10.1163/9789004692657_013

first gig goes a long way in determining a repeat performance (Woodcock & Graham, 2020).

The emergence of digital gig economy has been found to have some positive as well as negative implications, especially on gig workers. On the positive side, it has enabled Internet users to find work that they might not otherwise have been able to obtain (Wood, Lehdonvirta & Graham, 2018; Wood et al., 2019b). There is also much greater flexibility for platform companies, customers and workers. In the sense that platform companies can choose when and how they want to hire workers, clients and customers can reap the benefits of this flexibility by getting prompt and easy service delivery, while workers can supposedly choose what to do, how, when, where and for whom (Dokko, Mumford & Schanzenbach, 2015; Wood et al., 2018; Wood et al., 2019b). The flexibility offered allows workers, including those with other jobs, to generate new income or to supplement their primary incomes (Wood et al., 2018; Friedman, 2014). Furthermore, remote gig work has been perceived to be a means towards reaching more substantive entrepreneurial aims. This is because savings from earnings made in gig works could provide the initial capital to setup a business in the future. Also, the right attitudes needed to succeed as an entrepreneur could be developed while engaged in gig works (Wood et al., 2018).

Despite these and other possible benefits, there are a range of challenges that could unduly impact on the livelihoods of digital gig workers (Graham, Hjorth, & Lehdonvirta, 2017). The online labour markets have been carped for its orientation towards generating a disposable labour force (Anwar & Graham, 2021). According to Duggan et al. (2020), many digital platforms have a low entry requirement and deliberately recruit as many workers as possible, in order to create an oversupply of labour power, and therefore guarantee a steady supply of workers on demand to those who need them. Consequently, there exists a large temporary workforce, which can easily be hired and fired (Anwar & Graham, 2021). Gig platform companies have also been accused of sham contracting and shifting the burden of risk from firms to workers. This is because platform companies, though requiring certain behaviour from workers in order to control the quality of work, refer to employments as independent contracting, in order to avoid employee entitlements, such as superannuation (Anwar & Graham, 2021; Healy, Nicholson, & Pekarek, 2017). The jobs have also been criticised for being short-timed, low paying, precarious, unpredictable, stressful, and lacking career development and collective bargaining power (Duggan et al. 2020; Wood et al., 2019b; Anwar & Graham, 2021). Furthermore, the gig economy platforms have been reported to create a novel form of insecurity known as algorithmic insecurity, which relates to the vulnerability and fear that workers experience as a result of working in a system in which platforms use customer-generated ratings to score workers, and algorithms to amplify the consequences of those scores (Wood & Lehdonvirta, 2021).

Despite the divergent views on the merits and demerits of the gig economy, statistics have shown its wide acceptance among people from different parts of the world. The world's largest freelancing platform, Freelancer.com, claims to have connected over 30,325,814 employers and freelancers globally from over 247 countries and their Twitter account lists their location is everywhere. Also, Upwork.com, which hosts 12 million registered workers, talks about their worker pool as being global in scope (Woodcock & Graham, 2020). Yet, the economy is said to be only at the dawn of its developments (Bryant, 2020). The growth of the economy and its potential to bring changes that have effects on the economy, society, families, and people's lives (Petriglieri, Ashford, & Wrzesniewski, 2019) have led to increase in research and policy interest among stakeholders, especially in the high-income countries (Dokko et al., 2015). The paucity of research on the developing, low- and middle-income countries has also spurred some initiatives which led to a number of publications on the low- and medium-income countries, especially in the Southern Asia and Sub-Saharan Africa (Bukht & Heeks, 2018; Wood et al., 2019b; Wood, Graham, Lehdonvirta, & Hjorth; 2019a; Wood et al., 2018; Anwar & Graham, 2020).

These previous studies have helped in channeling a path in the forest of Gig economy research in the studied regions by providing very useful information such as the effect of platform-based algorithmic control on quality of work (Wood et al., 2019a), gig workers methods of exercising agency to earn and sustain their livelihoods in the gig economy (Anwar & Graham, 2020), development implications of the gig economy on labour (Anwar & Graham, 2021). Others are assessment of collective organisation among online freelancers (Wood et al., 2018), and possibilities of network embeddedness among gig workers and their clients (Wood et al., 2019b). The heterogeneity of the experiences, practices and labour processes within gig economies all over the world (Duggan et al., 2020), however, calls for more specific studies that could take into cognisance, the peculiarity of each country. Outcomes of such studies can lead to formation of specific research-driven policies that could better position the economy within the context of each country.

Nigeria is one of the developing countries with a massive adoption of the Internet and teeming, highly schooled yet mostly formally unemployed youth population. Nigeria has also been reported as one of the foremost countries with gig workers in the Sub-Saharan African Region (Anwar & Graham, 2020; Anwar & Graham, 2021). Furthermore, Nigeria is one of the few countries in the African region that are publicly stigmatised with substantial perpetration of the Internet scam. There is a need for ample studies about gig economy in the country to maximise its benefits to the gig workers in particular and the nation in general, despite the country's myriads of local challenges. There is, however, no known study that has been targeted on Nigeria's environment of the digital gig economy. The present study, to fill this research gap, seeks to focus primarily on the Nigerian digital gig economy environment, to understand its peculiarity and to identify some policy-related issues that can enhance the sustainability of this emerging economy in the country. To achieve the objective of the study, several specific objectives were pursued. These include determination of sources of awareness, motivating factors for involvement in digital gig works, personal positive and negative experiences of gig workers, perception of gig workers on the Nigeria's gig environment and suggestion for sustainability of the economy in the country. To achieve the objective of this study, the following research questions were explored.

1.1 *Research Questions*

1. How did Nigerian gig workers become aware of digital gig work practice?
2. What motivated Nigerian gig workers to get involved in the economy?
3. What constitute beneficial experiences of the digital gig economy to Nigerian workers?
4. What constitute unpleasant experiences of the digital gig economy to Nigerian workers?
5. How do Nigerian gig workers perceive the peculiarities of the economy in Nigeria?
6. What are Nigerian gig workers sentiment polarities based on their personal experiences and perceived peculiarity of Nigeria's environment of the digital gig economy?
7. What are their perceived means of sustaining the digital gig economy in Nigeria?

2 Methodology

This study employed a phenomenological qualitative method of research. An In-Depth Interview (IDI) method was used to gather qualitative information about the respondents' experiences with and perceptions of the Gig economy in Nigeria. A structured interview guide, having six (6) main questions, was designed to elicit information in respect to the research questions. The research instrument was assessed based on face and content validity. Snow-ball technique was used to select sixteen (16) Nigerian digital gig workers as informants in the interview. These informants, whose contacts were gotten through snow balling resided in different parts of Nigeria, namely Oyo, Lagos, Ondo, Plateau,

Delta, Anambra States of Nigeria. They were contacted remotely, through a telephone and appointments were booked for their interviews. The respondents were duly informed about the research objective, and they were allowed to give their consent to participate in the study before they were interrogated. The researcher ensured that no offensive language was used while carrying out the interview. Furthermore, confidentiality of respondents' identity was maintained. The questions were asked generally, for instance; what motivated you to get involved in digital gigs? Which positive experiences have you had as a digital gig worker? Which negative experiences have you had as a digital gig worker? From your own perspective, what are the peculiarities of digital gig work in Nigeria? The interview sessions were conducted with the informants, either on a face-to-face mode or through the mobile phone, by the researcher. The interviews were recorded on a voice capturing device and then listened to and transcribed on word processing document by two research assistants. Collected interview responses were analysed thematically. Sentiment analyses of informants' experiences were done both manually and automatically with Microsoft Excel and Orange Data Mining tool.

3 Research Findings

Demographic characteristics of the interview informants in the present study is as presented in Table 11.1.

As shown in Table 11.1, sixteen informants were interviewed, out of which 15 were male. Most (12) of the informants have bachelor's degree, three of them have postgraduate degrees while one has a Higher National Degree (HND). Most of the respondents offer writing jobs on digital gig platforms, there are also a few that offer web development, application development, transportation and voice-over artist jobs. Most of them have been engaged in gig jobs for three years. The platform used by our respondents are Fiverr and Upwork and then, Freelancer. It could also be found that some of our respondents get jobs sublet to them by some other Nigerians who are privileged to get their jobs directly from digital platforms.

4 Findings

4.1 *Getting to Know about Digital Gig Work Practice*

A question was posted to respondents to determine how they got to know about the gig economy. Their transcribed responses were first analysed with Orange data mining tool to get the word cloud representation of the contents and then

TABLE 11.1 Demographic characteristics of respondents

Respondent No.	Sex	Academic attainment	Gig service(s) rendered	Years of gig experience	Platform used
1	Male	PGD	Content Writing Creative Writing	5	From fellow Nigerians
2	Male	B. Sc	Creative Writing	4	Fiverr
3	Male	B.SC	Writing	3	Fiverr and Upwork
4	Male	B. Sc	Copywriting, Articles Writing and Web pages Content Writing	3	Upwork
5	Male	B. Sc	Content Writing	3	From fellow Nigerians
6	Male	B.Sc.	Software Engineering	3	Upwork
7	Female	HND	Content Writing Voice-over Artist	3	Upwork
8	Male	M.Sc	Website Development, Mobile Application Development, and User Interface/User Experience	6	Fiverr
9	Male	B.Sc.	Website Development	2	From Fellow Nigerians
10	Male	B.Sc.	Content Writing Copy Writing	4	Upwork Freelancers.com
11	Male	B.Sc.	Poetry Writer Also offers all possible services	6	Fiverr Upwork

TABLE 11.1 Demographic characteristics of respondents

Respondent No.	Sex	Academic attainment	Gig service(s) rendered	Years of gig experience	Platform used
12	Male	M. A.	Writing, Editing and Publishing	4	Upwork Fiverr Other Nigerians
13	Male	B. A.	Business Consultancy Writing	10	Freelancers Upwork Fiverr
14	Male	B. A.	Content Writing	3	Fiverr
15	Male	BLIS	Typing Application Development, Website Development and Graphics Design	3	Fiverr Freelancer
16	Male	B.Sc.	Transport Website Development	2	Uber, Taxify Upwork Other Nigerians

FIGURE 11.1 Word cloud representation of responses on awareness

manually to get their actual responses. The word cloud of their responses is presented in Figure 11.1.

As shown in Figure 11.1, the most prevalent words in the informants' responses are freelancing, job, friend, friends, started, school. The question posed was about freelancing jobs, hence the predominance of these two words in their responses. Other than these, a manual read-through of the responses supported the fact that most of the respondents got to know about freelancing jobs from their friend(s) as revealed in the following excerpts:

> A friend in the university.
>
> Respondent 1

> I got to know about freelancing job online from a friend and I searched more online.
>
> Respondent 3

> I got to know about freelancing from a friend.
>
> Respondent 4

> … I have this friend … , he encouraged my writing skills … He told me to go and open an account as a freelancer.… … So, I registered.
>
> Respondent 7

> I got to know about freelancing jobs from friends. They told me as a developer, they will not pay you much if you are being tied down by a company.
>
> Respondent 8

> I have friends who talk about it ... and then I studied more about it.
>
> Respondent 16

Apart from those who got to know about it through friends, there are a few others who found themselves in freelancing either through personal research or passion for writing as revealed by the following responses:

> ... I stumbled on freelancing. Through personal research....
>
> Respondent 11

> I got to know about freelancing jobs through browsing on the internet. You know sometimes when you are browsing you just come across stuffs....
>
> Respondent 15

> I kind of studied it.... I have ample amount of time to my side so I just thought about why do I not look for something else that can help me even more.
>
> Respondent 9

One of the respondents reported to have started freelancing out of passion at a time when he was not even aware of the gig economy:

> ... it started with passion to investigate things ... I link my writings to things happening around me and from there people started reading. I never knew it was freelancing then, I just write for people, and they pay ...
>
> Respondent 11

The prominence of the word 'school' shows the importance of school as a place where our respondents got to know about gig economy as shown by the excerpts:

> I have heard about it when I was in school.
>
> Respondent 4

> ... when I heard about freelancing, I was still in school.
>
> Respondent 9

.... in school....

Respondent 16

4.2 *The Motivation*

To determine the answer to this research question, respondents were asked what motivated them to get involved in providing digital gig services. Responses are presented first with word cloud representation as shown in Figure 11.2 and then thematically.

As shown in Figure 11.2, the words money, needed, motivated are very prominent among the other ones. A manual search through the responses shows that the motivating factor for getting involved in freelancing jobs was majorly money as shown by the following excerpts:

> ... when I realised that you can be earning money from it, it was appealing to me.
>
> Respondent 1

> The motivation was money. I needed money.
>
> Respondent 2

> It was the money that motivated me to get involved.
>
> Respondent 3

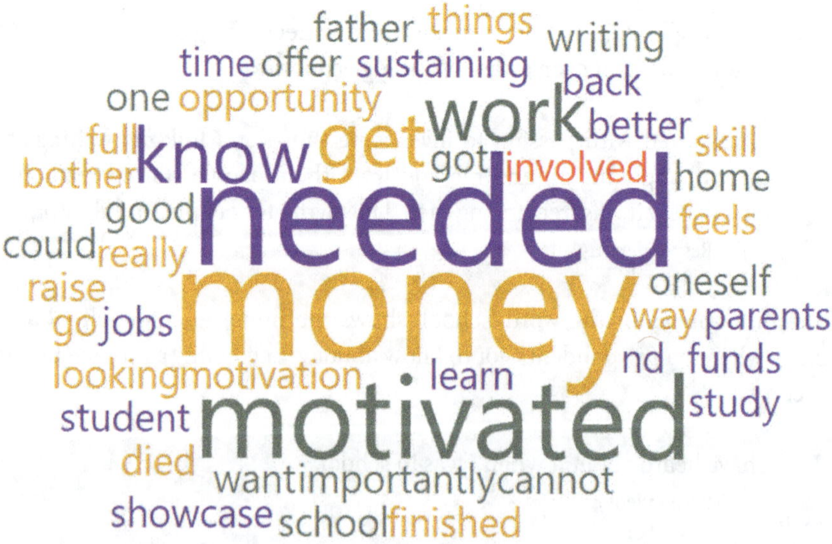

FIGURE 11.2 Word cloud representation of responses on motivation

> … I got motivated because it was an opportunity to learn, most importantly because I needed money. There were really no jobs as it were. It is a good way of sustaining oneself while looking for a better offer.
>
> Respondent 4

> … One of the things that motivated me to work then was that I needed money.
>
> Respondent 10

Some of the respondents also gave accounts of the unfavourable financial states that motivated them into getting involved in providing gig services, as shown in the following excerpts:

> You know how it feels as a student when you cannot raise funds and you do not want to bother your parents at home.…
>
> Respondent 5

> After I finished my ND, I could not go back to school full time because my father died.… so, I know I needed to work and study.
>
> Respondent 7

> The way the country is … you know outside the country, if you are a student, you can be doing something to get you money to feed yourself, you can even be paying your school fees but here as a youth, you can only face school.…
>
> Respondent 16

In addition to money, the desire to showcase one's skill was also reported as a motivating factor for getting involved in gig jobs:

> It is just to showcase my writing skill and get money out of it.
>
> Respondent 14, Male

4.3 *The Positive Experiences of Nigerian Digital Gig Workers*

To determine the answer to this research question, respondents were asked to relate their positive experiences as gig workers. Responses are presented first with word cloud representation as shown in Figure 11.3 and then thematically.

As shown in Figure 11.3, the prominent words include encouraging, good, work, writing, financial, time, amongst others. It could be inferred that the respondents have had some good and encouraging experiences with

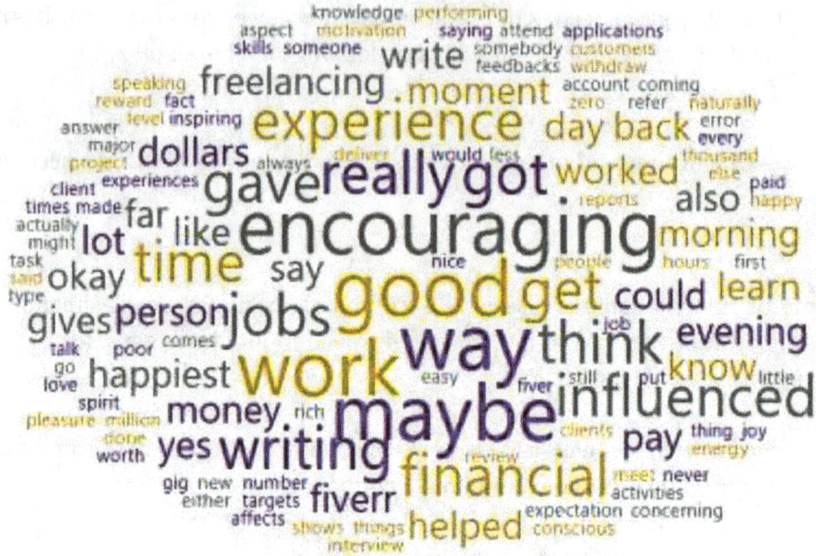

FIGURE 11.3 Word cloud representation of responses on positive experiences

the work, particularly in terms of finance and time. A manual study of the responses further buttresses these facts in addition to some other themes like clients' acceptance and appreciation of work done and opportunity for capacity building. Narrating their good experiences because of acceptance of jobs by clients, some of the responses are as presented in the following excerpts:

> My experience has been largely good, … my rejection rate has been very low. The first good experience was that the script I wrote was accepted even when I thought it would be rejected and I got another one. My second good experience was that I had course to write an essay for a Christian organisation. The client accepted it and paid an additional for an appreciation for a work well done. I also wrote a white paper for a crypto startup operation. The crypto currency pay was good, as an addition, I was given the crypto of the company.
>
> Respondent 1

> I could say that the people I have worked with have been nice … The jobs too have been easy. It is not that I deliver, and the person would say, 'No I do not like it'. It has always been good reports.
>
> Respondent 7

> Good experiences come from when you get a good review. It is really inspiring and encouraging.
>
> Respondent 12

> I think my good experience is that the feedbacks from my clients are good....
>
> Respondent 13

Some whose good experiences on the job were based on financial rewards stated:

> The only thing I can refer to as good experience is when you withdraw your money....
>
> Respondent 11

> The moment I got money out of Fiverr is my happiest moment.
>
> Respondent 14

> I think my happiest day during the work was the day I worked and got 100 dollars in just less than 3 hours ... Freelancing is so good that you can be poor in the morning and be rich in the evening. You can have zero number in your account in the morning and have a thousand dollars in the evening. That is how freelancing is.
>
> Respondent 10

> ... as far back as 2017, 2018, I made my first million on Fiverr because I did a work for someone and somebody else also gave me job. I got 4 jobs at the same time.... You could be doing 4 jobs at the same time and still meet up with the targets and expectations of the project. ...
>
> Respondent 8

> ... having a client coming back for more work shows that you know what you are doing. It was so encouraging writing and having to get paid with little energy you put into writing.
>
> Respondent 3

> ... The very first job I had, the money, I liked it....
>
> Respondent 16

Some other respondents also expressed opportunities of building up their skill capacity either with or without financial satisfaction on the jobs as shown in these excerpts:

> These Fiverr activities have done a lot on my writing skills.... May be in a way it has helped me to be more error conscious when I write. You never know when you go for an interview, it affects either the way you are speaking or most times what has helped you so far is the knowledge you had while performing the gig work ...
>
> Respondent 2

> ... The fact that I learn new things every time ... Also, the pay is a major motivation because if the pay is not there the spirit might not be there to that level of saying okay, I am happy with what I am doing ...
>
> Respondent 9

> Naturally, I love to type. Like I said, some of the applications that the person who gave me the task gave me gives me pleasure.... All that gives me joy doing them; Okay, concerning financial experience, it is not really encouraging.
>
> Respondent 15

> I think this is a Yes and No answer. It is yes because you get to learn a lot. It is a No, because the financial reward is not worth it. The financial aspect is not encouraging....
>
> Respondent 4

4.4 *The Negative Experiences of Nigerian Digital Gig Workers*

To determine the answer to this research question, respondents were asked to relate their negative experiences on gig jobs. Responses are presented first with word cloud representation as shown in Figure 11.4 and then thematically.

As shown in Figure 11.4, the prominent words are money, work, client, job, person, time amongst others. A manual study of the responses shows that there are diverse unpleasant experiences centered on these themes and some others. Many of the negative experiences could be centered on clients' rejection of jobs and attitude to gig workers as supported by the following excerpts:

> One thing is that most of the clients can be very annoying. I remembered there was a client I worked with in Tokyo, the client was frustrating. You will have to do a particular job almost ten times. You will follow what he says, and yet he will still complain, and the pay is not worth it.
>
> Respondent 5

FIGURE 11.4 Word cloud representation of responses on negative experiences

In freelancing, clients make every request that they cannot do themselves. If at least they can put themselves in the shoes of the freelancers, things will be better.

Respondent5

I have worked for someone for two weeks, after I sent the job, imagine someone telling me he cannot take the job he didn't take the job, then the offer was cancelled, and the money was refunded.

Respondent 2

… getting rejected by the client, when you have invested so much time in the work, and the client rejected the work.… very disappointing.

Respondent 3

After I had spent a couple of nights on a particular project, the client was like, what is the rubbish you have done? I needed to work on it again. He was later satisfied after like two other trials.

Respondent 9

> ... when clients decline your work and say they don't like it and you are not getting paid, that's another thing that has pissed many of us up.
>
> Respondent 14

Some respondents also complained of bad reviews received from clients:

> There are plenty of them, but I just want to share one.... I accepted about three jobs, and I did them. After doing them, I went to play. Around 5pm or so ... I checked my rating on the platform, I was in 4.98 ... Later, I was in 4.0 ... I thought it was still manageable, so I slept and when woke up ... I was already rated 3.80, ... I didn't check again throughout that day because it has affected me. I was just feeling more tired than I used to feel before. I think that is one of my bad experiences.
>
> Respondent 10

> This one has happened to me more than 10 times, they will put one star as the highest rating instead of five stars for you and once they put it you can't rate it again.
>
> Respondent 11

> Bad review. It leaves you broken. Review seems to be like an attack on your profession. Some clients can really hurt you with their words. So, you must struggle so hard. We are faced with clients who grow increasingly impatient, and they get pissed up when you don't meet up. It is putting more freelancers in anxiety mode. It can be overwhelming. Many freelancers don't have good fitness, so their anxiety piles up.
>
> Respondent 12

Some of the respondents recounted their experiences of being scammed and not getting financial remuneration for jobs done:

> I did a job for ... I completed the job; I sent it, and the guy ran away. The structure of freelancing makes it easy to be scammed.... ; Hmnn!
>
> Respondent 1

> ... the volume of Yahoo boys we have in Nigeria is not even up to the quarter of how these ... people scam. And it affects freelancers a lot.... I worked for a client for one month ... I withdrew the money, about 800

> dollars, … I discovered the client has charged back…. He went to his bank…. … that it was a fraudulent transaction. So, they renew his bank detail from Fiverr….. So, what Fiverr did was all other jobs that was done, I will not be paid until 800 dollars is completed or refunded. I have submitted, delivered and even left feedback.
>
> Respondent 11

> Yes, the unpleasant experiences I had are basically with Upwork, the money is not good. Even at the time when dollar is about 485 or 475, Upwork was still converting dollar to naira at 315 or so. It was low. The last job I did, I needed to go to studio for the person. I told the person, and he included the money on Upwork. By the time Upwork was going to convert the money, they did not pay me, and part of my workmanship went for the studio money due to the conversion. When I sent a mail about it, I was told that was the conversion to naira.
>
> Respondent 7

> My saddest moment is when they just withdraw money from my account. They can hack accounts too … They can just send you a document and you open it and once you open it, they have access to your computer (11).

> I think the disappointment is after doing your own job and you are not getting paid….
>
> Respondent 13

There were also accounts of unpleasant experiences because of workers' inability to secure gig jobs directly from platforms which resulted in doing jobs that have been sublet to them by fellow Nigerians who got jobs from digital platform.

> The lack of success in getting job directly is seriously frustrating … when you know that the people that are getting these jobs will be paying you peanuts.
>
> Respondent 1

> … many of my gig work were not gotten from Upwork like I said … it takes a lot of stress to get job and the fact that you get one, you might have

> applied 30 to 40 sometimes. So, most of the work is being sublet to us and by the time many get to us, the money is almost nothing.
>
> Respondent 4

> … with gig work especially in this part of the world, you are given a lot of work with small money and little time to be completed.
>
> Respondent 4

> In Upwork, you get people who are more understanding, but Nigerian clients are not understanding.
>
> Respondent 4

> One thing is that freelancing in Nigeria does not pay, … If you are working for someone, it does not really pay.… If you are getting gig work from a platform like Fiverr … that one pays very well.
>
> Respondent 5

Some of the informants also complained about some unpleasant experiences because of platform control:

> … then I could not register with my name and location. At that time, you must be on VPN and there was a time I forgot to turn on my VPN and my account was flagged, my account was blocked, and I lost a lot of money because my account was blocked.…
>
> Respondent 6

> … something about freelancing is blocking accounts. You might just wake up one day and Fiverr will say we don't want you again on our platform and they block your profile. Maybe you have a misunderstanding with a client and the client now reports you. Maybe you use a crossword or something. They can ask you to re-verify your information for just flimsy reasons.
>
> Respondent 11

Financial insecurity was also reported as one of the negative experiences on the digital gig jobs:

> For a while, you could get let say 5 jobs and for the next 4 or 5 months you might not get any job. Inconsistency is another problem in freelancing

> and gig. You might not get some jobs for a while. If you do not properly plan yourself by keeping the profits you make from 4 or 5 jobs, you might end up being broke.
>
> Respondent 8

> Okay, concerning financial experience, it is not really encouraging because most of the time some of these tasks that will be given to you require time.
>
> Respondent 15

4.5 *Perceptions on the Peculiarity of the Gig Economy in the Context of Nigeria*

Respondents were asked to comment freely on the Nigeria's climate of the gig economy. Some are of the opinion that the economy is new, growing, good but not for the feeble-minded ones:

> I think it is not too popular in Nigeria, people doing the work are not much in Nigeria and there are a lot of interesting things that can be done on the platform such as design, coding, and others.
>
> Respondent 3

> Uhm! Gig work in Nigeria is still growing.
>
> Respondent 4

> I think it is thriving. It is a good market that people are beginning to investigate and I think it is an unregulated market
>
> Respondent 11

> … freelancing in Nigeria is not for the feeble minded.
>
> Respondent 5

> It's a growing community … but it takes time … but you must be careful not to be lured into some other things because there are many vices. Some start as gig but before you know it, they are doing cybercrime …
>
> Respondent 16

Some also responded that engagement in gig work has helped to add values to the lives of Nigerian youths in various ways:

> There are a lot of connections. I know a lot of items through gig. It makes a lot of young people make ends meet. You could know people. It makes them make money instead of staying idle.
>
> Respondent 4

> Gig work generally … has given many writers the opportunity to be exposed to the world. I have many writers who have not taken any job, they are not working in any organisation and their life is based on Fiverr and they get at least 1,000 to 2,000 Dollars in a month. Which a normal Nigerian cannot earn in a month.
>
> Respondent 14

> It gives us opportunity to earn money from our own home, it gives us exposure, and it encourages us to do more research because if there is something I don't know that I must write about, I will have to make calls, send email and get information I want before I can start my writing. It saved many of us from depression generally, job depression.
>
> Respondent 14

Despite these possibilities, the nation's reputation has been perceived as a limiting factor in the efforts of these gig workers as can be seen by the following excerpts:

> … you know our identity as Nigerians sometimes limits our prospects especially when you want to be working remotely online. Whites see your identity and reputation as being a scammer. It's bad that we are blacks, there is already a stigma about blacks. It's not just the blackness but being Nigerians. We have that reputation of being scammers.
>
> Respondent 1

> I figured out that people pretend not to be a Nigerian by changing their identities using fake profiles and using VPN to change their locations.… A black Nigerian may pose as a white female.
>
> Respondent 1

> There is a stigma to Nigeria as a country, because Nigeria is known for some bad attitude by international communities. People especially the white men do not want to give Nigerians jobs because they believe they are scammers. It is something that is causing drawback on the platform.
>
> Respondent 2

> Also, a typical Nigerian would like to have a US account using a VPN just to make sure it is not showing a Nigerian location.
>
> Respondent 2

> The buyers see Nigerians as scammers, so most Nigerians don't use Nigerian name to get jobs. We have trust issues
>
> Respondent 3

> Getting job on Fiverr in Nigeria may be taken for a fraud.
>
> Respondent 9

> Some people buy mobile phone lines of other countries like Canada to pretend as if they are not based in Nigeria ...
>
> Respondent 16

> ... the nation itself. The fact that you are a Nigerian discourages them from giving you the job because they think everybody in Nigeria is a fraudster.
>
> Respondent 10

> It does not favor the third world country as it favors the Americans.... because of reputation and everything about the platform is about reputation.
>
> Respondent 10

Apart from the challenges faced by gig workers from the outside world due to the country's reputation, there are also the local challenges of societal resentment and stigmatisation of gig workers in Nigeria:

> I also know from friends that do freelance almost full time. People would think because this one is not going out, probably he is jobless or into yahoo.... People tends to see freelancers as jobless people.
>
> Respondent 7

> ... a lot of people are not educated about what it means to be a freelancer ... You are inside the house working so when they see you in a car, they call you a scammer. Even if you don't have a car and you are just living your life on a low income, your family will start calling you jobless, everybody around you will start saying you are not doing anything with your life, you are just wasting your time.
>
> Respondent 10

> … when you are going on the road, let us take this SARS for example, security people will stop you. They want to see your laptop and when they see you have some dollars you are in trouble…. , they start asking what you are doing because they don't understand and if you just tell them that it is for a foreign person, they say you are scammer.
>
> Respondent 10

> Even these policemen do not know anything about freelancing. Once they just see any foreign name on your system or phone, they decide that you are a Yahoo boy.
>
> Respondent 11

There is also a challenge within the community of practice of Nigerian digital gig workers, such that those who sublet jobs to others tend to be unfair as revealed by these excerpts:

> The thing about working with fellow Nigerians is that the pay is low. These guys get high pay for these jobs, but they slash it so that the writers at the end of the day will only get crumbs…. That has been my experience with Nigerians. The pay tends to be low, and the expectation tends to be high.
>
> Respondent 1

> Imagine I got a job for 20 dollars. 20 dollars is just 10 thousand naira, maybe I don't have time and I want to sublet the job at 1 thousand naira so what they do is that they keep 9 thousand sublet the job for 1 thousand and they demand for a lot of quality work.
>
> Respondent 10

> … there are times I see Nigerians on the platform looking for services, I personally avoid those people. I do not want to get involved with them.
>
> Respondent 4

Apart from these psychological challenges pointed out, very prominent are the challenges of infrastructure (electricity, data for Internet connectivity and the ban on Twitter).

> There is a certain level of difficulty with it because light can be an issue … Sometimes, you may miss deadlines because there is no light. I was robbed recently and lost my phone and laptop. I had to submit a work

that night and I could not because the electric power failed. I plugged my laptop and phones to charge that night, and both were stolen.

Respondent 1

No light. When there's no light, there is nothing you can do. If you are not rich enough to buy fuel, you might not really survive in it.

Respondent 3

Yes. Like power outages, data cost. The data charges here is higher compared to … western world…. , and we are also talking about the constant bad network of the network providers, and these clients give a short period of time.

Respondent 4

The … thing about Nigeria is electricity; as a freelancer you need 24/7 electricity because sometimes the client can give you a job on the run like they can just give you a job and tell you they want it in the next 5 or 10 or 15 minutes and sometimes you might want to make a lot of money and you access a lot of jobs and the transformer in your area suddenly gets spoilt….

Respondent 10

As a freelancer, … , you must be fast which means that the fastest guy gets the job, now you are using a network provider that is very slow, before I apply for a job, there are 10,000 other people waiting for that same job. Some of those 10,000 people are living in Dubai, US, Japan so such person will jump out before I see it. By the time I get there maybe what I will see is scraps.

Respondent 10

… we are in Nigeria where there is no light and you have gotten bid, … and maybe due to lack of light you are unable to meet up with the deadline and stuff like that.

Respondent 15

The Twitter ban dealt with a lot of freelancers because a lot of freelancers used to do what we call Twitter Ad so not been able to run Twitter Ad is going to cause a lot of issues.

Respondent 10

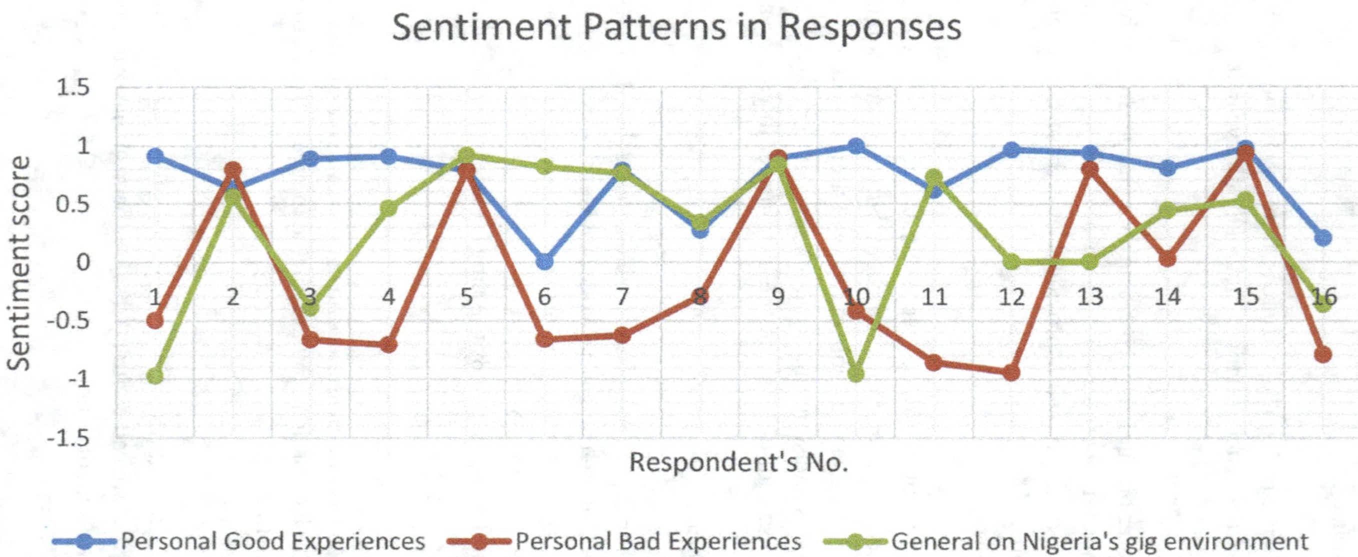

FIGURE 11.5 Sentiment polarities of gig workers' attitudes

4.6 *Sentiment Polarities of Gig Workers' Experiences*

The sentiment polarities of the informants' responses were examined to see how readily their positive or negative feelings could be determined from their responses. Figure 11.5 shows the plots of the sentiment scores of their responses.

As shown in Figure 11.5, out of the sixteen informants' responses in each case, the sentiment polarity of fifteen respondents were positive (greater than 0) for personal positive experiences, ten were negative (less than 0) in their responses on personal negative experiences while their statements on Nigeria's gig environment reflect nine (9) positive, two (2) neutral and four (4) negative sentiment polarities.

4.7 *Gig Workers' Perception on Means of Sustaining the Digital Gig Economy in Nigeria*

Respondents were asked about their perceived means of improving the digital gig economic practices in Nigeria. Their responses are categorised and presented in Figure 11.6.

As shown in Figure 11.6, respondents suggested several things that are required to improve the climate of the gig economy in Nigeria. These include introduction of minimum standard of payment, adequate provision of electric power, fast and affordable means Internet access, updating educational

FIGURE 11.6 Word cloud representation of responses on improving digital gig

curricula, enlightenment of the police, parents and youths generally about the opportunities of the gig economy, cleansing of Nigeria's reputation (name).

5 Discussion of Findings

The study showed that most of the informants in the present study got to know about the gig economy through their friends, especially in school. This result corroborates the importance of peers as agents of socialisation in digital inclusion decisions (Sasson & Mesch, 2014). The role of schools as a place for information sharing on gig economy is similar to that of previous studies (Tade, 2013; Aransiola et al., 2011; Omodunbi, Olaniyan, & Esan, 2016), that reported that institutions of higher learning are places to look out for when it comes to awareness, inclusion and perpetration of Internet scam. Furthermore, this finding is also similar to those of Koross (2016) and Okoti et al. (2019) that reported prevalence of online betting practices among youths in institutions of higher learning. This finding as corroborated by those previous studies imply that there are so many activities that go on among students in Nigeria's institutions of higher learning when it comes to their interest in and their activities towards making money from the Internet medium. This trend might not be unconnected with the submission of Aransiola et al. (2011) that the skills, tools and the level of education required in engaging in such online activities are easily available among students in Nigeria's higher institutions. These students might have also seen the potential of the Internet to enable them to make some money while in school, which the economic situation of the country might not offer them. For example, one of the informants pointed to the fact that their contemporaries in advanced countries are allowed to work and assist their parents in meeting some needs even while they are still in school, the Nigerian employment situation has not allowed this, but the Internet has proffered another opportunity for them to engage in economic activities even when they are still in school.

The predominant motivating factor for involving in gig services is the need for money. Some of the informants also expressed how gig economy has assisted them to cope with financial hardships which could have affected their academic pursuit negatively. This finding corroborates that of Aransiola et al. (2011) who reported that the incomes of majority of the Internet scam informants' parents were low. It also supports the assertion of World Bank (2016) as presented by (Wood et al., 2019a) that the growth of online labour platforms in low- and middle-income countries enables a new wave of online outsourcing that could lead to poverty reduction. This shows that gig economy has a lot of opportunities to offer Nigerian youths in enabling them to achieve some of their academic and social goals which might have been hampered due to financial incapacitation of their parents. Informants in the present study have attested to the fact that their involvement in digital gigs have brought some financial rewards. This, is one of the most important factors that lead to the positive experiences of freelancers. One of the informants related that he made his first million Naira on Fiverr because he provided a service that attracted more jobs at the same time. There were also reports of some other freelancers who were presently living on the earnings they get through digital gig services. In fact, one of the freelancers said that if the government knows how much people get through these services, the economy will be recognised and integrated in the mainstream of the nation's income. Furthermore, the study revealed that engagement in gig services has a way of improving workers' skill, confidence and expanding their capacity. Some informants related the cases of some of their colleagues who through digital gigs got permanent online jobs with international companies. For example, according to Respondent 1 'My younger sister got a job through LinkedIn and earns like a thousand dollars every month. That is close to 500 thousand naira, and it is a remote job that you can be doing at the comfort of your home'. Some also reported cases of some who started as freelancers but have grown their own businesses from the services they used to offer through digital gigs. This supports the fact that gig work has the potential to cultivate the right attitudes required to setup business and to succeed as an entrepreneur in a gig worker (Wood et al., 2018). Gig jobs, therefore, could be a means of cultivating discipline in those engaged in it.

Acceptance and appreciation by online clients are one of the foremost good experiences of gig workers. This corroborates the importance of clients in the algorithmic management of the new digital gig economy (Wood et al., 2018; Duggan et al., 2020). In the digital gig economy, clients are king even to the detriment of freelance service providers. There is a bias in the design and implementation of the digital platforms to generally favour the clients over the service providers. Little wonder then that the most valued experience of freelancers is the acceptance of services they render. This could be seen as a means of encouraging diligence and excellent delivery of jobs done by youth which could help them in future job deliveries. Conversely, what constitutes the most significant informants' negative experiences is also about clients, particularly, clients' oppressive behavior and negative reviews. Some of the informants' experiences with clients could be described as exploitative and servitude. Jobs are sometimes delivered by freelancers while clients refuse to make payments under the pretense that they are not satisfied. A particular informant related an experience where he delivered a job to a client, but the client refused to pay, claiming that he was not satisfied with the job. Unfortunately, the same job was found uploaded for sale on Amazon. This pattern appears to occur whenever there is no policy to guide the operation of digital gig platforms. In the words of *www.disobey.com/netslaves* as cited by (Terranova, 2000) 'The "NetSlaves" of the eponymous Webzine are becoming increasingly vociferous about the shamelessly exploitative nature of the job, its punishing work rhythms, and its ruthless casualization'.

Freelancers have also reported negative experiences of being scammed and the indiscriminate blocking of their accounts, by algorithmic control of digital platforms, which have led to financial loss. These experiences are similar to those reported by previous studies on African gig workers (Wood et al., 2018; Wood et al., 2019b; Anwar & Graham, 2021). It also corroborates the precarious tendencies of the emerging economy, particularly to gig workers (Duggan et al., 2020; Anwar & Graham, 2021; Healy et al., 2017). Other than these, attitudes of gig workers who sublet gig jobs to fellow Nigerians have been reported as being demeaning, while lack of financial security because of shortness and inconsistent flow of jobs is another challenge faced by gig workers. The present structure of the digital gig economy tends to encourage slavery as far as service providers' welfare is concerned. This corroborates the fact that despite the numerous benefits of this new economy, the digital platforms are being used to circumvent employment regulations, by operating informally in traditionally regulated markets at the detriment of gig service providers (Aloisi, 2016).

The perspectives of the informants on gig work in Nigeria are both positive and negative. On the positive end gig economy was reported to have created platforms for Nigerian youth to get connected to networks which they might not have been privileged to, they have also gotten exposure to useful resources and widen their scope of knowledge and skills. Financial gain, convenience of working from home and possibility of using idle time wisely have also been reported as positive perception of Nigeria's gig economy. This finding shows that gig economy has been contributing positively to the lives of Nigerians, particularly, the youths. The economy has also been reported by our informants to be new, growing but not for the feeble-minded ones. Nevertheless, the nation's reputation due to Internet scam stigmatisation is reported as a significant limiting factor to the success of gig economy in Nigeria. Nigeria has a huge population of youths whose financial needs are far from being met, some of these youths have embraced Internet scam, thereby denting the nation's reputation (Aransiola et al., 2011; Tade, 2013; Tade, 2013; Opesade, 2021a). Furthermore, many people, especially non-digital natives, particularly parents, law-enforcement agents are not knowledgeable about this emerging economy.

This has created local pressure on gig workers. Many of them face hostile reactions from people in society, some have also been mistaken for Internet scammers and punished unjustly. Some of the informants reported cases of harassment by law enforcement agents who apprehend freelancers and take them for Internet scammers. The Nigeria's ENDSARS protest that took place in October 2020 was partly a demonstration against police brutality against innocent Nigerian digital gig and start-up youths who were being mistaken for fraudulent scammers.

Apart from the challenges faced from external sources, this study also revealed levels of oppressive behavior within the circle of gig workers themselves. In this case, the ones who are privileged to get jobs from platforms sublet to others but at ridiculously low rates. This is a practice that further worsens the perception of workers about the emerging economy in Nigeria. Another unpleasant report on Nigeria's gig economy environment is that of inadequate infrastructure, particularly electricity supply and Internet connectivity. Nigeria is a developing country, one of its infrastructural maladies over the years has been irregular power supply (Opesade, 2021b).

The feelings of the informants to gig economy generally and specifically as mined from sentiment analysis of their responses revealed that they are very happy with their personal good experiences, less happy with Nigeria's environment of the gig economy and mostly unhappy with their personal bad experiences. This pattern further supports the usefulness of computational approach to identifying opinionated content (Jagdale, Shirsat, & Deshmukh, 2019; Singh, Piryani, Uddin, & Waila, 2013; Opesade, 2021c). To sustain and improve gig economy in Nigeria, it was suggested that there is a need to revive the reputation of Nigeria in the community of nations. Setting of minimum wage for gig workers, provision of adequate and constant electric power and internet access, enlightenment and education of the police and the general populace about the gig economy, review of academic curricula at secondary school level to create awareness of the economy at an earlier stage were also suggested.

6 Conclusion

It could be concluded from the present study that awareness of gig economy was mostly gotten through friends, especially in higher institutions of learning. The major motivating factor for rendering gig services is the need for money. Positive reviews, acceptance by clients, financial rewards, ability to build capacity and sharpen skills constitute workers' good experiences. They are however, dissatisfied by clients' oppressive attitudes, negative reviews, financial loss, indiscriminate blocking of accounts, oppressive behavior of fellow Nigerian gig workers who sublet jobs and inconsistent flow of income. Gig economy is an emerging economy in Nigeria. It has given a lot of benefits to Nigerian youths. It is, however, challenging for gig workers to work productively due to several psychological and infrastructural reasons. The informants' feelings about the gig economy could be appropriately mined from their responses. To sustain the economy in Nigeria, several reformations must be implemented.

7 Policy Recommendations

Considering the present mode of operation and experiences of gig workers in Nigeria, the potential benefits and possible sustainability and appropriate inclusion of Nigerian youths in the emerging digital gig economy. The following policy recommendations are made.

- It is high time that governments and adults in Nigeria understood the global revolution of the present information age. The Internet has created a generational difference in the way of living of the younger generation in an unprecedented manner. It is therefore, recommended that adults who are presently at the helms of the affairs get to learn and give room to positive exploitation of the Internet medium such as digital gigs engagement among the digital natives while curtailing its detrimental use in the form of Internet scam.
- Government of Nigeria should be opened to the emergence of the new economy and create amiable environment for its growth. This can be done by providing guiding policies for a fair structure of platform operations at the local and national levels, registration, monitoring and protection of Nigerian youths who are involved in digital gigs, provision of operation hubs where electric power and Internet could be assessed reliably and affordably.
- Provision of awareness, training and mentoring schemes for Nigerians' inclusion in digital gig should be provided by Nigerian government in partnership with reputable private organisations. This will help Nigerian youths to divert the use of their free times to profitable course and reduce vices and poverty in the country.
- Nigeria Police Force should educate their officers and acquire requisite digital forensic tools that could assist them in differentiating between Internet scam and digital gig evidence. Efforts should be made to encourage digital gigs and discourage Internet scam practices among Nigerian youths.

– Researchers, labour lawyers, economists should join the global communications on structuring the emerging gig economy in order to ensure fairness and welfare of all concerned.

References

Aloisi, A. (2016). Commoditized Workers. Case Study Research on Labour Law Issues Arising from a Set of "On-Demand/Gig Economy" Platforms. *Comparative Labor Law&Policy Journal, 37*(3). https://doi.org/10.2139/ssrn.2637485.

Anwar, M. A., & Graham, M. (2020). Hidden transcripts of the gig economy: labour agency and the new art of resistance among African gig workers. *Environment and Planning A, 52*(7), 1269–1291. https://doi.org/10.1177/0308518X19894584.

Anwar, M. A., & Graham, M. (2021). Between a rock and a hard place: Freedom, flexibility, precarity and vulnerability in the gig economy in Africa. *Competition and Change, 25*(2), 237–258. https://doi.org/10.1177/1024529420914473.

Aransiola, J. O., Ph, D., Asindemade, S. O., & Sc, M. (2011). *Understanding Cybercrime Perpetrators and the Strategies They Employ in Nigeria. 14*(12). https://doi.org/10.1089/cyber.2010.0307.

Barratt, T., Goods, C., & Veen, A. (2020). 'I'm my own boss …': Active intermediation and 'entrepreneurial' worker agency in the Australian gig-economy. *Environment and Planning A, 52*(8), 1643–1661. https://doi.org/10.1177/0308518X20914346.

Bryant, A. (2020). Liquid uncertainty, chaos and complexity: The gig economy and the open source movement. *Thesis Eleven, 156*(1), 45–66. https://doi.org/10.1177/0725513619898286.

Bukht, R., & Heeks, R. (2018). *Development Informatics Working Paper Series. February 2019*. https://doi.org/10.17323/1996-7845-2018-02-07.

Dokko, J., Mumford, M., & Schanzenbach, D. W. (2015). Workers and the Online Gig Economy. *The Hamilton Project*, 1–8.

Duggan, J., Sherman, U., Carbery, R., & McDonnell, A. (2020). Algorithmic management and app-work in the gig economy: A research agenda for employment relations and HRM. *Human Resource Management Journal, 30*(1), 114–132. https://doi.org/10.1111/1748-8583.12258.

Friedman, G. (2014). Workers without employers: Shadow corporations and the rise of the gig economy. *Review of Keynesian Economics*, 2(2), 171–188. https://doi.org/10.4337/roke.2014.02.03.

Graham, M., Hjorth, I., & Lehdonvirta, V. (2017). Digital labour and development: impacts of global digital labour platforms and the gig economy on worker livelihoods. *Transfer, 23*(2), 135–162. https://doi.org/10.1177/1024258916687250.

Healy, J., Nicholson, D., & Pekarek, A. (2017). Should we take the gig economy seriously? *Labour & Industry: A Journal of the Social and Economic Relations of Work*, *27*(3), 232–248. https://doi.org/10.1080/10301763.2017.1377048.

Jagdale, R. S., Shirsat, V. S., & Deshmukh, S. N. (2019). Sentiment Analysis on Product Reviews Using Machine Learning Techniques. *Proceeding of CISC 2017 Sentiment Analysis on Product Reviews Using Machine Learning Techniques*, *January*. https://doi.org/10.1007/978-981-13-0617-4.

Koross, R. (2016). University Students Gambling : Examining the Effects of Betting on Kenyan University Students ' Behavior. *International Journal of Liberal Arts and Social Science*, *4*(8), 57–66.

Nath, H. K. (2017). *The Information Society*. *March*. https://doi.org/10.20896/saci.v4i3.248.

Ng'weno, A., & Porteous, D. (2018). Let 's Be Real: The Informal Sector and the Gig Economy are the Future , and the Present, of Work in Africa. *Center for Global Development*, *Figure 1*, 1–8.

Okoti, D., Ogula, P. A., & Munyua, J. k. (2019). Extent of Students' Involvement in Sports Betting in Public Secondary Schools in Mumias East Sub-County, Kenya. *British Journal of Education*, *7*(9), 75–88.

Omodunbi, B., Olaniyan, O., & Esan, A. (2016). *Cybercrimes in Nigeria: Analysis, Detection and Prevention*. *October 2017*.

Opesade, A. O. (2021). *Twitter-Mediated Enterprise – Customer Communication : Case of Electricity Distribution Services in a Developing Country*. *6*, 1–17. https://doi.org/10.1177/08944393211019571.

Opesade, Adeola O. (2021a). Comparison of Sentiment-Lexicon-based and Topic-based Sentiment Analysis Approaches on E-Commerce Datasets. *International Conference on Advanced Engineering, Technology and Applications* (ICAETA).

Opesade, Adeola O. (2021b). Cybercrime and Cybercrime Policing in Nigeria : Findings from Oyo State Police Data on ICT-Related Cases. *University of Ibadan Journal of Science and Logics in ICT Research*, *6*(1), 1–17.

Petriglieri, G., Ashford, S. J., & Wrzesniewski, A. (2019). Agony and Ecstasy in the Gig Economy: Cultivating Holding Environments for Precarious and Personalized Work Identities. *Administrative Science Quarterly*, *64*(1), 124–170. https://doi.org/10.1177/0001839218759646.

Sasson, H., & Mesch, G. (2014). Computers in Human Behavior Parental mediation, peer norms and risky online behavior among adolescents. *Computers in Human Behavior*, *33*, 32–38. https://doi.org/10.1016/j.chb.2013.12.025.

Singh, V. K., Piryani, R., Uddin, A., & Waila, P. (2013). *Sentiment Analysis of Textual Reviews*. *December 2015*. https://doi.org/10.1109/KST.2013.6512800.

Tade, O. (2013). A Spiritual Dimension to Cybercrime in Nigeria : The ' Yahoo Plus ' Phenomenon. 2012, 689–705. https://doi.org/10.2478/s13374-013-0158-9.

Terranova, T. (2000). Free Labor: Producing Culture for the Digital Economy. *Social Text, 18*(2), 33–58.

Wood, Alex, J., Lehdonvirta, V., & Graham, M. (2018). Workers of the Internet unite? Online freelancer organisation among remote gig economy workers in six Asian and African countries. *New Technology, Work and Employment, 33*(2), 95–112. https://doi.org/10.1111/ntwe.12112.

Wood, A. J., Graham, M., Lehdonvirta, V., & Hjorth, I. (2019a). Good Gig, Bad Gig: Autonomy and Algorithmic Control in the Global Gig Economy. *Work, Employment and Society, 33*(1), 56–75. https://doi.org/10.1177/0950017018785616.

Wood, A. J., Graham, M., Lehdonvirta, V., & Hjorth, I. (2019b). Networked but Commodified: The (Dis)Embeddedness of Digital Labour in the Gig Economy. *Sociology, 53*(5), 931–950. https://doi.org/10.1177/0038038519828906.

Wood, A., & Lehdonvirta, V. (2021). Platform Precarity: surviving algorithmic insecurity in the gig economy. *SSRN Electronic Journal*, 1–48. https://doi.org/10.2139/ssrn.3795375.

Woodcock, J., & Graham, M. (2020). *The Gig Economy: A Critical Introduction*. Polity Press. https://doi.org/10.1080/00130095.2020.1831908.

CHAPTER 12

Decent Work, Informality and Pandemic: Empirical Insights from Ghana

Alex Anlesinya and Joseph Gerald Tetteh Nyanyofio

1 Introduction

Decent work is an essential aspect of people's life as it plays crucial roles in improving national and individual wellbeing (Anlesinya & Amponsah-Tawiah, 2020; Anlesinya, Amponsah-Tawiah, Adom, Damoah & Dartey-Baah, 2021) and eradicating poverty (United Nations, 2020). Decent work is defined as workers' overall "aspirations for opportunity and income; rights, voice and recognition; family stability and personal development; and fairness and gender equality" (International Labour Organisation [ILO], 1999, p. 3). During its 90th session of International Labour Conference on Decent Work and the Informal Economy, the ILO, recognised the resilience and dynamism of informal workers while agreeing to address the vulnerabilities that are associated with informal work and employment (ILO, 2002a, 2023) through a decent work agenda. Consequently, they highlighted the need to prioritise decent work for informal workers and not just the formal workers (Anlesinya & Nyanyofio, 2023; ILO, 2002b), and is in alignment with the United Nations' Sustainable Development Goal 8, which is concerned with ensuring inclusive growth and decent work for everybody.

The concept of informal sector work, which was originally developed in Ghana by a British economic anthropologist, Keith Hart in the 1970s (see Hart, 1970, 1972, 1973), means an unregistered employment and which often is not or insufficiently covered by formal arrangements like pensions, medical insurance, and paid sick or annual leave entitlements (Baah-Boateng & Vanek, 2020). Informal workers constitute about 60% of employment globally, 90% in developing countries, and 85.8% in Africa (ILO, 2018). In Ghana, the share of informal workers of all employment is 89% (Baah-Boateng & Vanek, 2020). Thus, it accommodates a significant number of developing countries' active working population (Omobowale & Omobowale, 2019; Omobowale, Oyelade, Omobowale & Falase, 2020).

Despite this, they continue to face significant decent work problems; with the outbreak of the Covid-19 pandemic further exacerbating their employment

 | DOI:10.1163/9789004692657_014

vulnerability. According to ILO (2020), the pandemic has affected about 76% of informal employment globally, and informal workers lost about 60% of their meagre earnings due to Covid-19 restrictions. This is a worrying situation as many informal workers have insufficient buffers (ILO, 2020), and limited access to finance (Megersa, 2020) and social security interventions (Baah-Boateng & Vanek, 2020). This suggests that the pandemic has created significant decent work challenges for informal workers and empirical knowledge could play a vital role in addressing decent work issues in the informal sector. However, decent work experiences of informal workers are less-researched empirically, with Monteith and Giesbert's (2017) study being a notable exception as previous related researches were limited to themes such as the role of informal workers/economy in economic growth (e.g. Debrah, 2007; Etim & Daramola, 2020), skills development (Magidi & Mahiya, 2021), characteristics of informal enterprises (Darbi, Hall & Knott, 2018), and drivers of informality (Etim & Daramola, 2020).

Hence, our study aims to, firstly, assess informal workers' general perception of decent work experience; and secondly, examine the impact of the Covid-19 pandemic on informal workers' decent work experience. We explored these objectives by integrating decent work perspectives from the fields of economics, sociology, and psychology, and used qualitative evidence from informal workers in Ghana. We used Ghana because of its historical and theoretical significance in the field of informal sector work and decent work. As earlier indicated, the theory of informal work was developed in Ghana (see Hart, 1970, 1972, 1973). Similarly, the ILO's agenda of decent work and local economic development was first piloted in Ghana in 2002 (see ILO, 2012), but there is no scholarly assessment of the decent work experience of Ghanaian informal workers.

The contribution of this chapter is in five-folds. First, it advances the limited informal sector decent work scholarship generally and specifically amidst a global pandemic. Second, it contributes to the integrated theory of decent informal work by integrating theoretical perspectives on decent work from the fields of economics, sociology, and psychology to bring to the fore key instrumental (economic) and intrinsic (psycho-social) drivers of informal workers' decent work experience. Third, it reveals the role of the Covid-19 pandemic in depleting buffers of decent work in the informal economy. Fourth, our empirical evidence re-echoes the need to prioritise decent work agenda for informal workers and further draws attention to the development of critical policy interventions which can serve as coping resources for informal workers against the depletion of their decent work attributes during and after the pandemic. Finally, it fills empirical voids on decent work literature in Ghana. The next sections present the literature, research method, empirical results, and discussion of implications and conclusion.

2 Theory and Literature Review

2.1 *Theoretical Frameworks of Decent Work*

The ILO's decent work agenda is anchored on four key pillars: quality job creation; protection of workers' rights; existence of social protection; and promotion of social dialogue (ILO, 1999). Thus, in simple terms, decent work means a better quality work/job and dignified employment, which further indicates the work gives the job holder guaranteed earnings, stability and security, safe working conditions, freedom, fair treatment, growth opportunities and pride in employment.

Decent work is central to sustainable development (Anlesinya et al., 2021) and advocates for developments that contribute to the elimination of dangerous working conditions, precarious employment, unemployment, child labour as well as forced labour (UNDP, 2015). In Sen's (1975) views, decent work is one of the fastest ways of achieving development because it enhances national productivity (i.e. the production aspect); its income aspect in the form of fair and adequate wage improves workers' purchasing power; and its recognition aspect in the form of workers' sense of fairness and wellbeing aids in achieving crucial psychological and social outcomes. This is similar to Anlesinya et al.'s (2021) evidence that decent work is multi-dimensional in nature and its psychosocial and economic dimensions contribute to better national economic and psychological wellbeing in developing countries.

Thus, decent work is viewed from the theoretical perspectives of three key academic fields: economy, sociology, or psychology (Monteith & Giesbert, 2017). The economic theory makes monetary remunerations like income, insurances, fringe benefits and pensions central to the decent work agenda because a work that is adequately rewarded is necessary for people to engage in utility-maximising behaviours (Dahl, Nesheim & Olsen, 2009). The limitation of this theoretical perspective, however, is its general neglect of non-monetary features and outcomes of work, which equally contribute to people's notion of a better quality work relative to monetary features. For instance, Achdut and Stier (2021) found that people attach more importance to non-monetary features of job quality (e.g. like their own skills and occupation, availability of standard employment contracts) than the monetary features of a job (such as wages). Jencks, Perman and Rainwater (1988) similarly found that non-monetary aspects of work make a job more desirable than the monetary attributes (earnings).

With respect to the perspectives of the sociological theory, attributes of a decent work include skilled work, occupational status, and autonomy (Green, 2006). However, this approach to evaluating decent work fails to adequately emphasise the preferences of the worker (Gallie, 1996). In contrast, the psychological perspective emphasises more of the non-monetary attributes of decent work (Deranty, 2009). Decent work is conceptualised based on the intrinsic versus extrinsic attributes of work as advanced by Herzberg's two-factor theory of job satisfaction. It suggests that conditions intrinsic to work like autonomy, achievements and recognition, responsibility, and challenging and interesting work give employees greater satisfaction but factors extrinsic to work like supervision and pay only prevent dissatisfaction (Herzberg, Mausner & Sydermann, 1959).

In the light of the above, our study draws on these different theoretical perspectives to permit a more holistic assessment of decent work among informal workers through their integrative roles. This is consistent with the approach of the ILO's 'Decent Work' initiative, which incorporates both characteristics and outcomes of work based on different but complementary theoretical perspectives.

2.2 *The Informal Sector – Emergence, Nature, and Theoretical Debates*

The concept of 'informal sector' was coined by Keith Hart, a British economic anthropologist through a series of researches in Accra among migrants from northern Ghana in the 1970s. Hart (1970; 1972; 1973) examined the strategies used by poor city dwellers in Accra to generate income. His researches on Ghana produced significant amounts of literature regarding the conceptual, methodological and policy debates in the circles of development studies and economics (Maloney, 2004; Rakowski, 1994). Subsequently, the term gained international acceptance after it was popularised by the ILO's Employment Mission to Kenya who used the term to examine economic activities in Kenya (ILO, 2002). From then, the term "informal sector" emerged as a field of study in different disciplines. The term is used interchangeably with informal economy or shadow economy.

Informal sector enterprises and their workers are usually not registered, and employment in this sector is not or is insufficiently governed by formal work arrangements (Baah-Boateng & Vanek, 2020). Informal sector workers are "self-employed (operate on own account) or employees in informal enterprises (i.e., unincorporated economic units that are not registered with national authorities) and, as a result, do not have access to social insurance, or are contributing family workers". It also includes employees of formal firms and households who do not benefit from social insurance (Carré, 2020, p. 53). Thus, it is thoseaspects of a country's economy that are not regulated (Omobowale et al., 2020).

However, it does not imply that there are no rules or norms that govern the activities of workers and operations of informal sector enterprises. The sector has its own informal rules, institutional arrangements and structures for mutual help and trust (ILO, 2002), and are considered as "legitimate" within the established norms, values, and beliefs within a country (Webb, Tihanyi, Ireland & Sirmon, 2009). Consequently, informal workers are individuals whose work and employment are not formally regulated, or are insufficiently governed by formal work arrangements, but are not illegal and illegitimate from the stance of the established informal institutions in a particular country.

A key debate in the informal economy literature is the kind of strategies that poor people in society employ to supplement their incomes (Debrah, 2007). This aspect of Hart's (1973) research work in Ghana started a recurrent debate about the characterisations of the informal economy between marginalists and structuralists. The marginalists consider the informal economy as peripheral (marginal) to socio-economic development (Leonard, 2000; Schneider, 2012). In their views, the informal economy is transitory so the organisation of its business model will be changed as modern capitalism develops. Besides, it only engages in activities and generates incomes in support of people's survival or subsistence. Relatedly, because it is a peripheral economy, it will disappear with the development of capitalism (Huang, Xue & Wang, 2020; Portes & Sassen-Koob, 1987).

However, the structuralists like the ILO, and the World Bank argue that the informal economy is alternative, vibrant, dynamic, and lasting forms of economic activity because it is a reservoir for the facilitation of local entrepreneurship development, job creation and growth (Leonard, 2000; Debrah, 2007). The above claims have been consistently affirmed, which suggest that the informal economy is a major source of employment, income, and livelihood for most people (see Baah-Boateng & Vanek, 2020; ILO, 2018; Omobowale et al., 2020). Hence, to structuralists, the informal sector is not the by-product of inadequate state intervention but rather a victim of excessive intervention by the state via focusing more on a small and inefficient formal sector. This, consequently, compels most people to meet their own needs outside the boundaries of the formal institutions and rules governing the formal aspect of a country's economy (Meagher, 1995). This is consistent with a study in Ghana by WIEGO (2021), which found that Ghanaian informal workers lack legal and social protections and face issues of harassment, eviction, and fines in the course of their work even though they make substantial contributions to socio-economic development in the country.

2.3 *Decent Work Issues in the Informal Economy*

Decent work issues are prevalent among workers in the informal economy. Self-employed, unregulated wage workers as well as domestic workers deserve better decent work experience, and not just formal sector workers (ILO, 2002). Unfortunately, many forms of work in the informal economy tend to lack decent work attributes so decent work deficit is high and common among informal workers. According to Baah-Boateng and Vanek (2020), Bulut (2015) and others, a significant number of types of work and employment in the informal economy are characterised by poor remunerated, dangerous working conditions, and absence of security of work, which in turn, increase the vulnerability of informal workers.

Earlier, ILO (2002) noted that "poor-quality, unproductive and unremunerative jobs that are not recognised or protected by law, the absence of rights at work, inadequate social protection, and the lack of representation and voice are most pronounced in the informal economy" (p4). Relatedly, Monteith and Giesbert's (2017) study in the capital cities of Uganda, Burkina Faso and Sri Lanka found that informal workers consider a work to be decent if it has a combination of instrumental features of work, like income, working hours, good health, and survival, as well as intrinsic characteristics of work like relationships, freedom and independence, and social recognition. While this research provides useful insights on the topic, there is a dearth of similar studies in Ghana.

2.4 *Covid-19 Impact on Perception of Decent Work in the Informal Economy*

The outbreak of Covid-19 in Wuhan, China, was declared as a pandemic on March 11, 2020 by the World Health Organisation (WHO). As of 18th October, 2021 over two hundred and forty million (240,061,454) were confirmed to have contracted the virus with nearly five million fatalities (4,887,600) globally. The African situation as of the same date was over six million (6,109,365) confirmed cases and over one million (149,041) deaths (WHO, 2021). Ghana's index case was reported on March 12, 2020; and as of October 18, 2021 recorded 129,440 confirmed cases and 1,167 deaths (Ghana Health Service, 2021).

Even though the Covid-19 pandemic affected workers in both the formal and informal sectors, informal workers are more vulnerable to decent work deficits and are exposed to greater risk of losing their livelihoods in the Covid-19 pandemic era. Informal workers lost about 60% of their meagre income and earnings due to Covid-19 restrictions (ILO, 2020), which makes it difficult for them to be able to earn daily income. The full and partial shutdown of their informal businesses has therefore pushed several of them below the poverty line (ILO, 2020; Omobowale et al., 2020) as a few days of absence from work increases their financial vulnerability since they will not be able to make their earnings and livelihood from their daily informal work operations (Megersa, 2020). A research in Ghana by WIEGO (2021) indicated that even though most informal workers are back to work after the lifting of the lockdown, they have not been able to recover their earnings or incomes.

This is a worrying situation because many informal workers have insufficient buffers (ILO, 2020), and limited access to finance (Megersa, 2020) and social security like pensions and medical insurance (Baah-Boateng & Vanek, 2020). Consequently, informal business owners are most likely to rely on their business capital to meet their personal consumption needs and for the survival of their families (ILO, 2020). Besides, the Covid-19 raises the threats of poor health and safety challenges inherent in formal work. Informal workers like traders operate in overcrowded places while street hawkers have very little or no access to handwashing facilities to enable them to comply with relevant prevention protocols to ensure their protection against the Covid-19 virus. Thus, the pandemic has made informal workers very vulnerable to health and economic shocks (ILO, 2020; Rogan & Skinner, 2020). Consequently our study aimed to empirically assess the perception of decent work among informal workers amidst Covid-19 pandemic focusing on Ghana.

3 Research Method

3.1 *Research Design and Sample*

We employed the abductive approach (using pre-determined codes based on the outlined theories and emergent codes) and qualitative method (Miles & Huberman, 1994). This helped us to capture insights from the experiences of informal workers and develop a deep understanding of their decent work experiences generally and in the era of a global calamity (Covid-19) Accra, Ghana specifically. According to Baah-Boateng and Vanek's (2020) analyses, the Greater Accra Region constituted more than half (56%; 889,099) of total employment in Ghana. Similarly, Accra contributes to about 80% of confirmed cases of the Covid-19 infections in the country (Ghana Health Service, 2021). Hence, we conducted our study in selected markets in Accra and its

TABLE 12.1 Profile of research participants

No.	Age	Gender	Education	Nature of business	Weekly working hours
P1.	71	Female	Middle School	Jewelry /cosmetics	66 hours
P2.	57	Female	Middle School	Sorghum/Cereals	66 hours
P3.	58	Female	Middle School	Corn Dough	66 hours
P. 4	56	Male	Senior High	Abattoir	66 hours
P5.	70	Female	No formal	Meat products	66 hours
P6.	74	Female	Senior High	Tea	66 hours
P7.	63	Female	Middle School	Provisions	66 hours
P8.	48	Female	Senior High	Vegetables	66 hours
P9.	71	Female	Middle School	Cassava and plantain	66 hours
P10.	52	Female	Middle school	Herbs	66 hours
P11.	37	Female	Primary	Fish Monger	66 hours
P12.	60	Female	Middle school	Distribution	66 hours
P13.	54	Female	Senior High	Rubber products	66 hours
P14.	43	Male	Junior High	Electrician	54 hours
P15.	42	Male	Technical	Carpenter	66 hours
P16.	34	Male	Senior High	Graphic designer	66 hours
P17.	39	Female	Junior Secondary	Merchant	66 hours
P18.	44	Female	Junior Secondary	Hairdresser	66 hours
P19.	39	Male	Junior Secondary	Footwear/ leatherworks	66 hours
P20.	42	Male	Junior Secondary	Hair stylist	66 hours

environs due to the sheer number of informal workers in the area; and the fact that Accra is Ghana's Covid-19 epicenter coupled with its historical and theoretical importance in the theory of informal economy. Using the purposive sampling method, we selected twenty (20) informal sector workers from different sub-segments of the Ghanaian informal economy for the study to organize two focus group discussions. Table 12.1 showed the demographic profile of the research participants. From the table, most of the respondents were women because traditionally women are dominant in informal works (see Anlesinya, Adepoju & Richter, 2019; Baah-Boateng & Vanek, 2020). Their overall level of education and long working hours is typical of the Ghanaian informal sector (see Baah-Boateng & Vanek, 2020).

3.2 *Data Collection*

As indicated, we conducted two (2) focus group discussions in two major markets in Accra as a means of gathering the study's data. We used the focus group discussion method because it has the capacity to develop interest and a rich debate among research participants to generate insightful data on the issues compared to other data collection methods (Ely, 1994). We were able to achieve this by leveraging the existing rapport between participants as well as by encouraging open and frank discussions (Ely, 1994). Following Monteith and Giesbert (2017), we asked respondents to indicate the aspects of their work they like the most and aspects they do not like. These helped us to ascertain their perception of decent and how it was impacted by the Covid-19 pandemic. The focus group discussions were conducted in compliance with research ethical guidelines, and Covid-19 prevention protocols; particularly, social distancing, and masking.

3.3 *Data Analyses*

We adopted a flexible coding protocol comprising of theory-driven codes and emergent codes, which ensured that we had increased ability to dig into the data via several assessments of the transcripts to generate new interpretations for both verification and contradiction (Miles & Huberman, 1994). The thematic data analysis technique was applied for the analyses to present the results using themes that emerged from the assessment of the transcripts (Creswell, 2014), as well as using specific quotes that are representative of major themes from the transcripts of the focus group discussions to support the analyses (Anderson, 2010). In all, we identified two major over-arching themes: (1) *Perception of decent informal work*, and (2) *Covid-19's impact of informal workers' decent work experience*. The data abstraction process and data structure is shown in Figure 12.1.

4 Empirical Results

In this section, we organised and presented the analyses and results under the two overarching research themes.

4.1 *Perception of Decent Informal Work*

Our first aim was to investigate the perception of decent work among Ghanaian informal workers. The analyses revealed that work characteristics that generate decent work experiences among informal workers are: adequate income and survival; fulfilling and meaningful work; health, safety and wellbeing; social recognition and mobility; and autonomy and control. However, the

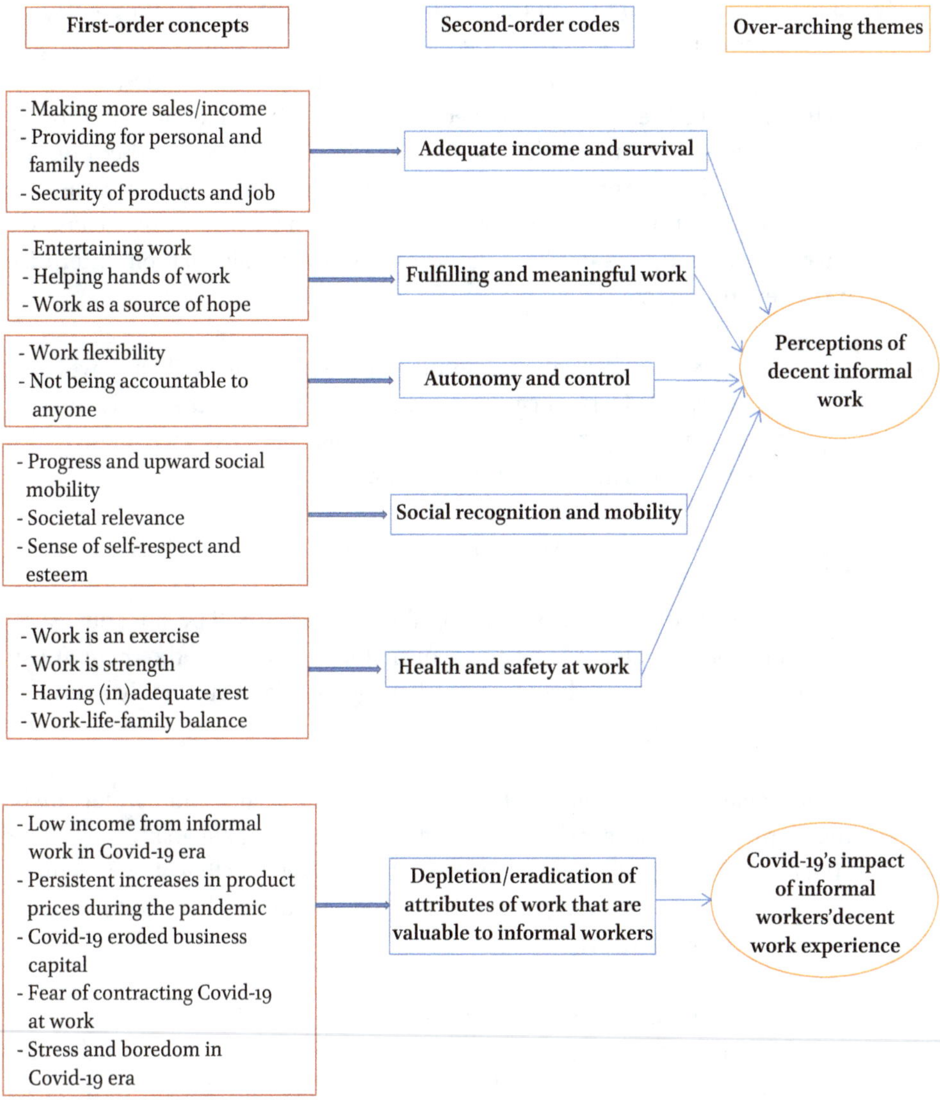

FIGURE 12.1 Data abstraction and data structure of decent work in the informal sector amidst Covid-19

majority attach more significance to adequate income and survival than the others.

4.1.1 Adequate Income and Survival

One of the features that are valuable for decent work experience among informal workers is adequate income and survival, and it concerns income generation from their work activities. Our respondents observed that they become happy with their work when they make more sales since it is an opportunity to earn more income to take proper care of themselves and their families in terms of the provision of basic needs of survival like food, clothes, shelter as well as meeting the educational needs of their children. This view is strongly shared across different genders and occupational segments of the informal economy in Ghana. For instance, a 34 year old male graphic designer was very emphatic in stating that "money is the main reason why we work because we have to take care of family". Similarly, a 56 year old male abattoir enterprise owner expressed that:

> You must eat when you get home and members of the family will also have to eat. At least you get excited when people buy the goods you sell. When our wives are earning a lot from their business and the men also support with their money, there is always food at home.

This was reiterated by a 39 year old female merchant who emphasised that:

> If you do not work, you will not be able to feed yourself because our wards must be educated. We take care of them, we eat, we clothe them. If you decide not to work because of this pandemic, all your family members will be hungry.

Another element of income and survival is physical security and protection of their products/shops against burglary. For instance, a male abattoir operator stated that 'security is a major concern at the market. Stealing of our products discourages us from coming to the market. If the little you have is stolen, then what will you work with?'

4.1.2 Fulfilling and Meaningful Work

Fulfilling and meaningful work is a work characteristic that is much cherished by informal workers. A fulfilling and meaningful informal work based on the viewpoints of our research participants is entertaining, a source of hope and provides the opportunity to exercise the 'helping hands of work' (i.e. excitement of helping people through work). On entertaining work and hope, they explained that coming to work is fun and is important to them as it gives them the opportunity to crack and share jokes among themselves, thereby making them happy. Hence, sitting at home and not coming to work deprives them of the benefit of work and happiness (i.e. entertaining themselves at work), which is an important source of hope that they will have better days ahead of them. According to a 57 year old female sorghum and cereals trader:

> What inspire some of us are the jokes we share among ourselves. You miss these jokes when you sit at home and so you feel like coming to the market to entertain yourself regardless of the very low sales you may make.

In a similar fashion, a 54 year old female trader in rubber products noted that:

> We are happy when people crack jokes. We watch what people do and are excited as well. We come to the market to have fun. The fun gives us hope that things will get better one day.

Besides, the opportunity to help and serve people through work is valuable to many informal workers (i.e. the helping hands of work). Based on the insights we have generated from our participants' responses, 'helping hands of work' means doing good work for or rendering good services to clients and resisting the urge to cut corners; sometimes charging below the required service/ product costs, and providing free service for minor works. They added that although money is very important, one's success or blessings from helping others through their work can be unimaginable. It makes them develop relationships that generate future benefits that are far and above what they would economically gained today since making money the centre of every relationship with clients has the tendency to destroy what could have been lasting mutual business relationships in the form of referrals, and bigger economically rewarding contracts.

In the views of a 43 year old male electrician:

> I feel sad when I get to see the kind of work other artisans execute for some clients. When someone's light goes off, you should not go and destroy other things while fixing another problem. Sometimes I refuse to take money for doing work for clients which I consider to be minor. I do it wholeheartedly and sometimes the person may even offer you some gifts based on that kind gesture.

Another respondent similarly expressed that:

> When you help people, your blessings come from different sources beyond your expectation. I am excited about helping people with my work. It is better to work and be blessed than to make money your focus before working for someone. If we decide to focus on money we may ruin relationships.
>
> Male, 34, Graph Designer

Likewise, a 39 year old male footwear/leatherwork artisan stated that:

> Sometimes when I look at what the work entails, I am unable to charge so I do it for free because it does not worry me. It does not affect me nor does it even make me lose. So, I do it for free. Through the person, I may get another client to work for. It happens often.

While there is a consensus among both genders about the features that make their informal work fulfilling and meaningful, female informal workers (especially traders) valued entertaining work more than their male counterparts; but the men (particularly, artisans) valued the 'helping hands of work' more than female counterparts (market traders). This implies that gender, personality, and personal values of informal workers may determine how they view their work as being fulfilling and meaningful.

4.1.3 Health, Safety, and Wellbeing

Health, safety, and wellbeing is an important source of decent work experience for informal workers. Health, safety, and wellbeing is constructed and expressed by informal workers severally as work is an exercise, work is strength, and better work-life-family balance. Many of the participants agreed that their work aids in improving their health and safety because it gives them the opportunity to engage in physical activities or exercises. For instance, a 54 year old female rubber products trader stated that 'the work is a form of exercise because you sweat when you go. As you work daily, your body becomes active'. Similarly, informal workers consider their work as a valuable source of strength. To them, 'coming to work gives you strength. We can't just sit at home. You will be ill if you are restricted from coming to work' (*male, abattoir owner*).

However, some constructed the importance of health, safety, and wellbeing in a negative sense by stating that they hardly get time to rest while others complained of not having quality time with their family. For instance, *a female, jewelry/cosmetics trader* lamented that 'we go to the market and sell and return home very late when the children are asleep. We are really suffering!'. Another, a 37 year old female fish monger, noted that 'I don't get to spend enough time with my family. I don't get home early like I used to so my children would be asleep by the time I get home. This has affected the way I used to discipline my children'. The above views are clearly supported by the average working hours of the respondents as shown in (table 12.1), where they reported working for 54–66 hours weekly.

4.1.4 Social Recognition and Mobility

Informal workers attach a great deal of value to the ability of their work to aid them achieve progress and upward social mobility; a sense of self-respect and esteem; and societal relevance. They belief it is possible for them to achieve societal recognition and progress by meeting the educational needs of their children up to the university level through their work, and consequently, raise their personal status as well in their communities. This view is also negatively expressed by some respondents in the sense that they expected higher respect for their work. As stated by a 70 year old meat product trader, 'as we progress, we are taking care of the children to attend university so they become successful men and women. I don't expect any of my children to sell at the market. I want all of them to succeed in life so that I will be respected'.

4.1.5 Autonomy and Control

Informal workers cherished the autonomy and control they have in their work. The benefits of work flexibility and not being accountable to anyone are very important to them. According to a female hairdresser, 'I am not accountable to anyone and that's why I like my work like the time I close too. There are instances where people work for other people and are unable to take care of their children because they are working for other people. That is not profitable. I like my work'.

The above features of decent informal work are summarised and mapped onto the main underlying theoretical perspectives in Figure 12.2.

4.2 *Covid-19's Impact of Informal Workers' Decent Work Experience*

Our analyses showed that the Covid-19 pandemic has negatively affected the decent work experience of informal areas through its impact on several of the features of a decent work in the informal sector work discussed earlier. The respondents unanimously expressed unhappiness about the inability to generate adequate income from their informal enterprises because the pandemic has caused their sales revenue to drastically reduce through (1) developing a sense of fear of contracting the virus among their clients and so many are reluctant to step into their informal workplaces; (2) causing the supply costs of their product to increase persistently; (3) causing formal sector workers, who are key patrons of their products and services, to lose their jobs; (4) placing restrictions on the opening and closing of marketplaces; and (5) low social occasions and activities.

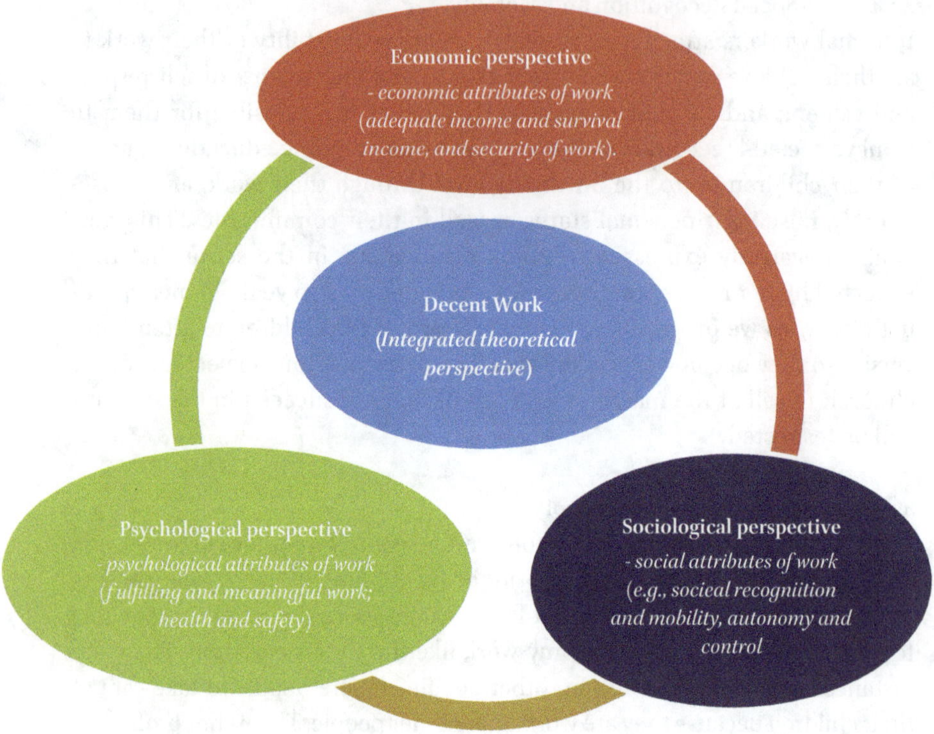

FIGURE 12.2 Integrated theoretical framework of decent informal work

In the words of the research participants:

> We are not happy with the work because of this pandemic. You don't even get enough money to cater for the children. It's been full of troubles- It's been like this since the pandemic started. Many people are scared to even enter the market. People get scared of you when they want to buy from you. The reason is that they cannot tell if the items they want to buy are contaminated
>
> Female, Meat Products

Agreeing with the traders, an electrician (artisan) said:

> The pandemic has adversely affected us. Unless the formal sector workers are paid, we do not get called to work for them. If you own a shop and these people are not paid, they cannot buy anything from you. If the person approaches your shop to buy something and you cough or sneeze,

> the person perceives you have Covid-19. The person will no longer buy from you. All these affect our work.

Expressing a similar sentiment, a female merchant stated that:

> The pandemic has affected our work negatively. People used to buy clothes a lot previously. There were many social and religious activities so I got a lot of customers but now people are scared so they don't invite a lot of people to their programmes. Prices of goods keep increasing as well. We don't get enough money to even do anything. We really need help.

Agreeing with her colleagues, a hairdresser said:

> Truly, the pandemic has adversely affected our work. The person may want to have their hair fixed but she will be scare of Covid-19. They don't come any longer so we could not get money to take care of our children or even to feed yourself. It has really affected us negatively.

For some, as noted, it is about the closure of the borders due to the Covid-19 pandemic that has affected their work. According to a male graphic designer:

> The closure of the borders prevented the importation of items we use. The cost of importation has increased. Prices of goods have increased. People are being laid off at various companies and this has affected the rate at which I get contracts to work on projects.

A male leatherworker had a similar experience. He noted that:

> My clients used to purchase my shoes a lot but their purchases have reduced because of Covid-19. Prices of item have increased too. They have a change of mind when you mention the price to them. We don't even know how to survive because we have children to take care of, including their education.

Many of our respondents lamented about the erosion of their business capital due to how product prices have been increasing in this pandemic. Expressing his concerns about the situation, a carpenter said:

> Prices of goods keep increasing daily. The problem is that my profit then reduces and that should not be the case. Secondly, people do not make

> payment when we work for them. You will never get it no matter how many times you follow-up.

For many others, the pandemic has caused them psychosocial stress and boredom due to staying at home as it deprived them of the opportunity to experience the usual entertaining aspect of their work as informal workers. For example, a female trader observed that 'we don't often hear these jokes when we are at home and this could lead to boredom'. A fish monger concurred with this, but linked it to the economic aspect of their work by stating that "I don't sell much too these days. We run at a loss when we count our money after selling. We are distress now". Further agreeing with the rest, a jewelry/cosmetics trader summed it up as "there's no better work at the moment. We are really suffering. We are no longer happy and we do not have peace".

5 Discussion of Implications and Conclusion

5.1 *Theoretical Implications*

While extant research has been conducted on the informal economy, issues of decent work of informal workers are less-researched. Accordingly, our study makes a crucial contribution to the literature on informal economy and decent work by providing the first empirical insights into the decent work experiences of informal workers in Ghana generally and in this Covid-19 pandemic era specifically. Our study shows that decent work perceptions of informal workers are influenced by different but interrelated factors. Informal workers' perceived decent work experience is high when an informal work is embedded with adequate income and survival; fulfilling and meaningful work; autonomy and control; social recognition and mobility; and health, safety, and wellbeing. These work features, which are valued by informal workers, indicate that decent work experience in the informal economy is driven by different extrinsic/instrumental and intrinsic conditions of work as they help them meet their economic and psychosocial needs and that of their family members. Our findings are similar to that of Monteith and Giesbert (2017), suggesting that better quality informal sector works have a combination of instrumental and intrinsic characteristics of work, and further echoes the need to view decent work generally, and particularly in the informal sector, as multi-disciplinary in nature (see Anlesinya et al., 2021).

That being said, our findings also suggest that the monetary work attributes (i.e. income generation) are more crucial than the non-monetary dimensions of decent work of informal workers because of their unique decent work vulnerability that is better buffered against with adequate income or remuneration. The unique decent work vulnerability of informal workers is based on the views that they do not have enough economic and psychosocial buffers due to absence of security of work, social protection (e.g., pension and insurance), inadequate earnings, exploitation, and unhealthy working conditions, among others. By this, our findings gave credence to Monteith and Giesbert's (2017) findings, which showed that informal workers ranked income as their topmost desirable feature of a better quality work but is inconsistent with the two-factor theory, which places more premiums on intrinsic attributes of work than the instrumental aspects (Herzberg et al., 1959), and some previous studies (e.g. Achdut & Stier, 2021; Jencks et al., 1988) that non-monetary factors make greater contributions to positive decent work experiences roles within the general working population.

Furthermore, our empirical evidence shows that informal workers perceived their decent work experience to be low amidst covid-19 pandemic because the pandemic has depleted, and in some cases temporary eradicated features of work that are valuable to informal workers as discussed earlier. Specifically, Covid-19 restrictions limit their ability to generate daily income from their work while at the same time increasing their psychosocial stress and boredom emanating from the erosion of their business and working capital, and deprivation of the benefits of the psychosocial attributes of their work. This unfortunate situation is happening in a sector that is already stressed by poor remunerated and dangerous working conditions, and lack of or limited access to economic and social protections. During these sufferings and low decent work experience, our research participants indicated that they have not received any support from the relevant authorities to cushion them against both economic and social hardships. This finding is therefore similar to ILO (2020) and Omobowale et al.'s (2020) assertion that Covid-19 restrictions have pushed several informal workers below the poverty line amidst limited access to finance (Megersa, 2020), and lack of social protections (Baah-Boateng & Vanek, 2020) including lack of participation in the government's Covid-19 relief programmes (WIEGO, 2021).

5.2 *Practical Implications*

Given that the informal economy is home to an overwhelming number of workers in Ghana, relevant authorities and stakeholders need to implement policy interventions to enrich informal work with both monetary and non-monetary work features to improve on the overall decent work experience of our gallant informal workers. These may include increasing equitable access to government's subsidized funding while developing their capacity to access affordable credit facilities from financial institutions. We further recommend that authorities should improve physical working conditions at identifiable places of informal workers, and ensure macroeconomic stability by arresting the drivers of the escalating prices of their products as persistent increases in general prices erodes their business capital and their meagre savings. Moreover, policy makers should educate informal workers on general health and safety practices (for example, the need to plan their working hours to ensure effective work-life-family balance), and the need to adhere to Covid-19 protocols because it can help boost their income generation to meet their social-economic needs by eliminating fear in people who are conscious of the virus to feel comfortable patronising their services.

5.3 *Limitations and Future Research Agenda*

While the use of the qualitative method was appropriate because it is the first research on decent work among Ghanaian informal workers, it would be useful for future studies to validate our exploratory insights on informal workers' perception of decent work using the quantitative or mixed method. Furthermore, although there is a strong consistency across different genders and occupations on most of the features, there are visible differences with respect to the fulfilling and meaningful work aspect of decent work in the informal sector. Future researches therefore should assess the differential roles of personal values and personality in decent work experience of informal workers. Moreover, this study focused only on market traders and artisans so future researches should be extended to other categories of informal workers like street hawkers. Besides, all our respondents were owners of informal enterprises so the views of employees in informal enterprises are not represented. Hence, future researches that comparatively assess perceptions of decent work between owners and employees of informal enterprises are highly recommended.

6 Conclusion

We assessed the perceptions of decent work among informal workers, and how Covid-19 pandemic affects their decent work experience by drawing on qualitative evidence from Ghana. Based on the findings, we conclude that perceptions of decent work in the informal sector in Ghana are driven by both intrinsic and instrumental attributes of work. However, catastrophic global situations (e.g. Covid-19 pandemic) remain major threats to informal workers' decent work experience since they can erode or eliminate work attributes that are valuable to informal workers, thereby deepening the prevalence of decent work deficits in the informal economy. We believe these findings could trigger the implementation of measures to improve decent work conditions for informal workers, especially in times of global calamities.

References

Achdut, N., & Stier, H. (2021). The role of monetary and non-monetary job quality components in determining welfare exit. *Journal of Social Policy*, *50*(1), 79–103.

Anderson, C. (2010). Presenting and evaluating qualitative research. *American Journal of Pharmaceutical Education*, *74*(8). https://doi.org/10.5688/aj7408141.

Anlesinya, A., Adepoju, O. A., & Richter, U. H. (2019). Cultural orientation, perceived support and participation of female students in formal entrepreneurship in the sub-Saharan economy of Ghana. *International Journal of Gender and Entrepreneurship*, *11*(3), 299–322.

Anlesinya, A., & Amponsah-Tawiah, K. (2020). Towards a responsible talent management model. *European Journal of Training and Development*, *44*(2/3), 279–303.

Anlesinya, A., Amponsah-Tawiah, K., Adom, P. K., Damoah, O. B. O., & Dartey-Baah, K.(2020). The macro talent management, decent work and national well-being nexus: a cross-country and panel data analysis. *International Journal of Manpower*, *42*(5), 777–793.

Anlesinya, A., & Nyanyofio, G. J. T. (2023). *Decent work, pandemic and informality: Empirical insights from Ghana.* A paper presented at Faculty of Business and Law Research Conference, De Montfort University, Leicester, United Kingdom, June 20, 2023.

Baah-Boateng, W., & Vanek, J. (2020). *Informal Workers in Ghana: A statistical snapshot.* WIEGO Statistical Briefs No 21.

Bulut, E. (2015). Glamor above, precarity below: Immaterial labor in the video game industry. *Critical Studies in Media Communication*, *32*(3), 193–207.

Carré, F. (2020). Informal employment in developed countries: Relevance and statistical measurement. In Chen, M., & Carré, F. (2020). *The Informal Economy Revisited-examining the past, envisioning the future* (pp. 52–59). Routledge.

Creswell, J. W. (2014). *Research design: Qualitative, quantitative and mixed methods approaches.* SAGE Publications.

Debrah, Y. A. (2007). Promoting the informal sector as a source of gainful employment in developing countries: insights from Ghana. *International Journal of Human Resource Management*, *18*(6), 1063–1084.

Dahl, S. A., Nesheim, T., & Olsen, K. M. (2009). Quality of work: Concept and measurement. In Guillén, A. M., & Dahl, S. Å. (Eds.), *Quality of work in the European Union: Concept, data and debates from a transnational perspective* (No. 67) (19–37), Peter Lang.

Darbi, W. P. K., Hall, C. M., & Knott, P. (2018). The informal sector: A review and agenda for management research. *International Journal of Management Reviews*, *20*(2), 301–324.

Deranty, J. P. (2009). What is work? Key insights from the psychodynamics of work. *Thesis Eleven*, 98(1), 69–87.

Ely, M. (1994). *Doing qualitative research: circles within circles*. London: Falmer.

Etim, E., & Daramola, O. (2020). The informal sector and economic growth of South Africa and Nigeria: A comparative systematic review. *Journal of Open Innovation: Technology, Market, and Complexity*, 6(4), 134.

Gallie, D. (1996). The quality of employment: perspectives and problems. In: Offer, A. (ed.), *In the Pursuit of Quality of Life*. New York: Oxford University Press, pp. 163–197

Green, F. (2006). *Demanding work: The paradox of job quality in the affluent economy*. Princeton, NJ: Princeton University Press.

Gullién, A. M., & Dahl, S. A. (eds), *Quality of Work in the European Union: Concept, Data and Debates from a Transnational Perspective*. Brussels: Peter Lang, 19–40.

Ghana Health Service. (2021). COVID-19 Situation Dashboard - Ghana. https://www.ghs.gov.gh/covid19/dashboardm.php.

Hart, K. (1970). Small-scale entrepreneurs in Ghana and development planning. *Journal of Development Studies, 28*, 705–16.

Hart, K. (1972). Employment, income and inequality: a strategy for increasing productive employment in Kenya. Geneva: ILO.

Hart, K. (1973). Informal income opportunities and the urban employment in Ghana. *Journal of Modern African Studies, 11*(1), 61–89.

Herzberg, F., Mausner, B., & Snydermann, B. (1959). *The motivation to work*. New York: Wiley.

Huang, G., Xue, D., & Wang, B. (2020). Integrating theories on informal economies: an examination of causes of urban informal economies in China. *Sustainability*, 12(7), 2738.

ILO. (1999). *Decent work*. Report of the Director-General. International Labour Conference, 87th Session. Geneva: International Labour Office.

ILO. (2002a). *Decent work and the informal economy: Sixth item on the agenda (report VI)*. The 90th Session of the International Labour Conference, International Labour Office Geneva.

ILO. (2002b). Decent work and the informal economy. Geneva: ILO.

ILO (2012). *Up-scaling local economic development: lessons from the Ghana decent work programme*. Turin – Italy: International Training Centre of the ILO.

ILO. (2018). *Informal economy: more than 60 per cent of the world's employed populations are in the informal economy*. Geneva. ILO Newsroom. https://www.ilo.org/global/about-the-ilo/newsroom/news/WCMS_627189/lang--en/index.htm.

ILO. (2020). COVID-19 crisis and the informal economy: Immediate responses and policy challenges. Briefing note. https://www.ilo.org/global/topics/employment-promotion/informal economy/publications/WCMS_743623/lang–en/index.htm.

ILO. (2023). *Decent work and the 2030 agenda for sustainable development.* Switzerland: ILO, Department of Communication and Public Information. (Accessed on May 1, 2023 from: https://www.ilo.org/wcmsp5/groups/public/---europe/---ro-geneva/---ilo-lisbon/documents/event/wcms_667247.pdf.

Jencks, C., Perman, L., & Rainwater, L. (1988). What is a good job? A new measure of labor- market success. *American Journal of Sociology, 93*(6), 1322–1357.

Leonard, M. (2000). Coping strategies in developed and developing societies: the workings of the informal economy. *Journal of International Development, 12,* 1069–85.

Magidi, M., & Mahiya, I. T. (2021). Rethinking training: the role of the informal sector in skills acquisition and development in Zimbabwe. *Development Southern Africa, 38*(4), 509–523.

Maloney, W. F. (2004). Informality Revisited. *World Development, 32*(7), 1159–1178.

Meagher, K. (1995). Crisis, informalization and the urban informal sector in sub-Saharan Africa. *Development and Change, 26*(2), 259–284.

Megersa, K. (2020). *The informal sector and COVID-19. K4D Helpdesk Report 890.* Brighton, UK: Institute of Development Studies.

Miles, M. B., & Huberman, A. M. (1994). *Qualitative data analysis: An expanded sourcebook.* Sage.

Monteith, W., & Giesbert, L. (2017). 'When the stomach is full we look for respect': perceptions of 'good work' in the urban informal sectors of three developing countries. *Work, Employment and Society, 31*(5), 816–833.

Omobowale, M. O., & Omobowale, A. O. (2019). Oju and Inu: Solidarity in the informal market space in Ibadan, Nigeria. *Journal of Black Studies, 50*(4), 401–420.

Omobowale, A. O., Oyelade, O. K., Omobowale, M. O., & Falase, O. S. (2020). Contextual reflections on COVID-19 and informal workers in Nigeria. *International Journal of Sociology and Social Policy, 40*(9/10), 1041–1057.

Portes, A., & Sassen-Koob, S. (1987). Making it underground: Comparative material on the informal sector in Western market economies. *American Journal of Sociology, 93*(1), 30–61.

Rakowski, C. A. (1994). Convergence and divergence in the informal sector debate: A focus on Latin America, 1984–92. *World Development, 22*(4), 501–516.

Rogan, M., & Skinner, C. (2020). The COVID-19 crisis and the South African informal economy: 'Locked out' of livelihoods and employment. *National Income Dynamics Study–Coronavirus Rapid Mobile Survey (NIDS CRAM), Cape Town.*

Schneider, F. (2012). *The shadow economy and work in the shadow: What do we (not) know?* Discussion Paper No. 6423, The Institute for the Study of Labor (IZA): Bonn, Germany.

Sen, A. (1975). *Employment, technology and development. A study prepared for the ILO within the framework of the World Employment Programme,* Oxford, Clarendon Press.

United Nations. (2020). Decent work and economic growth: Why it matters. Available at: https://www.un.org/sustainabledevelopment/wp-content/uploads/2016/08/8_Why -It-Matters-2020.pdf (accessed August 20, 2021).

UNDP. (2015). *Work for human development*. New York: UNDP.

Webb, J. W., Tihanyi, L., Ireland, R. D., & Sirmon, D. G. (2009). You say illigal, I say legitimate: Entrepreneurship in the informal economy. *Academy of Management Review, 34*(3), 492–510.

WIEGO. (2021). *COVID-19 Crisis and the Informal Economy: Informal Workers in Accra, Ghana.* WIEGO. https://www.wiego.org/publications/covid-19-crisis-and-informal -economy-informal-workers-accra-ghana.

WHO. (2021, October). *WHO Coronavirus (COVID-19) Dashboard.* WHO.https://covid19 .who.int/.

CHAPTER 13

Health Insurance and the Challenges of Public Response to Pandemics in Burkina Faso: Exploring the Role of the Informal Economy

Natéwindé Sawadogo

1 Introduction

Economic barriers are increasingly becoming the main challenge facing households regarding healthcare access in Burkina Faso.[1] Universal health coverage is yet to be extended to the majority of the population, especially the most vulnerable. Furthermore, access to community-based health insurance has been so far impeded by the financial challenges facing household to contribute. Yet, public health policy performances depend on the quantity and quality of health information. In case of epidemic outbreak, apart from mass testing, the standard sources of health information for decision-making are based on populations' demand for healthcare services. This paper analyses the state of the economic determinants of this demand focusing on the small traders of the informal sector.

The informal sector constitutes the large part of many African economies that public policy must take it into account if it is to succeed. In fact, the topic of informal sector has been a scholarly interest since the end of the 1970s. It continues to be so in current debates on economic development in low-income countries. Discussing the concept of informality in the light of the COVID-19 pandemic in Ghana, Akuoko et al. (2021) argued that neo-liberal approach to informality on the continent which has long considered it as an abnormality rather meant that the informal sector's contribution to the populations' resilience was largely neglected. Yet, in reality, many African countries show a different socioeconomic setup where informality takes the centre stage, to the extent that the effects of the pandemic in Africa is expected to take a specific pattern. In conceptualizing the concept of informality, the authors observed that "the theorization of the informal sector has gone from being labelled as 'hidden',

1 This chapter is the result of research conducted in the framework of the Africa Multiple Cluster of Excellence, at the University of Bayreuth, funded by the German Research Foundation, in line with the German Strategy for Excellence- EXC 2052/1 – 390713894.

 | DOI:10.1163/9789004692657_015

'black', 'second' to being recognized as a permanent and important aspect of urban lives globally" (Akuoko et al., 2021:2). However, the neo-liberal approach to informality as a transitional abnormal phenomenon to be absorbed by the formal sector resulted in governments focusing on the illegality of informal sector rather than its capacity for development. Since the evidence has challenged such view, the authors call for approaching the informal sector as a relevant factor for understanding other social processes such as resilience to shocks, and pandemics in particular. Benjamin et al. (2012) suggest that understanding the causes and consequences of informality is crucial given that the informal sector plays a dominant role in West African economies, particularly with regard to employment. Meagher (1997) studied the link between crisis, informalization and the urban informal sector in Sub-Saharan. Analysing the size of the informal economy in Sub-Saharan Africa Xaba et al. (2001) show that with 78 per cent is non-Agricultural Employment, 61 per cent in urban employment and 93 per cent employed in new jobs. Whereas in 1990, 21 per cent of SSA's 227 million labour force was working in the informal economy, by 1998 it was estimated to comprise 40–60 per cent of urban employment. During this period, while there was a decline or stagnation in the growth of formal employment, there was an increase in informal sector activities in the region. In some instances, the informal economy plays a far more significant role in the country's economy than the formal economy, as reflected in the number of economically active people working in the informal economy; in addition, the informal economy is making an important contribution to the country's economic growth, as the GDP data reflects; and growth in the informal economy, while being more rapid in urban areas, is also evident in rural communities. Hussmanns (2004) noted the informal economy plays an important role for employment creation, income generation and poverty reduction in many countries, especially developing and transition countries. The IMF (2021) notes that informal workers may be more vulnerable to negative shocks such as the COVID-19 pandemic, as they are likely to face greater income losses without the benefit of social protection. In their paper on self-Employment, wage employment and informality in a developing economy Bennett and Rablen (2012) observed that urban labour markets in developing economies exhibit considerable diversity, typically including significant segments of both voluntary and involuntary self-employment, as well as formal and informal wage employment. Onyebueke & Geyer (2011) through a thorough review focusing on Nigeria show how relevant it is to relate various processes in Africa with the informal economic realities of the continent. Meagher and Yunusa (1996), and Yusuff and Sherifat (2011) engaged in discussion of the concept because of its centrality in socioeconomic analysis.

Surprisingly, this context has been largely ignored in many African governments' response to covid-19 pandemic. In the absence of mass screening, it is the population's health seeking behaviour that will be determinant in the public response to the pandemic. The health seeking behaviour is likely to be in disfavour of public formal health facilities because of the lack a universal health coverage in countries, like Burkina Faso, thus not allowing public health authorities to diagnose the prevalence of the covid-19 virus among the population. Sociologists use the term "career" to make sense of this complex dynamic biographical and collective processes. In its objective meaning, for Hughes (1984:137), "a career consists of a series of status and clearly defined offices". Referring to work, Freidson defines the career-line of a worker as "the series of tasks or jobs performed over the course of a working life" (Freidson 2001:65). When defined in subjective terms, the term career refers to "the moving perspective in which the person sees his life as whole and interprets the meaning of this various attributes, actions, and the things which happen to him" (Hughes 1984:137). The term is applied both to things (Strauss 1992) and to human social and professional life (Becker 1963; Freidson 2001; Hughes 1984). In public policy analysis, some authors have found in the concept a handy shortcut for tracing the evolution of problems from their personal to their public status, and the consequences of such process on policymaking (Dingwall 2001). Knill and Tuson's summary is to the point. For them, "a public policy can be defined as a course of action (or non-action) taken by a government or legislature with regard to a particular issue. Although this definition is very broad, it emphasizes two constitutive elements. First, public policies refer to actions of public actors (typically government), although societal actors might to some extent be involved or participate in public decision-making. Second, governmental actions are focused on a specific issue, implying that the scope of activities is restricted to addressing a certain aspect or problem" (Knill and Tuson 2012:4). In other words, public policy "is concerned with how issues and problems come to be defined and constructed and how they are placed on the political agenda" (Parsons 1995: XV). The attainment of public status of an issue is very often seen with optimism in relation to the modalities of support and the efficacy of the response the problem thus defined may receive. This explains why some interest groups put every effort to gain public definition of problems they are concerned with. Yet, the optimism that the public character of a problem conveys overshadows the complexity and uncertainty of the public policy process *per se*. According to Mills, the distinction between personal problems and public problems raises fundamental methodological questions regarding the appropriate level for their statement and resolutions. In fact, similar to the above line of thinking about the career of problems, Mills uses the term "troubles" to designate the individually experienced stage of problems. For him "*Troubles* occur within the character of the individual and within the range of his immediate relations with others; they have to do with his self and with those limited areas of social life of which he is directly and personally aware" (Mills 1967:8). With respect to the above definition of public policy, at this stage, the problem does not involve the government but the individual and his immediate environment (such as family, friends, and neighbors).

On contrast Mills refers to the term of "issue" to designate the collective, public stage of problems' career. According to him "Issues have to do with matters that transcend these local environments of the individual and the range of this inner life. They have to do with the organization of many such milieu into the institutions of an historical society as a whole ... An issue is a public matter: some value cherished by publics is felt to be threatened" (Mills 1967:8). In reference to the definition of the concept of public policy stated above, issue corresponds to the stage of public definition of problems and the governmental involvement in the response to them. However, the fact that the public and its problems constitute a relatively autonomous level of reality raises important methodological issue that can constitute a challenge to public policy process, with the result of reducing the positive expectations that the evolution of a problem to public status usually conveys. Indeed, intelligence is considered as one of the main steps of public policy process. Through intelligence, public policy makers collect and process of all relevant knowledge and information that would enable them to identify and support selected alternatives for implementation. Access to information thus becomes a key challenge in public policymaking. The pandemic of covid-19 is a particular case of issue that is subject to public policy and could face important challenges regarding the access to the relevant information on the population. The paper sets out to address the following questions: What is the current health coverage opportunities offered to the population? What are the existing health insurance opportunities, and to what extent these opportunities are accessible to all citizens? What are the limitations of these existing opportunities and what are the implications for access in time of epidemic, such as that of the covid-19? What are the state of informal help regimes? How all of the above means for public response against the covid-19 pandemic in Burkina Faso?

These are important questions about which an understanding can inform appropriate measures for current and future pandemics in Burkina Faso and in Africa more generally. One reason why these are important questions is related to the relevance of economic determinants in explaining the demand for health services of the population supported by the literature. For example, Kremer and Miguel (2007) have shown in their study about primary school enrollment in a deworming program in Western Kenya that the demand for health services were sensitive to price, with only 18% in cost-sharing school compared to 75%

in schools which kept the free programme. Similarly, Cohen and Dupas (2010) and Dupas (2014) found similar results when studying the demand for new health products in rural Kenya. Subramanian and al. (2002) showed relationship between inequality and health (2002), while Swain (2016) demonstrated that economic disadvantage affects the ability to access clinical care. Comparable findings are provided by Barreto (2017), who has shown that inequality of health within a country relate to the distribution of accumulation of wealth within the society. Katikireddi (2016) drawing conclusion on the economic factors contribution to health noted that "ensuring economic policy is cognizant of effects on health is likely to become increasingly necessary for public health in the future". Tekabe (2012) cross country study confirmed these findings; and for Deaton (2003), income inequality is a health risk are as plausible for poor as for rich countries. Focusing on the covid-19 pandemic, Stojkoski and colleagues (2020) have showed that there are socio-economic determinants that contribute to the resulting coronavirus pandemic; among other determinant is government expenditure and testing power of countries; that means that sensitivity of demand to price is waived, that could have hindered health service demand.

Another reason for undertaking this study is the lack of study on the topic at present. We did not find any scholarly published paper on the role of health insurance on the control of the pandemic whether individually or state response, regarding Africa; outside Africa only two papers are found, with one by Clay and colleagues (2020) on broader issue in the past regarding the effects of medicaid implementation on pandemic influenza mortality, and how the expansion of insurance mitigate expansion of the disease among population. The other paper Woolhandler and Himmelstein (2020) concerns more directly COVID-19 and lack of the health insurance, particularly when many workers lose their jobs on the basis on which they accessed to health insurance. Both studies focus on the context of the United States. The aim of the present contribution is to explore how the context of health insurance coverage shapes pandemic control in an African context. We argue that economic constraints prevent demand for clinical services which would have provided complementary data on the prevalence of the pandemic among the population in the absence of systematic test of the population, and thus increasing the risk of exposure of other people in crowed promiscuous setting like markets. The paper is organized as follow. After this introductory section, methodological aspects are addressed. This is followed by the results section which covers macroeconomic determinants and household constraints regarding access to clinical care, before any diagnosis of covid-19 could be done. Finally, after the discussion section a conclusion is provided.

2 Methodology

Building on the state of the art regarding the economic determinants of health behaviour and its link with public policy, the study adopts a qualitative approach. Theoretically, Mills's conceptualization of personal troubles and public issues and their interdependences offered the guiding line for this research. Accordingly, we agree with Mills that when personal troubles evolve to a public issue "we may not hope to find its solution within the range of opportunities open to any one individual. The very structure of opportunities has collapsed. Both the correct statement of the problem and the range of possible solutions require us to consider the economic and political institutions of the society, and not merely the personal situation and character of a scatter of individuals" (Mills1967: 9). Individual households economic circumstances are examined and inferred to their chances of access to clinical services through which their health status regarding the coronavirus could be diagnosed and information fed into the health information system, that can inform policy action. Economic constraints of household appear therefore as a constraint, and challenges, for public response to the pandemic of covid-19, to the extent that economic constraints have the capacity to prevent households' demand for health services. The lack of demand reduces the information on the population that could be available to the government for proper policy decision-making.

To understand households' economic circumstances two methods were used for the data collection. The two methods are described as follow:

2.1 *Systematic Documentary Review*

This method is used to collect data on the existing macroeconomic policy and social security regimes. Regarding macroeconomic policy, focus is put on the evolution of the role of the state in social services provision in Burkina Faso. this involved what follows: a) inventory of macroeconomic policy from 1960 to 2021; b) inventory of social security regimes from 1960–202; c) analysis of the role of the state in social services financing; d) analysis of the role of citizens in social services financing. These data, which were analyzed using a reading grid, provided some insights on how vulnerable citizens are, in relation to access to some social services such as health services. This existing context also provided some understanding of the prevailing context of the covid-19 pandemic outbreak. In terms of analysis this situation is termed as a *process of detachment of the state* and *attachment of the populations* to the macroeconomic models, with the assumption that a strong attachment or dependence of the population to the model of the Market in healthcare provision would impede access to healthcare services, and therefore withdraw that population from the healthcare information system which would have provided some basis for evidence-based decision-making regarding the covid-19 pandemic.

2.2 *Questionnaire Survey*

The questionnaire survey involved a random sample of 503 vulnerable households of traders operating within Ouagadougou, the capital city of Burkina Faso. The survey was carried out in November 2020. The data collection concerned 10 markets in 5 districts of the city of Ouagadougou which were closed by the government on March 20, 2020, as a response to the COVID-19 pandemic. These are the Yonko Yaar and Toukin Yaar markets in district 4, Nabi Yaar and Toles Yaar in district 5, Bendogo Yaar and Quatorze Yaar in district 10, Karpala Yaar in district 11 and the Marché du 15 in district 12. A total of 503 traders were surveyed: 69 in Yonko Yaar, 65 in Toukin Yaar, 68 respectively in Nabi Yaar and Toles Yaar, 67 in Bendogo Yaar, 66 in Quatorze Yaar, 49 in Karpala Yaar and 51 at the Marché du 15. In practice, 10 surveyors organized in pairs with the most experienced surveyor as team leader proceeded to collect data on these markets. Regarding the survey selection method, the surveyors first contacted the market managers (Raag-Naaba). The surveyors then identified the participants with the help of market managers focusing on small traders with sheds who were more likely to be more affected by market closures. Among the 503 participants, 72.6% were females and 27.2% males, with an average age of 41 years. In terms of education, 53.5% were reported to be illiterate. Each household is made up of an average number of seven persons, with 95% being the respondent's children. The principal activity of 92.4% of the surveyed households is trade; 91.7% are reported to have not another secondary activity.

The analysis consisted in evaluating the current macroeconomic and personal economic circumstances of households and the possible impact of these circumstances on their demand for health services. The results of these analyses provided the bases for discussion about the policy challenges faced by the government of Burkina Faso in responding effectively to the covid-19.

3 Results

The results show that households have been resilient to the chock caused by the pandemic. From 2014 health policy measures started to reverse the trend in government's interventions in healthcare access that mitigated the negative impacts of several decades of privatization of healthcare services. Recent policy measures facilitated healthcare access for children aged less than five years and pregnant women, thus reducing households' health expenditures. Furthermore, the households in the informal sector suffered less from the restrictions due to the covid-19, as they benefited from the increase in domestic demand for goods and services in some of the branches of the economy.

3.1 *The Market for Healthcare in Burkina Faso: from Privatization to State Involvement*

Until the end of the 1980s, the Burkina Faso government's economic power ratio over its citizens was higher (World Bank 1990). Indeed before 1990, it was almost the only provider of health care services. Besides, although in practice individuals bought some medicines from out of pocket, in principle, the law made this function primarily that of the state (Kaboré 2002). This is visible from the budget lines which shows larger share for transfer and drug expenses. However, these power chances started to weaken from particularly 1987, with the advent of a new state of exception, which overthrew the revolutionary regime (1983–1987). The government's economic power sources, which were largely made up of internal assets weakened. In fact, from 21 million USD in 1970, the total external debt of the country skyrocketed to 866 million USD in 1988 (World Bank 1990). The country started also to trade with international financial institutions such the IMF whose contribution to the external debt passed from zero to three million USD for the same dates. Moreover, aid was increasing from 1986 with a higher pic in 1988, one year after the advent of the new military regime. These revenues from debt and aid enabled the government to substitute its weakening internal revenue sources and maintain its power ratio over its citizens. The problem is that the weakened economy of the country did not allow it to reimburse its debt, as expected by lenders. From the end of the 1970s, private lenders become dominant as source of capital to institutional financial institutions because of the economic crisis facing developed countries (World Bank 1990). As a result, the government's dependence on international economic and political actors increased, and correlatively the latter's power ratios over it became higher. These actors took this advantage of their power chances to obtain from Burkina Faso economic reforms that weakened the country's power ratio over its citizens. The government was pressed to adopt the market as framework of conduct for economic and social services exchange, with the effect of discharging itself from its social function in favour of the private sector. For example, even the small 7% of the state's budget share of health expenditure dramatically fell to less than 4% between 1991 and 1995 (Sawadogo, 2005)

As a result of the state's adoption of the Structural Adjustment Programme, there has been an increasing defunctionalisation (displacement) of the state in matter of health care provision and financing in Burkina Faso since 1991. In fact, private provision of health care has always existed in Burkina Faso. First practiced unofficially by French expatriates, it saw a boom since the country's adoption of the free market in 1991, which resulted in the setting up of an institutional framework for a private provision of health care services. The general deregulation measures, which followed the economic crises of 1972–1974, but which were blocked by the revolutionary regime (1983–87) in Burkina Faso, became generalized in the 1990s. Burkina Faso made its move to the market on 13th March 1991, opening a new area in the national health care system. In effect, medical practice has been liberalized and the different areas of professional practice were later defined in the Public Health Code by the law no.23/94/ADP of 19 May 1994. The Hospital law no.034/98/AN/ of May 1998 organized the health system by defining the different categories of health services. The Decree no.398/PRES/PM/MS of 19 July 2005, complemented respectively by the inter-ministry and ministerial by-laws no.2006/MS/MCPEA/MFB of 16 June 2006, no.200–060/MS/CAB, defined the conditions of professional licensing, and of the opening and operation of private health care centres. With respect to traditional medicine, 'After a lethargy from 1960 to 1970, the end of 1970 saw the issuing of the Order no.70–68 bis/PRES/MSP/AS of December 1970 related to the Public Health Code and the rules for its application; this act tolerate Traditional Medicine' (Bognounou et al. 2005:33); in 1994 then the law no.23/94/ADP on Public Health Code 'recognises Traditional medicine and Traditional Pharmacopeia as one of the components of the national health system' (Bognounou et al. 2005:34). Health statistics shows that more than 80% of the population use traditional medicine; in 2010 it was estimated that there was over 30.000 traditional healers in Burkina Faso, with more than 600 healers in Ouagadougou, the capital of the country. In addition, according to Soubeiga (1994:111) "Apart from their traditional activities of evangelisation, one of the common characteristics of Christian churches of different denominations established in Burkina Faso is that they appear more and more as places of care of illness". The marabous have been influential since the precolonial period, as explorers mentioned it. In terms of its size, informal drug selling is also another market for health care provision in both rural and urban areas. There is not yet a specific fiscal regime for the sector of private provision of health services. The private provision of health services is under a commercial fiscal regime. There is not yet a specific fiscal status for the sector. There are no rationalized pricing and prescription systems; there is a lack of quality standards regarding facilities, equipment, and personnel (Ouédraogo 2010). Policies, legislations, and the operation of public health services contributed to the development of private health care supply, particularly in urban areas.

Therefore, a functional reconfiguration took place. As the market policy recommends, for the citizens to meet their health care needs, instead of subsidizing their access, the state has embraced from then on, the function of negative regulator. Patients become consumers of both public and private health services. At the same time, the state becomes dependent on international financial actors. As Elias cogently put it, the character of power chances is that it enables its owner "on the one hand, the control he can exert over his opponent, and, on the other hand, the control it gives him over the course of the game as such" (Elias 1978:82). As it will be seen later, international financial institutions, particularly the World Bank, has since using their leverage to shape the market for health care service in Burkina Faso. The weakening of the state's power ratio over its citizens is revealed through the process of withholding of public support to the latter and their later configuration with other sources of support – and hence of dependences. This power started to change from 2014. New policy measures facilitated healthcare access for children aged less than five years and pregnant women, thus reducing households' health expenditures. Furthermore, the households in the informal sector suffered less from the restrictions due to the covid-19, as they benefited from the increase in domestic demand for goods and services in some of the branches of the economy.

3.2 *The Limits of Public Involvement and the Crisis of Alternative Solidarities*

Referring to power, Elias suggested that "when one-person (or group of persons) lacks something which another person or group has the power to withhold, the latter has a function for the former" (Elias 1978:78). What can be seen from the populations' side, is a defunctionalisation (or reconfiguration) of the state towards them on matter of health care, until 2014, through the withholding of the subsidies which were provided in so for their access to some of health care services. Indeed, in order for the private supply of health care services to exist there are at least two conditions. First, the State delegates all or part of its prerogatives on health care provision to a third party. In this case, the state pays this latter for the provision of the services to the population. Second is for the State to not only delegate all or part of its prerogatives on health care provision to a third party but also make patients responsible for the payment of the services they receive from the private provider. In this latter case, the public health care centres can continue free provision or ask for less or comparable payment. In Burkina Faso the State chose the second alternative, before a new opposite trend started in 2014.

In fact, health care has never been free for all irrespective of the kind of individual health problems in the modern history of the country. The difference is that the responsibility of the individual patient for the payment of health care services has significantly increased since the 1990s. In fact, between 1970 and 1983, there was no major change in term of scope of the category of beneficiaries of the formal social security system. Instead, the changes were organizational. For instance, Law n° 13/72 AN of 28/12/1972 on the code of social security created the National Social Security Fund (Caisse Nationale de Sécurité Sociale) which gather Family benefits (*Prestations Familiales*), Work accidents and Professional illnesses (*Accidents du Travail et Maladies Professionnelles*-AT & MP) Old age insurances (Assurances Vieillesse-AV)). At the date of 2001, only 11% of the population was covered by this mechanism, meaning that like most countries in Sub-Saharan Africa, 90% of the informal sector workers are excluded. Public social security arrangements cover the small population of employees of the formal sector. However, the weakening of the state's economic power over its citizens did not result in an increase in the economic power of the individual. As the above analysis shows, the majority of the population cannot afford their health care on their own. They still need support from a third party. New interdependencies have to be formed. In this context, due to the lack of adequate healthcare financing mechanisms in order to pay for treatment during illness, the poor resort to various forms of informal means such as loans, dissolution of savings or the selling of essential resources (Bationo et al. 2012). Then, at first, the state sought to balance this discriminatory coverage by seeking to promote primary health. However, until the early 2000s, in practice, the tendency was rather for the state to discharge itself from the social protection of the population in the context of high external pressure for economic reform (Zagré 1994). In the area of health, in Burkina Faso, like in most West African country, this was done through the implementation of the primary health program in the framework of the Bamako Initiative. The Bamako Initiative is the West African initiative design in the late 1980s to implement primary health care laid down in the late 1970s by the WHO. In the name of involving communities in their own health care and discharging the state from the burden of social expenses, the Bamako Initiative introduced user fees and cost-recovery mechanism through out-of-pocket payments and user fees alongside management responsibilities for the communities at existing health facilities (Sawadogo 2005). Social changes in rural communities and the consequences of privatization resulted in the impoverishment of large sections of the population. Besides, the withdrawal of the state from the health sector resulted in poorer qualities of health services. As a result, not only primary health care providers were not accessible for all, but also the targeted financing mechanism still excluded many poor.

The community-based health insurance (or *mutuelles de santé*) emerged at the beginning of the 1990s as the result of individual responses to the problem of access and quality of health care. These community health insurances are diverse and include community health insurance companies, help societies, insurance societies, specific prepayment schemes, mutual solidarity funds, professional mutual, solidarity banks and system of risk sharing. But beyond this diversity they all set to assist and help the poor and the vulnerable including access to adequate health care services. The community-based health insurance covers low-income workers with informal labour relations. Membership fee is reported to be between 1000 and 2400 fcfa (between euro 1.50 and euro 3.00) and consists of the pooling of these funds to help reimburse the health benefits collectively. The main characteristic of this form of solidarity is that usually it is reached only in small groups or among close relatives. At the village level, collective mobilisation becomes challenging because of the increase in conflicting polarities which are generally present in large groups. The mutuals have a potential reach as the informal sector workers are around 90%. However, in practice, the mechanism covers much less (about 1%). The number of Mutual Health Organizations (MHO) has significantly increased during the past decade. For instance, whereas in 1997 there were 6, in 2005 their number rose to 146 MHOs and cooperatives. Since 2000, the government has tried to support local community-based health insurance with the aim to extend nationally and help set up a national network of mutual health organisations. Since that period International Labour Organization has been helping the government to expand the community-based system to the national level. In this connection, the decree no. 2008–736 of Feb 2009 established the Committee (Comité de Pilotage) to develop a National Health Insurance System like Ghana's. In 2008, a permanent NHIS was adopted by the Ministerial council, and in March 2009 the NHIS was officially approved; in 2009 the *Comité de pilotage* was yet to design the benefits package for a Universal Health Insurance system. The Universal Health Insurance system (Assurance Maladie Universelle – AMU) relies on community-based health insurance for higher reach; full implementation is expected to be completed by 2015, while the system is stated to be launched in 2011. This is a general trend in the region, which Ouédraogo captured well when she said that "A promising approach of many governments in sub-Saharan Africa is the extension of mutual health insurance schemes to the national level. Through their integration in public social security arrangements these national schemes can exploit the potential of MHIS and reach previously excluded population segments" (Ouédraogo 2012:430).

The AMU is designed as compulsory health insurance for the formal sector and as voluntary health insurance for the informal sector; The formal sector will be covered by social security financing institutions such as the *Caisse Nationale de Securité Sociale* (CNSS), *Caisse Autonome de Retraite des Fonctionnaire* (CARFO), while the informal sector will be covered by the *mutuelles de santé*. It is believed that "The integration of mutual health insurance schemes (MHIS) into public social security arrangements is a new and innovative approach taken by many governments in Sub-Saharan Africa to include people of low income within public social protection measures" (Ouédraogo 2012:429). The programme will use a single benefit package but different pricing measures (urban/rural, poor/rich). The system plan to use the generic provided by the state central drug agency (*Central d'Achat de Médicaments Génériques*). There are also private commercial insurances (main insurances including, SONAR, FONCIAS, UAB, GA, Colina Assurance), but they cover a minority of privileged, being less than 1% of the population. The question of significant importance for the present purpose is that of how one can make sense of this dynamic of integration, which shows an apparent willingness from the part of the state to democratize social security protection so as to cover all the sections of the society. On further examination of the dynamic of the institutional design, there appears a striking matching of the level and pattern of integration of the social security regime and the decrease in the pattern of interdependences between the governors and the governed. Since the end of the 1980s, there has been an increasing trend in the individualisation of health care expenses in Burkina Faso. Although in theory fees in public health centres are less than in private ones, the unavailability and the substandard nature of services, as the long time required to receive services will play in favour of important development of private health care supply. The reconfiguration of the patient's function as user to consumer is complete as the above analysis shows. Citizens pay for their own health care through different models, with out-of-pocket still being the largest model of financing health care in Burkina Faso. New financial institutions have emerged to offer financial services to the populations in order to pay for their health care, at the same time the function of the state in that matter decreased.

3.3 *Fragile Personal Opportunities Amid State Crisis and Disappearing Community Solidarities*

Like many citizens, the population concerned by the study interred the COVID-19 pandemic period with almost no direct social support. The withdrawal of the state from social sectors, and particularly the health sector, continued to present. However, new policy measures facilitated healthcare access for children aged less than five years and pregnant women, thus reducing households' health expenditures. At the same time, the private sector of health care has been expanding. Until the mid-1980s there was almost no private medical centre in Burkina Faso. There were only nineteen pharmacists and a few private nursing clinics. The number of private health centres increased from 58 in 1990 to 250 in 2000, and 380 in 2009; of the 380 centres in 2009, 54.6% are in Ouagadougou, 22.4% in Bobo-Dioulasso, the second biggest city of the country (Ouédraogo 2010). Since 2009, this number plateaued because, between 2009 and 2014, there was a simple variation in the order of around 30, whereas this variation was 192 between 1990 and 2000 and 130 between 2000 and 2009. From 2009, the number of private health centres plateaued but still remains important, as in 2014 there were 407 private health centres. This figure was 544 in 2018 according to the latest health census (Ministry of Health 2019). This is a perfect indicator of the relative disappearance of the state as a social support agent to its citizens. This privatization of individual troubles is reinforced by the lack of a universal health insurance system, and the inability of many citizens to subscribe to the developing community and formal private insurance systems. Though flexible, the fact that community insurance systems require regular income source prevent many citizens in the informal sector, such as those concerned by the study, from subscribing. However, the data did not support a significant loss of income during the COVID-19 pandemic restrictions.

Of the 503 participants in the study, there were 72.6% females and 27.2% males, with an average age of 41 years. In terms of education, 53.5% were reported to be illiterate. Each household is made up of an average number of seven persons, with 95% being the respondent's children. The principal activity of 92.4% of the surveyed households is trade; 91.7% are reported to have not another secondary activity. When one consider the type of trade in which the participants are involved, one can see the precarious nature of these activities in the face of the multiple demands households are confronted to. To the question of the area in which they practice their trade, 22.1% said to be in the trade of seasoning 22.5% in clothing and 15.9% in fruit and vegetables; all together more about 70% have precarious activities. The evidence about such precariousness is that around 90% of the households do not have precautionary savings, 83% reported to receive no state direct support, and more that 90% do not receive support from a parent, while almost none of the participants receive a friend's support. The evidence shows that participants are left to their own. Nonetheless, 91.3% against 8.3% household reported to have access to health services, with an average household size of seven people.

4 Discussion and Conclusion

Public policy is a function of intelligence (Knill and Tosun 2012; Foucault 1976; 1989; 2004), whether one adopt a positivist or a constructionist approach (Parsons 1995). In the area of health, the availability of intelligence for public policy purpose is in turn a function of demand for health services whether for preventive or curative purposes as shown earlier by Foucault (Foucault 1976; 1989; 2004) and supported by recent empirical studies. Then, demand for these health services is a function of the economic circumstances of households (Barreto 2017; Cohen and Dupas 2010; Deaton 2003; Dupas 2014; Katikireddi 2016; Kremer and Miguel 2007; Subramanian and al. 2002; Swain 2016; Tekabe 2012; Stojkoski and colleagues 2020). The study predicted that intelligence constraints for government regarding policy making on the covid-19 based on the assumption that the economic circumstances of the surveyed households are likely to drive them away from the health apparatus through which knowledge about the prevalence of the pandemic among the population is gained. This withdrawal of household from the mechanisms of knowledge of the state would be supported by macroeconomic context of the country and the household individual economic circumstances. The evidence failed to support these assumptions. Small traders in Ouagadougou have been resilient to the covid-19 pandemic's shocks. It is still obvious that the state involvement remains weak. Like the general population of the country, the households have been freed by the public health system until very recently, through the structural adjustment measures that led to the privatization of health care provision in most of African countries (Zagré 1991). As the state relinquishes from the social and particularly the health sector, private agencies open for profit health care centres as to be become particularly in cities the dominant providers of health care services. At the same time, household have been proposed alternative community health insurance coverage which the precarious nature of households' income sources does not allow to subscribe amid disappearance of traditional solidarities. In sum, until very recently, one could support the statement that "the very structure of opportunities has collapsed" (Mills 1967: 9). The state interventions in the healthcare sector witnessed some improvement from 2014. These findings challenge the handy shortcut that some authors have found in the concept of public issue to anticipate societal supportive outcome in relation to a give problem in society (Dingwall 2001). The optimism that the public character of a problem conveys overshadows, as has been shown, the complexity and uncertainty of the public policy process. Following Mills, the distinction between personal troubles and public issues raises fundamental methodological questions regarding the appropriate level for their statement and resolutions. In absence of mass systematic testing, the COVID-19 pandemic is likely to continue challenging government measures as these latter lack a large part of the evidence-base for their formulation and implementation. The result of this process is the widening of health disparities among the population. In a country where most of the population are poor and lacks universal health insurance public response that is appropriate to pandemics is likely to succeed when control measures are not limited to those who attend health facilities. Social and economic processes mediate the population's attendance to health facilities in a way that a large part of it, mainly the elderly, is excluded from the health surveillance mechanisms. This excluded section of the population can sustain the pandemic for long time.

References

Akuoko, P.B., Aggrey, V., Amoako-Arhen, A. (2021). Ghana's informal economic sector in the face of a pandemic. *Social Sciences & Humanities* Open 3 (2021) 100094 https://doi.org/10.1016/j.ssaho.2020.100094.

Anselm L Strauss, L. A, Baszange, E. (éd.), (1992), *La Trame de la Négociation, Sociologie qualitative et interactionnisme*, L'Harmattan, Paris.

Barreto, L.M., (2017), Health inequalities: a global perspective, *Ciência & Saúde Coletiva*, 22(7):2097–2108.

Bationo, B.F. et Ouédraogo, L–M, (2012). 'Solidarity in the extension of micro health insurance – the problem of enrolment in mutual health organisations in Burkina Faso' In: Hans Jurgen Rosner, Gerald Leppert, Philipp Degens, Lisa-Marie Ouédraogo, éds. 2012. *Handbook of Micro health insurance in Africa. Zurich*, Lit Verlag, pp. 415–427.

Becker, S.H., 1963, *Outsiders: Studies in the Sociology of Deviance*, New York: The Free Press

Bennett, J., Rablen, M. (2012). Self-Employment, Wage Employment and Informality in a Developing Economy, Working Paper No. 12-02, Centre for Economic Development & Institutions Brunel University.

Bognounou, O., Guinko, S., (2005), *Ethnobotanique-médecine traditionnelle*, Rapport, Ouagadougou.

Clay, K., Lewis, J., Severnini, R.E., Wang, X., (2020), The Value of Health Insurance during a Crisis: Effects of Medicaid Implementation on Pandemic Influenza Mortality, *IZA Institute of Labor Economic Discussion Paper* No. 13200.

Cohen, J. and P. Dupas (2010). "Free Distribution or Cost-Sharing? Evidence from a randomized malaria experiment." *Quarterly Journal of Economics* 125: 1–45.

Cohen, J., P. Dupas and S. Schaner (2015). "Price Subsidies, Diagnostic Tests, and Targeting of Malaria Treatment." *American Economic Review* 105(2): 609–645.

Cohen, Jessica, Günther Fink, Kathleen Maloney, Katrina Berg, Matthew Jordan, Theodore Svoronos, Flavia Aber & William Dickens (2015). "Introducing rapid diagnostic tests for malaria to drug shops in Uganda: a cluster-randomized controlled trial". *Bulletin of the World Health Organization*, Volume 93, Number 3, 133–208.

Deaton, A., 2003, Health, Inequality, and Economic Development, *Journal of Economic Literature* (XLI) : 113–158.

Dingwall, R. (2001) *Aspects of Illness*. Aldershot: Ashgate Publishing Limited.

Dupas, P. (2009). "What matters (and what does not) in household's decision to invest in malaria prevention?", *American Economic Review* 99(2): 224–230.

Dupas, P. (2011a). "Health Behavior in Developing Countries", *Annual Review of Economics*, 3: 425–449.

Dupas, P. (2011b). "Do Teenagers Respond to HIV Risk Information? Evidence from a Field Experiment in Kenya", *American Economic Journal: Applied Economics*, 3 (1), 1–36.

Dupas, P. (2014a). "Short-Run Subsidies and Long-Run Adoption of New Health Products: Evidence from a Field Experiment". *Econometrica* 82(1), pp. 197–28.

Dupas, Pascaline (2014b). "Getting Essential Health Products to Their End Users: Subsidize, but How Much?" *Science* Vol. 345, Issue 6202, pp. 1279–1281, 12 September 2014.

Dupas, P. V. Hoffmann, M. Kremer and A. Zwane. (2016). "Targeting health subsidies through a non-price screening mechanism: Evidence from a Randomized Controlled Trial in Rural Kenya". Mimeo, Stanford University.

Dupas, Pascaline, and Jonathan Robinson (2013). "Why Don't the Poor Save More? Evidence from Health Savings Experiments". *American Economic Review* 103(4): 1138–71.

Elias, N., (1978). *What is sociology*? London: Hutchinson.

Freidson, E., (2001), *Professionalism. The third logic*, Cambridge, Polity Press.

Hughes, C. E., (1984), *The Sociological eye. Selected papers*, New Brunswick, Transaction, Inc.

Hussmanns, R. (2004). Measuring the informal economy: From employment in the informal sector to informal employment, *Working Paper* No. 53, Policy Integration DepartmentBureau of Statistics International Labour Office.

IMF (2021). Measuring the informal economy, *IMF policy paper*, February 2021.

Makoni, L & Tichaawa, T. M. (2021). Impact Analysis of the COVID-19 Pandemic on the Informal Sector Business Tourism Economy in Zimbabwe. *African Journal of Hospitality, Tourism and Leisure*, 10(1):165–178. DOI: https://doi.org/10.46222/ajhtl.19770720-93.

Meagher, K. (1997). Crisis, Informalization and the Urban Informal Sector in Sub-Saharan Africa. *Development and Change*, 26, 259–284.

Kaboré, B., (2002), *Histoire politique du Burkina Faso 1919–2000*, Paris, L'Harmattan.

Katikireddi, V.S., (2016), Economic opportunity: a determinant of health?, *The Lancet*, S2468–2667(16)30004–4.

Knill, C. and Tuson, J., (2012), *Public policy. A new introduction*, Palgrave Macmillan, Hampshire.

Meagher, K., Yunusa, M-B. (1996) Passing the buck structural adjustment and the nigerian urban informal sector, UNRISD Discussion Papers.

Miguel, Edward, and Michael Kremer (2004). "Worms: Identifying Impacts on Education and Health in the Presence of Treatment Externalities", *Econometrica* 72 (1): 159–217.

Mills, C. W., (1967), *The sociological imagination*, Oxford, Oxford University Press.

Ouédraogo, J-B., (2010), 'L'émergence du secteur privé et les perspectives d'avenir', Communication *Conférence sectorielle sur la santé dans le cadre du cinquantenaire*, Ouagadougou, Décembre 2010.

Ouédraogo, L–M., (2012), 'Access for all' and 'reaching the poor'? Integrating of mutual health insurance units into public social security arrangements-benefits and risks for mutual schemes', in Rosner, H.J., Leppert, G., Degens, P., Lisa-Marie Ouédraogo, L–M., eds., 2012, *Handbook of Micro health insurance in Africa*, Zurich, Lit Verlag, pp429-

Onyebueke, V., Geyer, M. (2011) The informal sector in urban Nigeria: Reflections from almost four decades of Research, SSB/TRP/MDM 2011 (59).

Parsons, W., (1995), *Public policy. An introduction to the theory and practice of policy analysis*, Cheltenham, Edward Elgar.

Strojkoski, V., Utkovski, Z., Jolakoski, P., Tevdovski, D. and Kocarev, L., 2020, The socio-economic determinants of the coronavirusdi sease (COVID-19) pandemic *medR* XIV preprint doi: https://doi.org/10.1101/2020.04.15.20066068.

Sawadogo, N., (2005), *Dynamique et enjeux de la planification sanitaire au Burkina Faso: cas du district de Pissy/Ouagadougou*, Mémoire Cycle PRAT, IPD/West Africa-Sahel, Ouagadougou.

Soubeiga, A., (1999), 'Quête de guérison, conversion, évangélisation.' in Otayek, R., *Dieu dans la cité*, Bordeaux, Centre d'Etude D'Afrique Noire, pp. 111–128.

Subramanian, V. S., Belli, P., and Kawachi, I., (2002), The macroeconomic determinants of health, Annu. Rev. Public Health 2002. 23:287–302.

Swain, R., G., (2016), How does economic and social disadvantage affecthealth?, Focus, 33 (1): 1–6.

Tekabe, L. F., (2012), Health and Long Run Economic Growth in Selected Low Income Countries of Africa South of the Sahara. Cross country panel data *analysis*, Master Thesis, Södertörns University.

Woolhandler, S. and Himmelstein, U.D., (2020), Intersecting U.S. Epidemics: COVID-19 and Lack of Health Insurance, *Annals of Internal Medicine, Ideas and Opinions*, https://doi.org/10.7326/M20-1491.

World Bank, 1990, *World Development report 1990*, Oxford, Oxford University Press.

Xaba, J.; Pat Horn, P., Motala, S. (2001) The Informal Sector in Sub-Saharan Africa, Employment Sector 2002/10 Working Paper on the Informal Economy: International Labour Organization.

Yusuff, O. S., A Theoretical Analysis of the Concept of Informal Economy and Informality in Developing Countries, European. *Journal of Social Sciences*, 20(4), 624–636.

Zagré, P., 1994, *Les politiques* économiques *du Burkina Faso. Une tradition d'ajustement structurel*, Paris, Éditions Karthala.

Index

Adequate income and survival 258-259
Adogan 88, 91
Adolescents 3–4, 47–61,
African economy 1–3
Apprentice 4, 134–136
Artisan 150, 171–176, 189–194

Bode market 130–140
Border communities and markets 106–110, 122, 124–126
Business networking 3, 65, 67-68, 73–75

Coconut fruit 87–88,
Coconut meat 88–93
Covid-19 250–260, 273–278
Credit 4, 118, 148–151, 164–165, 267

Economic survival 60, 65, 192
Emancipated adolescent 3, 47–53

Fiverr 221–222
Freelancing 221–225, 237

Gig economy 220–235, 242–247
Graduate artisans 171–173

Health preference 4, 107–121
Health Insurance 129, 217, 273, 277–278
Herbs 4, 56, 121–122, 129–140

ILO, International Labour Organisation 169, 250
Informal capital 149–151, 154

Keke 23–25, 26–28, 31–37

Mechanic village 64–65, 66–70
Motorcycle 9–15, 25, 35, 38, 64

Patriarchy 23, 26

Traffic space 47–50
Tricycle 3, 11–14, 23–30

Upwork 221–222
Usury 148–150

www.ingramcontent.com/pod-product-compliance
Lightning Source LLC
LaVergne TN
LVHW010625300926
849162LV00001B/63